Linguistic Studies
in Romance Languages

Proceedings of

the Third Linguistic Symposium

on Romance Languages

R. Joe Campbell
Mark G. Goldin
Mary Clayton Wang
Editors

Georgetown University Press, Washington, D. C. 20007

PREFACE

This volume contains the papers and alternate papers presented at the Third Linguistic Symposium on Romance Languages, held at Indiana University, Bloomington, on March 29-31, 1973. The symposium was sponsored by the Department of Spanish and Portuguese, the Latin American Studies Program, the Research Center for the Language Sciences, the Department of French and Italian, and the Committee for Research and Development in Language Instruction, all of Indiana University.

The first Linguistic Symposium on Romance Languages took place at the University of Florida in February 1971. The handbook of that symposium stated its goals:

> . . . to bring forth novel contributions in the description of Romance languages, to draw attention to phenomena that might be of importance in the constant re-examination of our theoretical views, and to suggest formulation of more adequate methods for foreign language teaching.

LSRL was such a success that a number of the participants resolved that it should be the first of a series. Accordingly, the second symposium was held in April 1972 at the University of Illinois, Urbana, under the title Conference on Diachronic Romance Linguistics, and LSRL III followed in March 1973 at Indiana University. The proceedings of the first LSRL are published as <u>Generative Studies in Romance Languages</u> (Jean Casagrande and Bohdan Saciuk, eds.; Rowley, Newbury House, 1972) and the proceedings of the Illinois conference, <u>Diachronic Studies in Romance Languages</u> (Mario Saltarelli and Dieter Wanner, eds.; The Hague, Mouton) are in press.

The LSRL series owes its success to the enthusiam and excitement of the linguists whose field is the intersection of modern linguistic theory and the Romance languages, and to the feeling of

community among them. In organizing LSRL III, we have had the
enthusiastic support of a number of people, and it is our pleasure to
thank them for their efforts. In addition to those participants who
presented papers at the symposium, we would like to thank William
Cressey, Marta Luján, Richard Kayne, Dieter Wanner, David B.
Pisoni, Daniel Quilter, David L. Wolfe, and Jean Casagrande for
adding their insights as discussants, and Edward N. Burstynsky and
Josep Roca-Pons for their roles as session chairmen. We would also
like to express our thanks to the members of the program committee
for their collaboration in choosing the papers to be presented: Jean
Casagrande, William Cressey, Daniel Dinnsen, David Fagan, Andreas
Koutsoudas, Michael Mazzola, María-Luisa Rivero, Mario Saltarelli,
Albert Valdman, David L. Wolfe, and Dieter Wanner.

In addition to the linguists and Romanists who helped make the
symposium a success, we would like to thank the Department of Spanish and Portuguese, the Latin American Studies Program, the Research Center for the Language Sciences, the Department of French
and Italian, and the Committee for Research and Development in Language Instruction for their sponsorship. We are grateful to many individual faculty and staff members, students, and friends for assistance
with the details of transportation, registration, and conviviality. We
would especially like to mention Gregory Brown, Trini Campbell,
Mal Compitello, Thomas Creviston-Cox, Margaret Dean, Violeta
Demonte, Augustine Domínguez, Thomas Giometti, Ellen Horn, Mark
Long, Roberta Yankiver Long, Barbara Lotito, Paul Rose, David
Stead, Sylvia Straub, and Margarita Suñer.

Finally, we want to try to verbalize what may not fit into the normal mold of the words 'thank you': the kind of gratitude you owe someone for special effort on your behalf before you think you have earned
the right to it. We thank John V. Lombardi, chairman of the Latin
American Studies Program at Indiana University, for his sympathy,
his practical advice, and his timely and persistent forcefulness--in
short, for his 'godfather' role in supporting LSRL III.

RJC
MGG
MCW

CONTENTS

ON THE CONDITIONED LOSS AND RESTITUTION OF LATIN -s̲

ERIC P. HAMP

University of Chicago

1. G. Bernardi Perini (1972) in his 'Appunti per la storia e la preistoria di -s̲ latino' has reviewed carefully and lucidly the recurring debate on this complex question and has brought to it welcome points of clarification and decision. He has seen certain aspects much more clearly than I did when I considered the matter more than a decade ago (Hamp 1959). While I still hold Proskauer's (1910) work in high regard for its time, I must immediately grant that Bernardi Perini's criticism is well founded when he insists on the inherent skewing in representation of the vocalisms induced by the structure of the inscriptions; Proskauer overlooked the true nature of her sample and proceeded then to misevaluate the possibility of a preceding long vowel. I failed to notice this distortion. Bernardi Perini is quite justified, then, in asserting (258) that -s̲ was lost regardless of the quality or quantity of the preceding vowel.

I agree with Bernardi Perini, too, in accepting (262) Belardi's (1965) argument that in context Cicero's opposition of subrusticum to politius[1] referred to a chronology of stylistic value. Bernardi Perini is further right in insisting, in light of the other facts, that Cicero need not be interpreted restrictively from his examples (263-65) with respect to the vowel length preceding the -s̲. Everything, then, conforms well to Bernardi Perini's assertion (270) of la caduta di -s̲ dopo vocale lunga. There is no conflict between the inscriptions, known metrics, and the critical testimony of antiquity.

This said, I believe we may now carry the argument one stage farther than Bernardi Perini left it. In passing, I must first remark that I do not follow his reasoning (274) that the timbre -us̲ could

1

develop only after the restitution of -s, a point on which I am pleased
to say that Bernardi Perini now (per litt.) agrees with me. Surely
if the pair of alternants (contextually induced) had developed -o ~ -os,
with the closing of the vowel we may arrive at -o ~ -us; then with the
elimination of the first variant, i. e. the 'restitution' of -s, we arrive
immediately at -us. In this respect I see no reason to alter my view
as previously expressed (1959).

For me, the strongest point in Bernardi Perini's argument is to
be derived from his remarks (276) regarding length in final syllables
--an argument which he does not drive as far as he might. He correctly perceives that the preservation of final long vowels in Latin
cannot be without connection with the conservation of final-syllable
length before only -s. But we may link these two facts even more
closely than Bernardi Perini does, and at the same time the non-
phonetic explanation advanced by him becomes unnecessary. We need
only suppose that after -s was lost in certain contexts vowels were
shortened before all final consonants, including s. Thus the contextual
instances where -s was lost were able to preserve their vocalic length.
Later, when -s was once again generalized from the instances or contexts where it was not lost, it came to stand once again, unlike other
consonants, after long vowels. On the other hand, the long-vowel
variant was preferred when the -s was restored because it gave a
much better means of preserving many inflexional distinctions. In
fact, since underlying -os had by now become [-us] (see the preceding paragraph above), it may be that [-os] was immediately and directly interpreted by speakers as underlying -ōs.

We may therefore envisage the following chronology of alternations:

    I   -os,   -ōs (i. e. no alternation)

    II > -o ~ -os, -ō ~ -ōs

    III > -o ~ -us, -ō ~ -os

    IV (>   -ō ~ -ōs)

    V > -us,   -ōs

Thus we may say, paradoxically, that the best argument for the
earlier loss of -s after long vowels is the apparent preservation of
length before -s.

As for the context where -s was lost, now that we see that the
preceding vowel did not have any distinguishing effect, it seems best
to follow the formulation of antiquity (e. g. Cicero) at least in major

part. I would propose, both on phonetic grounds[2] and on analogy with
known developments in internal syllables in Latin, that -ṣ was lost
before initial voiced consonants and that it was preserved before
initial vowels. It would be reasonable that at first -ṣ was also preserved before initial voiceless stops, at least in fast speech, despite
Cicero's <u>Omnibu princeps</u>.

Finally, we must thank Bernardi Perini for rescuing Otrębski's
(1924) morphological arguments from oblivion. I share Bernardi
Perini's judgments about many of them (282); certainly points 3 and 4
gain improved motivation by the hypothesis of an early phonetic loss
of -ṣ.[3]

2. We may now formulate these assumed changes as a succession
of excerpts from grammars expressed in the terms of generative
phonological rules. At first the grammar of Latin contained no such
rules applicable to the class of segments in question [Vs#]. Then it
developed the rule (at stage A)

A. (1) $\text{s} \rightarrow \text{zero} / \text{V} \_\_ \# \begin{bmatrix} -\text{voc} \\ +\text{voice} \end{bmatrix}$

(assuming that the context was first before voiced consonants).[4]
Next, another rule(s) was added changing vowel quality (height)

B. (1) $\text{s} \rightarrow \text{zero} / \text{V} \_\_ \# [??]$[5]

   (2) $\begin{bmatrix} \text{V} \\ -\text{low} \end{bmatrix} \rightarrow [+\text{high}] / \_\_ \text{C}\#$

This rule merges <u>o</u> with <u>u</u> and <u>e</u> with <u>i</u> in this position; it may easily
be part of the set of rules adjusting the quality and height of non-initial
syllabics.[6] Probably the context for rule (2) should better be stated
$\begin{bmatrix} -\text{length} \\ \_\_\_\_\_ \end{bmatrix} \text{C}\#$.
After this, yet another rule was added:

C. (1) $\text{s} \rightarrow \text{zero} / \text{V} \_\_ \# [??]$

   (2) $\text{V} \rightarrow [+\text{high}] / \begin{bmatrix} -\text{length} \\ \_\_\_\_\_ \end{bmatrix} \text{C}\#$

   (3) $[+\text{length}] \rightarrow [-\text{length}] / \_\_ \text{C}\#$

Subsequently (3) was revised to allow length before -ṣ; i.e. the rule
was complicated by one feature further.

D. (1) s → zero / V __ # [? ?]

(2) V → [+high] / $\begin{bmatrix} \text{-length} \\ \underline{\hspace{1.5em}} \end{bmatrix}$ C#

(3) [+length] → [-length] / __ [-strident] #

Rule (3) in this form is probably related to the compensatory lengthening before spirants upon loss of nasal in that position. Therefore the context is better formulated [-continuant] instead of [-strident]. If *n had been preserved sufficiently late before final -s, its absorption accompanied by vowel lengthening would have laid the groundwork for this revision (and generalization) of rule (3).[7]

Finally, representing the chronology of Cicero's politius to sub-rusticum[1] (and of course whatever chronological linguistic or dialectal realities this stylistic trait rested on), rule (1) was eliminated:

E. (1) V → [+high] / $\begin{bmatrix} \text{-length} \\ \underline{\hspace{1.5em}} \end{bmatrix}$ C#

(2) [+length] → [-length] / __ [-continuant] #

We see then that by comparison with stage C, with the addition of one feature to old rule (3) the language has now eliminated old rule (1). We may view this dropping of a rule between stages D and E as a kind of simplification. With this simplification we arrive at the sort of Latin depicted by the schoolbooks.

I have already claimed (1959) that the practice of the poetae novi was a stylistic move in the direction of realism. We may now add to this the assertion that this literary change and the necessarily presupposed linguistic change were moves in the direction of grammatical simplicity. Even if the 'restitution' of -s appears to be a return to an older state, it is not like an insistence on whom in English, or on a liberal use of subjunctives, or on the use in katharévousa Greek of long disused declensions or datives or perfects. All of the latter represent proliferations of form, additional complexities to the grammatical rules. In our case we have a clear and simple instance of simplification, of rule elimination. Latin may be said to have undone a bit of the complexity it had been accumulating over the past few centuries.

3. Because in my earlier attempt (1959) I accepted Proskauer's finding that -s was lost in early Latin only after certain vowels I was unable to find a direct correlation between that early event and the known loss of final -s at an early date in Eastern Romance.[8] In

Eastern Romance -s was lost after vowels regardless of their length (but not in Italian monosyllables), and the loss after long vowels (as in the feminine plural) is particularly noticeable and filled with consequence. As a result of Bernardi Perini's findings and as a corollary to my above argument and formulation, we are now in a position to reverse my statement of 1959, to make a much more positive link with the Romance phenomena, and to derive an interesting implication for the detailed mechanism of linguistic change which is not without purport for more general theory.

Stage E above has been formulated for the Classical Latin outcome, in which the old alternation (rule (1) of D) has been eliminated and the underlying forms in -Vs# then surface. The observed outcome in Western Romance is also to be derived from E with the same underlying forms. Let us now consider a dialect variant derived from D wherein rule (1) yields the alternation -V ~ -Vs, from which -V is chosen (lexicalized) as the underlying form.

Apart from the fact that (if this V were as general as has just been implied) with underlying -V the old (D) rule (1) would apply vacuously, we may suppose that whatever pari passu was chosen as the underlying form the old rule (1) was also eliminated from this grammar. That is to say, some underlying forms in -Vs (e. g. in -V̄s) could have subsisted, but e. g. -V̄s could have been supplanted by -V̄; the resulting details would be different, but the general principle would be the same if the old rule (1) were eliminated.

Additionally, if underlying - V̄s had been set aside in favor of -V̄, the form of the rule seen in E (2) would be simpler since there would now be no need to specify the feature context [-continuant]. For such a dialect, which we see is the exact precursor of Eastern Romance, with underlying -V̄ in the instances discussed, the following rules apply:

E'. (1) $V \rightarrow [+high] / \begin{bmatrix} -length \\ \underline{\hspace{1.5em}} \end{bmatrix} C\#$

(2) $[+length] \rightarrow [-length] / \underline{\hspace{1em}} C\#$

In this respect, the rule structure of Eastern Romance was simpler than that of Western Romance.

We see, nevertheless, how by lexicalizing different alternants in the two dialect areas the same rule structure, in nearly the same form, applies. And we succeed thereby in deriving both major variants of Romance from the same Early Latin grammar. Each therefore preserves an aspect of archaism, and neither requires the assumption of a separate departure.

6 / ERIC P. HAMP

NOTES

[1]Quin etiam, quod iam subrusticum uidetur, olim autem politius, eorum uerborum quorum eaedem erant postremae duae litterae quae sunt in 'optimus' postremam litteram detrahebant nisi uocalis insequebatur. Ita non erat ea offensio in uersibus quam nunc fugiunt poetae noui.

[2]Voicing assimilation of [s] to [z] before a voiced consonant and then absorption of the [z] in voiced surroundings are two phonetic developments that are natural and widely attested in languages.

[3]Points 3 and 4 relate to the loss of the inherited IE -ās in the genitive sg. and nominative pl. of ā-stem (first declension) nouns.

[4]Incorporating Bernardi Perini's mention of *sizdō, *poznō, which I agree in finding highly pertinent, we might revise the context of rule (1) (after lengthening to yield *sīzdō, pōznō) to read

$$V \_\_ (\#) \begin{bmatrix} -voc \\ +voice \end{bmatrix}.$$

[5]At some stage generalization (= rule simplification by elimination of features) may have taken place in speech matching what we find in metrics and in Cicero's statement; alternatively, the metrical convention may have been just a simplification of the more complex linguistic rule. For Cicero the material in the bracket was simply [-voc].

[6]Those rules, which I deal with on another occasion, are not so complex as the handbooks tend to make them seem.

[7]I am indebted to Bernardi Perini for having called my attention to the important role of *-ns, which I would see not so much as restituting the -s as perhaps restoring the privilege of occurrence of long vowels.

[8]Eastern Romance here means roughly Italian and the Balkans (= Romanian plus the Albanian contacts). W. von Wartburg, Die Ausgliederung der romanischen Sprachräume (Bern 1950), 20-31 assigns the Piedmont, Liguria, Lombardy, Emilia, Venetia to Western Romance.

REFERENCES

Belardi, W. 1965. Di una notizia di Cicerone (Orator 161) su -s finale latino. Rivista di cultura classica e medioevale = Studi in onore di A. Schiaffini, 114-42.
Bernardi Perini, G. 1972. Appunti per la storia e la preistoria di -s latino. In: Dignam Dis a Giampaolo Vallot, pp. 247-84. Padova.
Hamp, Eric P. 1959. Final -s in Latin. Classical Philology. 54.165-72.

Otrębski, J. 1924. Z dziejów języka łacińskiego (o zachowaniu się wygłosowego -s̲ po samogłosce długiej). Wilno. (résumé: Le traitement de -s̲ final après une voyelle longue en latin, pp. 107-15.)

Proskauer, C. 1910. Das auslautende -s̲ auf lateinischen Inschriften. Strassburg.

MORPHOLOGIZATION OF PHONOLOGICAL RULES: AN EXAMPLE FROM CHICANO SPANISH*

JAMES W. HARRIS

Massachusetts Institute of Technology

1. Introduction. It is widely held, I believe, that purely phonological rules can become morphologized in language change; in other
words, a rule that at one historical stage requires no morphological
information in its environment may at a later stage require such information. The best known example is probably umlaut in German.
At an early stage, the rule could be stated entirely in phonological
terms, roughly as follows:

$$V \rightarrow [\text{-back}] / \underline{\quad} C_0 i, \, j$$

Vowels are fronted by a following high front vowel or glide. In time,
however, the phonological motivation for umlaut was obscured or lost
entirely, and the rule became dependent on morphological conditions.
   Although my impression is that I have heard, and participated in,
a fair amount of loose discussion of phonological rules becoming
morphologized, it is nevertheless surprisingly difficult to find in
print explicit discussions of specific examples. The case just cited,
umlaut in German, is, as far as I know, the only one that has pro-
voked extended and explicit discussion in the generative literature.[1]
That a double standard exists with regard to the morphologization of
phonological rules--nearly everybody assumes it can happen but almost nobody writes about it explicitly--can be substantiated by the
fact that Kiparsky could state in 'Historical linguistics' (1971) that
'examples of [one type of rule opacity] are commonplace [emphasis
mine, J.W.H.]. This case is simply the initial stage of the process
of morphologization, by which rules lose their phonological conditioning

and begin to be dependent on abstract features in the lexicon' (634).
The example following this passage is, not surprisingly, German umlaut. On the other hand, the subject of morphologization is not mentioned at all in King's Historical Linguistics and Generative Grammar,
which provides thorough and penetrating coverage of work in the field
right up to the date of publication (1969). [2]

No doubt the main reason why there is a paucity of explicit discussion of specific examples of rule morphologization in the generative
literature is that generative grammar has not officially included a
theory of morphology. In the absence of such a theory, it may not be
clear, in specific cases, what the difference is between a phonological
rule and a morphological rule, and it may thus be difficult to talk
about a phonological rule becoming a morphological rule. Again we
find a double standard: although morphology has remained relatively
unexplored up to the present in generative grammar, it is my impression that few generative grammarians doubt that a grammar has a
component that accounts for the form and composition of words. [3]

I will be concerned in this paper with the diphthongization of mid
vowels in Chicano Spanish. I will argue that the diphthongization rule
in Chicano is a morphologized version of the ancestral phonological
rule of diphthongization still represented in standard Mexican Spanish
and other dialects. The argument contains the following components:
(a) the standard rule is indeed phonological rather than morphological,
(b) the corresponding rule in Chicano is in part morphologized, but
certain effects of the ancestral rule have not been 'lexicalized' by
restructuring of underlying representations, and (c) the terminology
'phonological rule' versus '(partially) morphologized rule' makes
sense as used here, or, in any event, the distinction drawn between
the two rules is substantive rather than terminological.

Invaluable historical data are available that suggest that the phenomena of diphthongization in Chicano are in the initial stages of a
process of rapid change. Thus this dialect deserves careful watching
at present and in the near future, as an excellent laboratory specimen
for the theory of linguistic change.

In sum, the present paper has the following threefold purpose: (1)
to call attention to Chicano Spanish, in the hope that the excellent
studies of it begun by Aurelio Espinosa (1930, 1946) and continued by
Rogelio Reyes (forthcoming) will find worthy successors, (2) to add
one example to the tiny sample of cases of rule morphologization discussed in detail in generative studies, and (3) to make a small contribution to the nascent but long overdue study of morphology in generative grammar. [4]

2. Diphthongization in standard Spanish

2.1. The simple cases. The diphthongization of mid vowels is a
common and pervasive feature of Spanish. The beginning language
student encounters it early on, under the rubric of 'stem-changing
verbs'. Verbs of this type are illustrated in (1). Second person
plural forms are enclosed in parentheses since not all speakers use
them.

(1)   'heat'   'cook'

    a. Present indicative

	Singular	Plural	Singular	Plural
Person: 1	caliénto	calentámos	cuézo	cocémos
2	caliéntas	(calentáis)	cuéces	(cocéis)
3	caliénta	caliéntan	cuéce	cuécen

    b. Present subjunctive

caliénte	calentémos	cueza	cozamos
caliéntes	(calentéis)	cuézas	(cozáis)
caliénte	caliénten	cueza	cuézan

Orthographic ue and ie represent phonetic [we] and [ye], respectively.
(The stem-final c ~ z alternation in 'cook' is purely orthographic; both
letters spell [s] in Latin American and [θ] in Castilian Spanish.) As
can be seen, the stems of these verbs alternate between calient-/cuez-
and calent-/coz- . The diphthongal alternant occurs when stress falls
on the stem, and the monophthongal alternant occurs when stress falls
to the right of the stem. Present indicative and subjunctive paradigms
have both alternants; all other paradigms have only unstressed stems.[5]
    What textbooks regularly fail to point out is that e ~ ie and o ~ ue
alternations are not restricted to verb paradigms, or in fact to any
other morphological category or derivational type. Consider the
following sets of forms, which include all the main 'parts of speech'
except certain inherently unstressable ones (e.g. articles):

(2) Stressed diphthong   Unstressed monophthong

    a. caliénte 'hot' (Adj)   calentadór 'heater' (N)--cf.
                              caliént- ~ calent- 'heat' (Vb)
    b. cuénta 'count, count-   contáble 'countable' (Adj)--cf.
        ing' (N)   cuént- ~ cont- 'count' (Vb)

c. meriénda 'light
supper' (N)

merendéro 'place to eat meriéndas'
(N)--cf. meriénd- ~ merend⁼
'eat a light supper' (Vb)

d. viéjo 'old' (Adj),
'old man' (N)

vejéz 'old age' (N)

e. fuéra 'outside' (Adv)

forastéro 'from outside' (Adj),
'outsider' (N)

f. nuéstro 'our' (Poss
Adj)

nosótros 'we, us' (Pron)

g. siéte 'seven' (Det, N)

seténta 'seventy' (Det, N)

h. nuéve 'nine' (Det, N)

novénta 'ninety' (Det, N)

i. diéz 'ten' (Det, N)

decéna 'set of ten' (N)--like dóce
'twelve'/docéna 'dozen'

j. pués (Conjunction?)

pos (unstressed variant of pués)[6]

This list could be extended as long as anyone wished, with no difficulty.

As will have been noticed, not all unstressed e's and o's alternate
with stressed diphthongs. In fact this alternation is slightly exceptional. There are countless instances of stressed, undiphthongized e and
o in Spanish words, as can be seen in (1) and (2) above; e.g. calentémos,
cocémos, calentadór, merendéro, vejéz, nosótros, dóce, etc. There
is no morphological restriction on non-diphthongizing e and o, both of
which occur in all possible form classes. To give only one contrast
between diphthongizing and non-diphthongizing mid vowels, there is a
verb coser 'to sew', which is identical to the verb 'cook' illustrated
in (1), except that 'to sew' does not diphthongize:

(3) Present indicative

cóso   cosémos
cóses   (coséis)
cóse   cósen

Present subjunctive

cósa   cosámos
cósas   (cosáis)
cósa   cósan

Furthermore, there is no phonetic difference between the e's and o's
that diphthongize and those that do not. For example, cocémos/
cosémos and cozámos/cosámos are absolutely homophonous pairs.
In short, what we must say at this point about standard Spanish is
simply that there are mid vowels that alternate with diphthongs and
otherwise identical mid vowels that do not alternate with diphthongs,
the latter being in the majority.

The data discussed so far can be summarized in the following rule,
which although quite informal is sufficiently precise for present purposes. [7]

(4) Diphthongization (standard Spanish)

$$\begin{bmatrix} e \\ o \end{bmatrix} \rightarrow \begin{bmatrix} ye \\ we \end{bmatrix} \ / \ \overline{\quad} \ [+\text{stress}] \quad \text{MINOR RULE}$$

The fact that (4) is a minor rule reflects the slightly exceptional nature of diphthongization. Those e's and o's that do diphthongize are assigned the rule feature [+diphthongization rule] in the lexicon, as exceptions (in that they undergo a minor rule); non-diphthongizing e's and o's are not assigned this lexical feature. [8]

It does not follow from anything said so far that all instances of the diphthongs [ye] and [we] in phonetic representations are the result of rule (4). There are many examples of these diphthongs, both stressed and unstressed, that do not alternate with e and o, or with anything else. A small sample is given in (5):

(5) Stressed   Unstressed
     diéta 'diet'   dietético 'dietetic, dietary'
     siluéta 'silhouette'   silueteádo 'silhouetted'

In such examples, the diphthongs occur within a single morpheme, diet- and siluet-, which is segmentally invariable--there is no *det- or *silot-. I would postulate the underlying representations /dyet-/ and /silwet-/ (or at least nothing more abstract than /diet-/, /siluet-/), and similarly for all such non-alternating diphthongs. Obviously the examples in question have nothing to do with rule (4). [9]

The diphthongs [ye] and [we] can also appear both stressed and unstressed in phonetic representations, accidentally as it were, because of the juxtaposition of two morphemes each of which contains one element of the diphthong:

(6) Stressed   Unstressed
     variémos 'vary' (1st   variedád 'variety'
       pers plu pres subjunct)
     limpiémos 'clean' (1st   límpie 'clean' (3rd pers sing
       pers plu pres subjunct)   pres subjunct)

Variémos is morphologically vari+e+mos, and variedád is vari+e+dad. A general rule of glide formation changes i+e to [ye]. Limpiémos is limpy+e+mos, and límpie is limpy+e. [10] Obviously, examples like these also have nothing to do with rule (4).

To summarize and conclude this section, standard Spanish has a rule of diphthongization, formulated roughly in (4), that controls e ~ ye and o ~ we alternations. These alternations are somewhat

exceptional and are determined idiosyncratically, i. e. lexically.
There is no correlation whatsoever between diphthongization, or its
absence, and morphological categories. Stress is the conditioning
factor for the diphthongal member of the alternation (nothing could
show this more clearly, at least for Mexican Spanish, than (2j),
pués ~ pos). Finally, the 'psychological reality' of rule (4) is hardly
open to question: unsolicited testimonials are available like that of
the Spanish philologist Vicente García de Diego who remarks that the
alternation between stressed diphthongs and unstressed monophthongs
is a 'juego . . . del que tiene nuestra lengua una conciencia viva'
(1961:243).

As a postscript let us briefly consider the suggestion, which has
been made independently a number of times, that Spanish does not
have a rule of diphthongization like (4), but rather that non-diphthongizing mid vowels are represented as underlying simple vowels and the
alternating pairs e ~ ie and o ~ ue are represented as underlying
diphthongs; no (relevant) rule applies to the former, and an 'anti-
diphthongization' or monophthongization rule converts the latter into
simple vowels when they are unstressed. Although I have not seen
the arguments formulated carefully, it is presumably thought to be a
virtue of the anti-diphthongization proposal (henceforth AP) that no
arbitrary diacritic such as [+diphthongization rule] is needed to distinguish non-diphthongizing from diphthongizing mid vowels since these
are now distinct in underlying representations. I do not believe that
the AP is tenable, and will sketch the outlines of several arguments
against it, but without going into much detail. Observe first that the
AP does not entirely escape the objection that presumably motivated
it in the first place, namely the use of diacritic exception-marking
features. Unstressed diphthongs of the type illustrated in (5) and (6)
must somehow be exempted from the anti-diphthongization rule. This
cannot be done, say, by representing non-alternating and alternating
underlying diphthongs as /ye, we/ and /ie, ue/, respectively, or conversely. In the first place, such distinct representations would be at
best merely a notational trick, since no motivation can be given, as
far as I know, for the choice of one or the other set of representations
for one or the other type of diphthong. Worse, the trick cannot work
anyway, since unstressed surface diphthongs must be derived from
both /ie/ (vari+e+dád) and /ye/ (límpy+e), as shown in (6). In short,
the AP cannot avoid appeal to non-phonological distinctions. An
a priori argument against the AP can be formulated on the basis of
considerations of 'naturalness' or 'markedness': a good many linguists would probably agree that, all other things being equal, a
system containing the five underlying vowels i, e, a, o, u plus a
diphthongization rule is 'better' than a system containing the same
underlying vowels plus two underlying diphthongs and a

monophthongization rule. However one feels about this weak argument, there are compellingly strong non-aprioristic, empirical, reasons to reject the AP. Consider third conjugation verb forms such as partír (infinitive), partímos (present indicative and preterit), partído (past participle), etc. The underlined i is the so-called 'theme vowel' of the third conjugation--cf. first conjugation hartár, hartámos, hartádo. The statement of a number of important generalizations requires that the underlying representation of the third conjugation theme vowel be /i/--see Harris (1969:104-16), Brame and Bordelois (1973), and Harris (forthcoming). In certain forms, however, this theme vowel surfaces as the (stressed) diphthong ie: partiéndo (present participle or gerund), partiéra (past subjunctive), etc.--cf. first conjugation hartándo, hartára. Now, it is a relatively straightforward matter to specify the (partly morphological) environments in which this thematic i is lowered to e, with subsequent diphthongization, under stress, to ie, by rule (4). On the other hand, I see no way in which the AP could accommodate these data without a massive loss of generalizations.

2.2. More complex cases. In the overwhelming majority of instances of e ~ ye and o ~ we alternations, the monophthong appears unstressed and the diphthong stressed, as described in the previous section. There remains a small residue of cases in which the diphthongal member of these alternations may appear both stressed and unstressed, in phonetic representations.[11] Examples of unstressed alternating diphthongs are found regularly in three classes of morphologically complex words: diminutives of adjectives and nouns, superlatives of adjectives, and certain types of derived verbs. A sample is given in (7), where underived base words are in the left column; the morphologically complex diminutives, superlatives, and derived verbs in question are in the middle column; and other related forms are in the right column:

(7)

	Stressed diphthong	Unstressed diphthong	Mid vowel
a.	ciégo 'blind (man)'	cieguíto (Dimin) ieguísimo (Superl)	ceguéra 'blindness' cegár 'to blind'
b.	diéstro 'skillful'	diestrísimo (Superl) adiestrár 'to make skillful'	destréza 'skill'
c.	viéjo 'old (man)'	viejíto (Dimin) viejísimo (Superl) aviejár 'to get old'	vejéz 'old age'
d.	muéble 'piece of furniture'	muebl(ec)íto (Dimin) amueblár 'to furnish'	mobláje '(set of) furniture'

Diminutive and superlative affixation is as freely productive as any kind of derivational process ever is in any language; the type of verb derivation illustrated is also productive, though less often actually used. [12]

In Harris (1969:125-26) I accounted for unstressed alternating diphthongs, in the derivational classes mentioned, as illustrated in (8):

(8) [[vej] it+o]$_N$ [[vej] isim+c]$_A$ [a[vej] a+r]$_V$ Inner cycle:
　　 véj　　　　　 véj　　　　　　 véj　　　　　 Stress
　　　　　　　　　　　　　　　　　　　　　　　　 Word level:
　　 véj ſto　　　 véj ſsimo　　　 a véj ár　　　 Stress
　　 viéjſto　　　 viéjſsimo　　　 aviéjár　　　 Diphthongization
　　 viejſto　　　 viejſsimo　　　 aviejár　　　 Erase non-right-
　　　　　　　　　　　　　　　　　　　　　　　　 most stresses

The internal constituent structure shown in (8) imposes cyclical assignment of stress. No other rules apply cyclically, and the rule of diphthongization is the same stress-governed one given in (4). No such internal structure is postulated for underived nouns and adjectives (e. g. viej+o, whose -o is a gender marker), or underived verbs (e. g. ceg+a+r, whose -a- is an empty conjugational-class marker and whose -r is the infinitival inflection), or words of non-productive derivational types (e. g. vej+ez, ceg(u)+era, mobl+aje, whose suffixes are distributed idiosyncratically, that is lexically--there is no *vej+aje, *ceg(u)+ez, or *mobl+era).

It is important to observe at this point that the constituent structure postulated in (8) is not ad hoc, i. e. concocted solely to explain away certain phonetically unstressed diphthongs. Instead, the same constituent structure also provides the basis for a natural account of another, totally independent, phonetic anomaly in exactly the same three types of derivationally complex words. This is the anomalous non-application of a rule (mentioned just below (6)) that changes unstressed high vowels to glides when contiguous to another vowel. Consider the examples in (9):

(9) Sofía (proper name), diminutive Sofiíta [sofiíta] *sofyíta]
　　　 *[sofíta]
　　 frío 'cold', superlative friísimo [friísimo] *[fryísimo]
　　　 *[frísimo]
　　 israelí 'Israeli', aisraeliar 'to Israeli-ize' [aisraeliár]
　　　 [aÿsraelyár][13]

Constituent structure and (phonological derivations are as in (10):

(10) [[sofi] it+a]$_N$ [[fri] isim+o]$_A$ [a[israel+i] a+r]$_V$ Inner cycle:
      sofí   frí   ìsrael f   Stress
                                                          Word level:
      sofí íta   frí ísimo   a ìsrael f ár   Stress
                                                          Glide BLOCKED
      <u>sofiíta</u>   <u>friísimo</u>   <u>aisraeliár</u>   Stress erasure

In underived nouns, adjectives, and verbs, and in non-productively
derived words, where no internal constituent structure is postulated,
glide formation is not blocked, within a morpheme or across a boundary, even in cases in which the vowel in question is stressed in the
underived form:

(11) <u>frío</u> 'cold'   <u>frialdád</u> [fryaldáδ] 'coldness'
      <u>Perú</u> 'Peru'   <u>peruáno</u> [perwáno] 'Peruvian'
      <u>vacío</u> 'empty(ness)'   <u>vaciár</u> [basyár] 'to empty'

In spite of recently proposed alternatives to a word-internal stress
cycle in English (e.g. Ross (1972), Schane (1972)), and with the reser-
vations to be voiced directly, I persist in believing that the derivations
illustrated in (8) and (10) are essentially correct. Restricting our
attention to the major topic, diphthongization, the following facts can
be adduced in support of this view. For an impressionistic start, to
the extent that native-speaker intuitions concerning the 'derivationally
complex' words in question can be elicited, it can be said that native
speakers feel that such words (e.g. <u>viejíto</u>) contain a virtually intact
phonetic representation of the base word (e.g. <u>viéjo</u>), in a sense in
which lexically derived words (e.g. <u>vejéz</u>) do not. The proposed
constituent structure provides a natural reconstruction of this intuition.
More to the point technically is the fact that there is no case in which
a diminutive or superlative has a simple vowel while the underived
form has a diphthong, or conversely. For example, no set like
<u>viéjo</u>/*<u>vejíto</u>/*<u>vejísimo</u> or *<u>véjo</u>/<u>viejíto</u>/<u>viejísimo</u> (or worse, ran-
domly distributed mid vowels and diphthongs as in <u>viéjo</u>/<u>viejíto</u>/
*<u>vejísimo</u>, *<u>véjo</u>/*<u>vejíto</u>/<u>viejísimo</u>, and so on) exists, or indeed
could even possibly be improvised as a joke by the productive process
in question. Even more crucially, in cases with polysyllabic roots
(e.g. <u>merend-</u>), it is precisely the vowel that is diphthongized under
stress in the appropriate base form (e.g. <u>meriénda</u>) and no other
vowel, that appears as a (phonetically unstressed) diphthong in the
complex derived word (e.g. <u>meriendíta</u>, but *<u>merendíta</u>, *<u>mierendíta</u>,
*<u>mieriendíta</u>, as opposed to lexically derived <u>merend+éro</u>, <u>merend+ár</u>).
Exactly this complex set of facts follows automatically from the proposed constituent structure. This would not be the case on an account
in which 'lexical' ('concatenative') derivation is not distinguished from

'freely productive' ('hierarchical') derivation, and in which the appearance of phonetically unstressed diphthongs in the 'productively
derived' words in question is not directly predicted from the diphthongization, under stress, of a particular vowel in the appropriate
base form.[14] In short, the description proposed above achieves
descriptive adequacy.

Of course, the study of derivational processes, and of morphology
in general, is in its infancy in generative grammar. It is altogether
possible, even likely, that as we grope toward a fuller understanding
of generative morphology, the proposals made above will be superseded. It is easy to envision, but hard to formulate precisely, some
alternative way of capturing the genuine (I believe) insight that words
like, say, viejíto contain an 'island' consisting of (the phonetic representation, almost, of) the independent word viéjo.[15]

Incidentally, the data presented here suggest a constraint that
could be formulated as a necessary (but not sufficient) condition on
the no doubt too powerful current theory of phonological cycles.
Stated loosely, it might be proposed that (a) material contained in a
word-internal cycle must exist as an independent word (with the
possible addition of inflections, e.g. gender and number in Spanish),
and (b) the meaning of the containing word must be predictable. All
the relevant Spanish examples clearly conform to both parts of this
constraint, but much more investigation would be necessary to determine the precise form of such a condition that would be tenable in
general.

In order to give a comprehensive description of words like those
in (7), it has been necessary to partially bury the main point of this
section, namely that diphthongization, i.e. application of rule (4) in
standard Mexican Spanish is in ALL cases phonologically rather than
morphologically conditioned (although the phonological conditioning
factor, stress, does not necessarily appear in all outputs of (4) in
phonetic representations). That point should be clear now. The environment of rule (4) contains a single phonological feature [+stress],
and no morphological restriction. Its status as a minor rule re-
stricts its application to lexically marked items, but this lexical
restriction completely cross-cuts morphological categories. The
same rule applies in the (phonological) derivation of complex words
like those illustrated in (8), no differently than in morphologically
simpler words, as a word-level rule, whenever its (phonological)
environment is met, namely to lexically marked stressed mid vowels,
again across morphological categories.[16]

3. Diphthongization in Chicano. It will be perfectly legitimate to
imagine, for expository simplicity, that Chicano Spanish is exactly
like standard Mexican Spanish, except as explicitly noted herein.[17]

The one relevant systematic difference is illustrated in (12) with a number of inflected forms of the verb that means 'fly':

(12) infinitive: vuelár
     past participle: vueládo
     gerund: vuelándo
     present indicative: vuélo   vuelámos
                         vuélas   (2nd pers plu not used)
                         vuéla   vuélan
     imperfect: vuelába, vuelábas, etc.
     preterit: vuelé, vuelátes [sic], vueló, etc.
     past subjunctive: vuelára, vueláras, etc.

The following surprising fact is illustrated in (12): if ANY form of ANY a-theme (first conjugation) verb has the diphthong [we], then ALL forms do, regardless of the position of stress. What is surprising about this is that first conjugation ue-stems are unique in this respect. All other types of Chicano verbs have the same e ~ ie and o ~ ue alternations as in standard Spanish. Specifically, in Chicano both of the expected e ~ ie and o ~ ue alternations occur in the second and third conjugations, and, strikingly, the expected e ~ ie alternation occurs even in the first conjugation (although the o ~ ue alternation does not occur in the first conjugation). Examples are given in (13), with two present indicative forms for each verb. [18]

(13) second conjugation, e ~ ie: tiéne   tenémos
     second conjugation, o ~ ue: puéde   podémos
     first conjugation, e ~ ie: piénsa   pensámos
     first conjugation, o ~ ue: MISSING; only ue, stressed and
                                   unstressed

At first glance, it may seem that the peculiarity of Chicano first conjugation stems with the diphthong ue in all forms is that part of the effect of the ancestral diphthongization rule has been lexicalized. That is, in all stems of this type, the diphthong ue has been incorporated into the underlying representation. For example, the stem 'fly' is no longer /vol-/ as in standard Mexican, but rather /vwel-/, or at the extreme of abstractness /vuel-/. However, forms of the sort illustrated in (14) show that this cannot be the case:

(14) vuel- 'fly'   volador 'flying', 'flyer'
     cuel- 'strain'   colador 'strainer'
     cuent- 'count'   contador 'counter'; (pagar) al contádo '(to
                      pay) in cash--counting it out' (cf. past
                      participle cuentádo)

suelt- 'loosen'   soltúra 'looseness'
rueg- 'beg'   (hacerse del) rogár '(play) hard-to-get--
                  demand to be begged' (cf. inf ruegár)

The ue diphthongs in the strictly verbal stems of (14) are clearly
alternating diphthongs, and they alternate with precisely the simple
vowel o, in non-verb forms. There can be no question about the re-
latedness of the stems of the verbs in (14) to those of the non-verbs--
they are one and the same stem. Ruegar versus hacerse del rogar
makes this transparently clear. To take another example, Chicano
speakers judge cuelar and colador to be related in exactly the same
way as 'to strain' and 'strainer' in English.

What then is the form of the Chicano rule(s) of diphthongization?
The relevant Chicano data are identical to those of standard Mexican
except that Chicano diphthongizes in one additional case, namely unstressed first conjugation verb stems with /o/. Therefore the grammar of Chicano incorporates the standard (phonological, stress-
conditioned) rule of diphthongization, plus some additional principle
to diphthongize /o/ in first conjugation verb stems when it is unstressed, as well as when it is stressed. This additional principle
must be incorporated into the familiar stress-governed rule as a
special case, rather than being stated as an independent rule. The
argument is elementary: the 'special' diphthongization of /o/ gives
the same output [we] as the ordinary case. If an independent rule
were set up, this result would be fortuitous; there would be no
account of the fact that the output is precisely [we]--which is after
all rather odd since [we] shares almost no features with o--rather
than, say, [ye], [wo], [upa], [pti], or whatever.

Thus the single Chicano diphthongization rule must say in effect
'those instances of e and o marked [+diphthongization rule] are diphthongized if (a) they are stressed, and if (b) o is in a first conjugation verb stem (stressed or unstressed).' Still stating the structural
change informally as in (4), the rule can be given as in (15):

(15) Diphthongization (Chicano)[19]

$$
\begin{bmatrix} e \\ o \end{bmatrix} \rightarrow \begin{bmatrix} ye \\ we \end{bmatrix} \Big/ \left\{ \begin{array}{l} [\text{+stress}] \qquad \qquad \text{(a)} \\[2em] \Big[\cdots \big[X[\text{+back}]C_0 \atop 1\ \text{conj} \big]_{\text{Stem}} \cdots \Big]_{\text{Verb}} \quad \text{(b)} \end{array} \right\}
$$

MINOR
RULE

The status of (15) as a minor rule correctly prevents its application to non-diphthongizing first conjugation stems like forz- 'force', whose back vowels do not have the lexical feature [+diphthongization rule].

There is no motivation that I can imagine for postulating internal constituent structure for first conjugation ue-stem verbs in Chicano, whereby the unstressed diphthongs would be produced, mutatis mutandis, as in (8). The utterly ad hoc nature of such constituent structure is revealed by the fact that it would have to be set up solely for first conjugation ue-stems and for no other underived verb forms (recall (13)). In sum, rule (15) succinctly and correctly expresses the generalization that in Chicano, the diphthongization of mid vowels is controlled partly by phonological conditions, case (a); and partly by morphological conditions, case (b).

4. Historical notes and conclusion. It has been argued in the previous sections that standard Mexican Spanish has a relatively simple, strictly phonological, rule of diphthongization, while Chicano Spanish has a more complex version of the rule whose additional complexity lies in an extra morphological condition. Making the entirely non-controversial assumption that the standard version of the rule is the direct lineal ancestor of the Chicano rule, it is fair to ask why the grammar of Chicano got more complicated. A facile, and I believe correct, answer can be given without much thought: the increase in complexity of the rule is more than compensated for by a concomitant .ncrease in paradigmatic uniformity.[20] Compare present indicative paradigms in standard and Chicano Spanish:

(16) Standard   Chicano
      vuélo   volámos   vuélo   vuelámos
      vuélas   vuélas
      vuéla   vuélan   vuéla   vuélan

In Chicano, but not in standard, the verb stem is segmentally invariable. In Chicano present subjunctive paradigms (and in fact all paradigms except present indicative), not only the segmental composition of stems, but also the position of stress is also invariable:

(17) Standard   Chicano
      vuéle   volémos   vuéle   vuélenos [sic]
      vuéles   vuéles
      vuéle   vuélen   vuéle   vuélen

A mystery remains, however. The regularization of stems in the present indicative, that is, the elimination of surface monophthong-diphthong alternations, has occurred only in first conjugation stems with the diphthong ue. Why just this? Why not e ~ ie alternations in the first conjugation? Why not either or both alternations in the other conjugations? The answers to these questions are not immediately obvious, to say the least.

According to Reyes (forthcoming, and personal communication), some Chicano dialects still retain the phonological rule (4) of diphthongization, although the partially morphologized rule (15) has made considerable inroads. Espinosa (1946) presents quite a different picture. He points out that (at the time he was writing) verbs with vowel alternations had undergone almost no changes in New Mexican Spanish (83), and adds that 'formas analógicas como juegámos, piensámos, ruegó, etc., son rarísimas, y si se encuentran pertenecen al lenguaje infantil' (85). Espinosa's fantastically massive and detailed field work was done, if I am not mistaken, in the first decade of this century. Thus it has taken, at most, only about half a century for the appearance of unstressed diphthongs in verb forms to change from an 'extremely rare' child-language over-generalization to the widespread adult phenomenon that it has become in Reyes's generation. Note, incidentally, two things about Espinosa's only examples: (a) they are all first conjugation verbs--he does not say whether or not the same thing happens in other conjugations, and (b) the example piensámos corresponds to pensámos in Reyes's speech, since in his generation only the o ~ ue alternation has been leveled in favor of ue in unstressed verb stems.

It is a stroke of luck that we have Espinosa's highly regarded and reliable description of the state of New Mexican Spanish shortly after the turn of the century. This enables us to gauge with unusual accuracy the time depth of the change that is evidently still going on in the Chicano rule of diphthongization. We have caught Chicano Spanish in the act, red-handed as it were, of initiating the same kind of change that French underwent, in certain forms, over a period of time extending through the twelfth to the sixteenth centuries (Pope 1952:348-64). One example will suffice (whose simplicity may give an erroneous impression of the intricacies of the maze from which it is extracted). Compare the present indicative paradigms of the verb 'love' given in (18):

(18) | Middle French | | Modern French | |
|---|---|---|---|
| áim | amóns | áime | aimóns |
| áins | améz | áimes | améz |
| áint | áiment | áime | áiment |

In middle French, the stem alternation áim- ~ am- shows the result of regular sound change in stressed and unstressed vowels. In modern French, the alternation has been leveled, with aim- occurring both stressed and unstressed in verbs (but not necessarily in non-verb forms, e.g. amóur, amánt). Although this sort of leveling has been widespread in French, it has not succeeded in eliminating all stem alternations in French verbs, as is well known. The parallel with Chicano is obvious. The question is 'What will happen next, and eventually, in Chicano?'[21]

NOTES

*Except as explicitly noted, the description of Chicano Spanish given here is based on the speech of one informant from New Mexico, Rogelio Reyes. Reyes is a deluxe informant since he is both a native speaker and a linguist. My indebtedness to him is total; I could not have written this paper without him. It should be noted that I will henceforth use the term Chicano without qualification, in spite of the fact that there is considerable dialect variation within Chicano Spanish, and the description does not necessarily carry over to dialects other than Reyes's.

[1]I am referring primarily to Zwicky (1967), which offered a morphological account of German umlaut, and to Bach and King (1970), which criticized Zwicky's treatment and argued for a phonological explanation. There are also numerous less detailed references to German umlaut in historical contexts in recent generative studies.

[2]More recently, Vennemann (1972:218-19) mentions briefly an example from Sanskrit, and Hooper (1971:6-10) discusses a portion of the material to be presented in the present paper, from a quite different point of view.

[3]Reference to strictly morphological rules is made in François Dell's 'Les règles phonologiques tardives et la morphologie dérivationnelle du Français' (1970). For some preliminary observations on the 'morphological component' see Morris Halle's 'Prolegomena to a theory of word formation' in Linguistic Inquiry 4 (1973). Strictly morphological rules are also discussed in Harris (forthcoming).

[4]I hope I am wrong, but it does not seem hazardous to speculate that the study of morphology in a generative grammar, unlike the study of phonology and syntax, will reveal little about the human faculté de langage beyond the fact that languages have a morphological system that is complex but not very interesting.

[5]Calient- ~ calent- belongs to the 'first conjugation' (verbs with thematic a); cuez- ~ coz- belongs to the 'second conjugation' (thematic e). For convenience I will ignore 'third conjugation' verbs (thematic i), in which most diphthongizing stems have a third alternant with a high vowel, e.g. duerm- ~ dorm- ~ durm- 'sleep'; and two have a diphthong-high vowel alternation (no mid): adquier- ~ adquir- 'acquire' and inquier- ~ inquir- 'inquire'. (The third '-quire'

verb, 'require', has the three alternants requier- ~ requer- ~ requir- expected in the third conjugation.) Vowel alternations in i-theme verbs are discussed in detail in Harris (1969:104-16), Brame and Bordelois (1973), and Harris (forthcoming). I will also ignore the unique a-theme verb with a ue ~ u alternation, jueg- ~ jug- 'play'.

[6]Pués has several senses or functions. The one intended here is its use as a clause-initial 'fumble word' or hesitation signal. Contrasts like the following are common in standard Mexican Spanish, but not in other dialects:

¿Quién lo hizo? ⎡Pués, éste, . . . yo no fui.⎤
⎣Pŏs yo no fui.   ⎦

Who did it? ⎡Wéll, úh, it wasn't me.⎤
⎣Wĕll it wasn't me.   ⎦

It can hardly be maintained that pos and (the relevant sense of) pues are different words; the contrast illustrated is clearly a matter of different sentence-stress.

[7]In Harris (1969:161-63) this rule is formulated somewhat more carefully: a glide is inserted that agrees in backness with the original vowel, the latter being simultaneously fronted. It may be preferable to consider that the é of both yé and wé is epenthetic, the glides being the reflexes of the original vowels, that is:

$$
\begin{bmatrix} +stress \\ -high \\ -low \end{bmatrix} \quad \emptyset \quad [-syllabic]\ \acute{e}
$$

1   2   1   2

However, the improvement, if there is any, hardly smites one; and in any event the details of the 'structural change' of the diphthongization rule are neutral with respect to the main issues at hand, which concern the environment of the rule.

[8]This is notationally, but not substantively, different from the position I took in Harris (1969:116-18, passim). There, the diacritic [D], mnemonic for 'diphthongizing', rather than [+diphthongization rule] is assigned lexically. The corresponding rule, rather than being declared a minor rule, has the feature [D] in its environment. Despite recurrent misinterpretation, I did not then and do not now identify the diacritic feature [D] with the phonological feature [tense]. I devote several pages to precisely the argument that this identification cannot be made in a synchronic description. The last paragraph of this section (116-18) is, however, apparently unclear. I will now translate it into the plainest English I can: 'The diacritic [D] is correct; the phonological feature [tense] is incorrect. But I will henceforth write [tense] anyway. It should be understood that I really mean [D], however. The only reason I introduce this terminological muddle is that "tense" and "lax" are the words everybody I know uses when they are chatting casually about the subject.'

[9]Except to render the rule 'opaque' by case (ii) of Kiparsky's (1971:621ff) definition of 'opacity': given a rule A→B/C__D, there are instances of B in environments other than C__D.

[10]The distinction between the stem-final /i/ of vari- versus the /y/ of limpy- is suggested by the position of stress (penultimate) in verb forms like present indicative varío [barío] versus límpio [límpyo]. For further discussion see Harris (1969:122-25).

[11]These cases must not be confused with non-alternating diphthongs, as in diéta/dietético, siluéta/siluetear, mentioned in the previous section.

[12]For example, from hielo 'ice' (cf. helar 'to freeze', which guarantees that the diphthong is an alternating one), one can freely invent as a nonce form the morphologically impeccable though unused verb ahielar, whose meaning is perfectly predictable: 'to cause to become like ice'.

[13]If frío can have a diminutive, it is certainly fritto [frítto], phonetically distinct from frito [frítto] 'fried'. Aisraeliar, like its English gloss, is not found in dictionaries, but it is phonologically, morphologically, and semantically acceptable. The base word israelí, when incorporated into the verb aisraeliar, both begins and ends with high vowels apparently in the environment of the glide formation rule; yet neither is changed to a glide, as shown in (10). The subsidiary stress on the initial syllable of [ì]sraelí, assigned in the first cycle of (10), is a well-known phenomenon, although the rules assigning such stresses have not been studied carefully.

[14]Analogous remarks can be made concerning the words in (9), (10), and (11).

[15]Similar 'islands' occur in other freely productive forms. For example, (a) forms of the future and conditional paradigms of verbs incorporate the corresponding infinitives, with all and only the morphological and phonological peculiarities of the infinitives as independent words (e.g. ser 'to be' is suppletive--cf. future seré, conditional sería); (b) forms with the nominalizing suffix -miénto share the peculiarities of the verbal base, e.g. just as there is free variation in the infinitive podrír/pudrír 'to rot' there is also free variation in the nominalization podrimiénto/pudrimiénto--but not in the noun podredúmbre/*pudredúmbre 'rot'.

[16]The examples are nouns, adjectives, and verbs. We can add to this list adverbs formed from adjectives by suffixation of -ménte '-ly', a derivational process just as freely productive as its English counterpart; e.g. ciégaménte 'blindly'. In this case, both stresses are retained, at least in careful speech, although the first is probably reduced to secondary or tertiary.

[17]Specifically, what I want to disregard, because it has no bearing on the formulation of the diphthongization rule itself, is that the

lexical assignments of the minor-rule-triggering feature [+diph-thongization rule] do not match exactly in Chicano and standard Mexican, although they come very close. For example, the verb stem entreg- 'hand over, deliver' diphthongizes in Chicano but not in standard Mexican (Chi. entriégo, Std. entrégo); conversely the verb stem forz- 'force' (Std. fuérzo, Chi. fórzo). I would guess that the number of discrepancies of this sort is on the order of a dozen, with some dialectal variation.

[18]Other forms are identical to those of standard Spanish, in all relevant respects, e. g. undiphthongized infinitives tenér, podér, pensár, undiphthongized past participles tenído, podído, pensádo, and so on. Chicano present subjunctive forms have not been illustrated so far because of an additional wrinkle: unlike the corresponding standard forms, Chicano first person plural present subjunctive forms are stressed on the stem; e. g. vuélenos (Std. volémos), piénsenos (Std. pensémos), puédanos (Std. podámos), and so on. Of course, diphthongs are expected in these Chicano subjunctives, given the position of stress. (Chicano -nos for standard -mos as the first person plural person-number morpheme after an unstressed vowel is interesting, but has nothing to do with diphthongization.)

[19]Case (b) of (15) apparently rules out, at least for Chicano, the alternative mentioned in note 7 for standard Spanish, wherein a more careful statement of the structural change involves insertion of stressed é. This does not work in Chicano since the output we is not always stressed. We might speculate, however, that stress should not be mentioned in the output of either the standard or the Chicano version. Instead, some (as yet unformulated) universal principle might automatically shift stress off of V_1 onto V_2 in either $\hat{V}_1V_2$ or V_2V_1 clusters in case V_1 is changed to a glide (this principle is of course not applicable if V_1 is unstressed).

It is also possible that the Chicano data argue against the alternative, for Chicano, of an anti-diphthongization rule that monophthongizes basic diphthongs when they are unstressed. There is no problem with this alternative in restating the structural change of the rule, or with changing the environment of case (a) to [-stress]; but it is much more difficult, though not impossible in principle, to restate the environment of case (b) as 'everywhere EXCEPT ue in first conjugation verb forms'.

[20]The notion of paradigmatic uniformity has received a fair amount of attention lately, e. g. in Kiparsky (1971), King (1972), Laferriere (1972), Harris (1973).

[21]In a letter received after this paper was written, Reyes has informed me that he has recently encountered a dialect of Chicano (spoken by adults, not a child-language phenomenon) that has taken the next step. In the more innovative dialect, not only has the

o ~ ue alternation been leveled to ue as in Reyes's speech, but also the
e ~ ie alternation has been leveled to ie (e. g. the verb forms piensár,
piensádo, piensándo, piensámos, piensába, piensé, etc., but cf. the
noun pensamiénto), but only in the first conjugation. Formally, this
amounts to removing the feature [+back] from the environment of
case (b) of rule (15). It is interesting to ponder the implications of
the fact that precisely this was the 'next step', in one dialect.

REFERENCES

Bach, E. and R. D. King. 1970. Umlaut in modern German.
    Glossa. 4.3-21.
Brame, M. and I. Bordelois. 1973. Vowel alternations in Spanish.
    Linguistic Inquiry. 4.111-68.
Dell, F. 1970. Les règles phonologiques tardives et la morphologie
    derivationnelle du Français. Unpublished Ph. D. dissertation,
    Massachusetts Institute of Technology.
Espinosa, A. M. 1930. Estudios sobre el español de Nuevo Méjico,
    Parte I, Fonética. Biblioteca de dialectología hispanoamericana
    I, Buenos Aires.
_____. 1946. Estudios sobre el español de Nuevo Méjico, Parte II,
    Morfología. Biblioteca de dialectología hispanoamericana, II,
    Buenos Aires.
García de Diego, V. 1961. Gramática histórica española. Madrid,
    Gredos.
Halle, M. 1973. Prolegomena to a theory of word formation.
    Linguistic Inquiry. 4.3-16.
Harris, J. W. 1969. Spanish phonology. Cambridge, Mass.,
    MIT Press.
_____. 1973. On the order of certain phonological rules in Spanish.
    In: Festschrift for Morris Halle. Ed. by S. R. Anderson and
    P. Kiparsky. New York, Holt, Rinehart, and Winston.
_____. Forthcoming. Vowel alternations in Spanish verb stems.
    To appear in Linguistic Inquiry.
Hooper, J. B. 1971. Some observations on linguistic change in a
    natural generative grammar. Unpublished paper, UCLA.
King, R. D. 1969. Historical linguistics and generative grammar.
    Englewood Cliffs, N. J., Prentice-Hall.
_____. 1972. A note on opacity and paradigm regularity. Linguistic
    Inquiry. 3.535-38.
Kiparsky, P. 1971. Historical linguistics. In: A survey of lin-
    guistic science. Ed. by W. O. Dingwall. University of Maryland,
    Linguistics Program.
Laferriere, M. 1972. Surface phonetic structure in change. Paper
    read at the North East Linguistic Society Meeting, October 21-22,
    Amherst, Mass.

Pope, M. K. 1952. From Latin to modern French with especial consideration of Anglo-Norman. Manchester, Manchester University Press.

Reyes, R. Forthcoming. Studies in Chicano Spanish. Unfinished Ph. D. dissertation, Harvard University.

Ross, J. R. 1972. A reanalysis of English word stress. In: Contributions to generative phonology. Ed. by M. K. Brame. Austin, University of Texas Press.

Schane, S. A. 1972. Noncyclic English word stress. Paper read at the Winter LSA Meeting, Atlanta.

Vennemann, T. 1972. Rule inversion. Lingua. 29.209–42.

Zwicky, A. M. 1967. Umlaut and noun plurals in German. Studia Grammatica. 6.35–45.

SPANISH STRESS AND LANGUAGE CHANGE

BOHDAN SACIUK

University of Florida

Language change is viewed within the framework of generative grammar as the result of rule addition, rule loss, rule reordering, rule simplification, lexical restructuring, and lexical simplification.[1] Lexical simplification may involve the reduction of the number of idiosyncratic features present in a lexical entry, or the change of a marker associated with a lexical entry (King 1969:62, 129). Lexical simplification may also consist in changing the stratal affiliation of a given formative from the marked case, i.e. [-Native], to the unmarked case, namely [+Native] (Saciuk 1969b:521-25).

In Saciuk 1969a and 1969b it was claimed that the formatives that make up the lexicon of a language belong to several subsets. The division of the lexicon into lexical strata is based on the fact that the subsets of formatives undergo particular subsets of phonological rules. Thus, the [+Native] formatives are subject to the [+Native] rules, that is, the rules associated with this lexical stratum. The [+Native] rules do not apply to [-Native] formatives, because a different subset of phonological rules is applicable to the members of this lexical stratum.[2] Recently, Nessly (1971) and Kreidler (1972) have indicated the need for lexical strata and suggested improvements in this theory. Wanner (1972:14) on the other hand, came to the conclusion that:

> Lexical stratification, a device for describing relations between lexical items by exploiting the abstract potential of phonological theory, is not a part of a phonological description of any language. It violates conditions on empirical falsifiability and reveals itself as inconsequential for the phonology as a

28

whole. None of its implications can be evidenced in a natural
language. Consequently lexical stratification should be abandoned as a concept.

Some of the criticisms raised in Wanner (1972) are well taken, [3]
but others are not so easy to accept; for example, the claim that two
speakers of the same language or dialect that exhibit the same surface
forms must have the same underlying representations. However, the
underlying forms that a speaker of any language will have in his grammar are based on his linguistic experience, i. e. on the alternations
with which a given formative is associated in his system. The underlying representations may change as new alternations are introduced
into his grammar. This restructuring of the lexicon is very important
and constant in the early years of life, during language acquisition,
but it also may and does take place later in life, although at a much
lesser scale. [4] Schane (1972:352) claims that a similar process may
occur within a language, not only an idiolect. He proposes:

> If a language acquires a substantial learned vocabulary whose
> direct source is the same as the indigenous vocabulary, and
> if as a consequence there are alternations between nonlearned
> and learned forms, then that language will have a highly ab-
> stract phonology.

It seems to me that a grammar of Spanish must somehow relate
the words given in (1).

(1) segundario 'secondary'   secundario 'id.'
     muelle 'soft'   mole 'id.'
     lefble 'readable, legible' legible 'id.'
     llamear 'to flame'   flamear 'id.'
     población 'populating'   populación 'id.'

The words (and there are other doublets of this kind) in both columns
are exactly the same in meaning (in one or more definitions), obviously containing identical formatives in identical combinations.
Nevertheless, the phonetic representations are different in both
columns. We would be missing a generalization about the phonological system of Spanish if we followed Wanner's suggestion and
'relegated' the statement of the very close relationship between
these words 'to its appropriate place, the lexicon.' In a sense,
within the proposal of lexical strata the lexicon plays an important
role. The lexical entries must include the information as to the
stratal membership of each particular formative. Formatives may
be either (a) always [+Native] (i. e. unmarked), (b) always [-Native]

(i. e. marked), or (c) [+Native] in some words and [-Native] in others.[5] In the case of the words in (1), those in the left column contain a [+Native] root, while in those on the right the root is specified as [-Native]. The segmental composition of both the [+Native] form and the [-Native] form is identical. The rules associated with each stratum cause the difference in phonetic forms.

After this brief exposition of the concept of lexical strata, we are ready to look at Spanish stress and how it is related to lexical simplification.

Harris (1969) noticed that, with very few exceptions which can be easily and regularly accounted for, the main stress in Spanish verb forms always falls on the penultimate vowel. With a minor alteration,[6] the rule that he proposed for main stress assignment in Spanish verbs can be formulated as

(2) MSR (for verbs)
$$V \longrightarrow [1 \text{ stress}] / \underline{\quad}((\text{[+past marker]})C_oV)C_o{}^\#]_V$$

This rule will assign primary stress to the penultimate vowel in formatives specified [+Verb]. The rule also states that a [past marker] may occur optionally between the final vowel or syllable (shown as C_oVC_o) and the vowel that carries the stress, the latter being in antepenultimate position in such cases. The 'past markers' that may occur optionally are the 2nd person plural Preterite /ste/, the Imperfect /ba/ and the Past Subjunctive /ra/ or /se/. The outer set of parentheses in this rule is needed for stressing monosyllabic verb forms, while the inner set indicates that the [past marker] is optional. This rule accounts correctly for the main stress in all Spanish verb forms.[7]

The vast majority of Spanish nouns and adjectives are also stressed on the penultimate vowel, e. g. mucáma 'maid', dáma 'lady', corréa 'belt', crestúdo 'heavy-crested', entéro 'entire', and thousands more. Besides, there is a very large set of nouns and adjectives that in their phonetic representations carry stress on the final vowel, but which will have to be derived from underlying representations with a final lax /ĕ/, which is deleted by the ĕ-Deletion Rule after the application of MSR, as shown convincingly by Foley (1965, 1967), and by Harris (1969). Words like amór 'love' (</amorĕ/, cf. pl. amóres), paréd 'wall' (pl. parédes), cardinál 'cardinal' (pl. cardináles), and a large number of others will be stressed on the penultimate vowel, just as all of the verb forms. Thus, we need a rule similar to the MSR for verbs to assign stress to non-verb forms. Note that, in addition to nouns and adjectives, other words will also be stressed on the penultimate vowel, e. g. péro 'but', ustéd 'you' (< /ustedĕ/), etc. This rule is

(3) V ---> [1 stress] / ___$(C_0V)C_0\#]$

and, by using the 'angled brackets' convention, it can be collapsed with the previously given rule for verbs into

(4) MSR (normal case)
     V ---> [1 stress] / ___$(<([\text{+past mark. }])>C_0V)C_0\#]_{<V>}$

Spanish also contains a considerable number of nouns and adjectives with primary stress on the antepenultimate syllable. Many of them have corresponding verb forms which, as we would expect, exhibit regular penultimate stress. A minute set of examples of these forms is given below, together with their related verb forms.

(5) límite 'limit'   limíte 'to limit' (Pres. Subj.)
     cómputo 'computation'   compúto 'I compute'
     legítima 'legitimate' (f.)   legitíma 'he legitimates'
     íntegro 'integral'   intégro 'I integrate'

There are many more pairs like these. [8] Foley and Harris in their analyses of Spanish account for the stress of these antepenultimately stressed nouns and adjectives by including in the grammar of Spanish the so-called 'Latin Stress Rule', that is, a rule which assigns stress on the basis of the tenseness or laxness of the penultimate vowel. According to this rule, which was first formulated in distinctive features by Foley (1965), stress is assigned to the penultimate vowel if this vowel is tense or if it is followed by two consonants of which the second is not a liquid, otherwise the antepenultimate vowel is stressed (1965:90). While Foley assumed that this Latin Stress Rule applied to all Spanish words, including verbs, Harris noticed the regularization of stress in verbs mentioned earlier. Harris's formulation of the Latin Stress Rule is

(6) LSR (Harris)
     V ---> [1 stress] / ___$(C_0(\check{V}C_0^1(L))V)C_0\#]_{N, A}$

Both Foley and Harris had to include in their rule the specification that if the lax penultimate vowel is followed by one consonant and a liquid then the antepenultimate vowel is stressed, but if it is followed by two consonants, 'of which the second is not a liquid', then this lax penultimate vowel will be assigned stress. They were forced to do this, because they noticed that although íntegro, múltiple, óctuple, álgebra, etc. are stressed antepenultimately, words in which a lax penultimate vowel is followed by two consonants (the second of which is not a liquid) are penultimately stressed. It is clear that the words

in this second group have to come from underlying representations
with lax penultimate vowels, because when they are stressed penultimately they undergo the Diphthongization Rule. In related forms,
when these lax vowels are not stressed, they cannot undergo Diphthongization. Examples of this are

(7) vergüénza 'shame'   vergonzóso 'shameful'
    compuérta 'flood-gate'   portál 'town-gate'
    caliénte 'warm'   calentár 'to warm'
    infiérno 'hell'   infernál 'hellish'
    contiénda 'contest'   contendér 'to contest'

An examination of the nouns and adjectives that are stressed
antepenultimately shows that all of them are somehow peculiar,
namely, they consistently do not undergo those rules of Spanish that
apply to the members of the [+Native] stratum of this language. Most
of them fail to undergo the Vowel Lowering which applies to lax high
vowels in [+Nat] formatives and specifies them [-high]. If the forms
in (5) were to undergo this [+Nat] rule they would result in phonetic
*[límete], *[kómpoto], *[lexítema]. This rule would apply vacuously
to íntegro, since the penultimate lax vowel is already [-high]. Many
of the words belonging to this class do not undergo the [+Nat] rule of
Syncope that deletes lax vowels in interconsonantal position. In addition to not undergoing Vowel Lowering and Syncope, límite, cómputo,
legítima are exceptions to another [+Nat] rule, namely, Lenition,
which voices intervocalic stops. Three of the words listed in (5)--
límite, cómputo, and íntegro--have obvious [+Nat] doublets: línde
'limit, boundary', cuénto 'count, computation', entéro 'whole, entire'. The [+Nat] rules mentioned above apply to these [+Nat] words.
    It seems clear that there must be a connection between stress
assignment in nouns and adjectives and the lexical strata of Spanish.
The Latin Stress Rule applies to [-Nat] nouns and adjectives, while
the Main Stress Rule given in (4) applies to verbs of all strata and to
all [+Nat] words.
    Before formulating the final version of the Main Stress Rule of
Spanish, let us return to the 'two consonants' constraint placed on
LSR by both Foley and Harris. Harris does not give any reasons for
including this restriction, but only mentions the fact that a consonant
+ liquid cluster does not behave like a cluster of two consonants,
giving as examples for this the forms íntegro and múltiple (1969:121).
Foley, however, cites four forms as examples of a class of words
that motivate the 'two consonant' restriction. The forms given by
him are haciénda 'estate', sangriénto 'bloody', saneamiénto 'sani-
tation, improvement', and remiéndo 'patch' (Foley 1965:89). Since
in their analyses the LSR applies to both [+Nat] and [-Nat] forms,

Foley and Harris assume that the two consonant cluster is responsible for the penultimate stress in these words. It turns out that this constraint is an unnecessary complication of the rule. Thus far I have not been able to find cases that would clearly indicate that it is needed in the Main Stress Rule of Spanish. Words like those presented by Foley as motivation for this complication are just [+Native] and receive penultimate stress because of this stratal specification.

The final simplified version of the Main Stress Rule can be formulated as

(8) Main Stress Rule (final version)

$$V \longrightarrow [1 \ stress] \, / \left\{ \begin{array}{ll} \underset{[-Nat]}{\boxed{}}^{(C_0(\check{V}C_0)V)C_0\#]} \ _{N,\,A} & \text{(a)} \\[2em] \underset{[<\alpha Nat>]}{\boxed{}}^{(<([+p.\,m.\,])>C_0V)C_0\#]} \ _{<V>} & \text{(b)} \end{array} \right\}$$

The stratal features indicate that part (a) applies to nouns and adjectives that belong to the [-Nat] stratum, while part (b) applies to [+Nat] (i. e. unmarked) nouns and adjectives and to all verbs, as well as to prepositions, stressable pronouns, etc. Part (a) stresses [-Nat] nouns and adjectives according to the quality of the penultimate vowel.

The Main Stress Rule as formulated in (8) captures the generalization that in Modern Spanish stress has been regularized to a very large extent and that an overwhelming majority of Spanish words are penultimately stressed. Although Harris' version of the MSR reflects this generalization for verbs, it fails to do so for nouns and adjectives. As a result of this, Harris is faced with a problem, which he states as follows:

Stress on a penultimate lax vowel in a 'weak' syllable. Here there are problems. It is not obvious how the LSR can assign stress in nouns like the following, in which diphthongization indicates an underlying lax vowel and this lax vowel is followed by a single consonant: Venez[wé]la (cf. venez[ŏ]láno), ag[wé]ro (cf. ag[ŏ]rár), trop[yé]zo (cf. trop[ĕ]zár), ab[wé]lo (cf. ab[ŏ]léngo). Further examples of this sort can be found easily. In most cases the historical reason for the apparently aberrant placement of stress is known, but there seems to be no residue that would provide a synchronic explanation. With a little ingenuity one could of course incorporate into the synchronic grammar relevant aspects of the historical development of these forms. However, without independent synchronic motivation, that is, without evidence for the underlying representations and rules

postulated aside from stress placement, such a move would be
totally ad hoc, and any 'explanation' provided thereby would
be illusory. (Harris 1969:119)

The Venezuéla type of words are indeed a problem for Harris and
for the proponents of the Latin Stress Rule for the assignment of
stress in all Spanish nouns and adjectives. But these words are
easily accounted for and explained under the analysis of Spanish main
stress that incorporates the notion of lexical strata. In fact, they
may be used as supporting evidence for this theoretical concept and
the analysis presented here.

Venezuéla, abuélo 'grandfather', agüéro 'prediction', tropiézo
'stumbling block', and many other nouns and adjectives like them do
contain underlying lax penultimate vowels. There are no synchronic
reasons for assigning them to the [-Nat] stratum, and therefore these
words will be specified [+Nat], i. e. they will be unmarked for stratal
membership in the lexicon. Being [+Nat] they will undergo part (b)
of the MSR, which will place stress on the penultimate vowel. Since
the penultimate vowel in all of them is lax, it will later undergo the
Diphthongization Rule, thus producing the correct phonetic forms. It
is clear that the penultimate syllable in these words has to contain a
lax vowel and not a diphthong or two vowels in the underlying forms
(which would make the LSR work correctly) because in the related
forms (given above by Harris) in which this vowel is not stressed or
in related [-Nat] words it appears phonetically as the corresponding
mid vowel.

Thus, the incorporation of the notion of lexical strata simplifies
the Main Stress Rule, and captures generalizations about stress in
Spanish that were not evident before. It explains why penultimate
stress is the normal or unmarked stress in this language. It also
explains why words of the Venezuéla type are stressed penultimately,
and why all verbs have regularized penultimate stress.

Data from language change give additional support to the analysis
of Spanish stress presented here.

It has been proposed above that lexical simplification may take
the form of changes in the stratal affiliation of the formatives listed
in the lexicon. [+Native] is the normal or unmarked case of stratal
specification, [-Native] being marked and therefore more costly.
Thus, if there would be restructuring in the lexicon with respect to
stratal membership of lexical entries, we would expect it to be in
the direction of decreasing the complexity of the lexicon. That is,
our notion of lexical strata predicts that lexical entries will tend to
change from [-Native] to [+Native], i. e. from marked to unmarked.

This prediction is confirmed by dialectological data. In Spanish
dialects (both American and peninsular) there are numerous cases of

nouns and adjectives that occur very frequently with penultimate
stress, although originally they were proparoxytonic. Many of them
appear with antepenultimate stress in standard, educated, and more
careful dialects and idiolects. Alonso (1930:349-61) lists the most
frequently occurring paroxytized nouns and adjectives that illustrate
this ongoing sound change. Some of them are:

(9) arábe, cranéo, heróe, opálo, paralísis,
    celébre, idolátra, almibár, condór,
    albumína, vertébra, análisis, caratúla,
    fabríca, Gerónimo, trafágo, pristíno,
    plátano

The words in (9) in which the penultimate stressed vowel does not
diphthongize (e.g. cranéo, condór) are restructured not only to the
unmarked case of the stratal feature [Native], but also the mid vowel
changes from the marked 'lax' mid vowel to the unmarked 'tense'
mid vowel. According to Chomsky and Halle (1968:405) [+tense]
vowels are more highly valued (i.e. less complex) than [-tense]
vowels which have to be marked for the feature [tense]. In fact, the
underlying representations of all of these words would be made less
highly complex by being simplified to include a tense rather than a
lax penultimate vowel. In all of them there would be no synchronic
reason for positing a lax penultimate vowel.[9] Of course, one could
say that the only restructuring taking place in these words is the
change in the tenseness of the penultimate vowel. But then this would
be an ad hoc solution which would work, but it would not explain why
it is natural for words in Spanish to be penultimately stressed. This
alternate solution would also fail to account for words of the Venezuéla
type.
     There are also many Spanish nouns and adjectives like período,
etíope, cardíaco which become penultimately stressed in the majority
of the dialects (periódo, etiópe, cardiáco). However, these are not
examples of lexical simplification. They exhibit a tendency of Spanish to minimize VV sequences. Perhaps we could say that this is a
conspiracy in Spanish, since there are three other rules, at least,
that eliminate contiguous vowels (Glide Formation, Vowel Simplification, Vowel Deletion). In the words mentioned, just as in maíz >
máiz [májs], país > páis [pájs], two adjacent vowels with no conso-
nant(s) between them are converted into one syllable by the creation
of a diphthong. The two rules operating here (Stress Shift and Glide
Formation) are late phonological rules that apply to formatives of all
strata. In the dialects that contain the Vowel Raising Rule (unstressed
o, e > u, i), oceáno [osjánu], alveólos [alβjólus] are also the result
of this process and not of lexical simplification.

That penultimate word stress is the normal, unmarked case in Spanish can be easily seen by giving a list of nonsense words to native-speakers of this language. They will tend to pronounce these nonsense words with paroxytonic stress. The same tendency is evident in many words borrowed from other languages which were oxytonic or proparoxytonic in the other language, but became nativized in Spanish, thus acquiring penultimate stress. To take just three examples: Guarani ñandutí > Sp. ñandúti; Aztec kóyotl > Sp. coyóte; Eng. Róbinson > Sp. Robinsón (the literary character in Defoe's novel; [-Nat] Róbinson for the English surname).

The present analysis of Spanish stress predicts that if stress became regularized in Spanish, then this language would have penultimate stress across the board (just as in Polish). Support for this prediction can be found in the Aragonese dialect of Spanish, which has a very strong and generalized tendency towards the regularization of paroxytonic stress. Alonso (1930) and Zamora Vicente (1967:221) give Aragonese forms such as: estomágo, sabádo, tabáno, pildóra, tetúlos (títulos).

More data could be brought in to motivate the concept of lexical strata, and the analysis of Spanish stress proposed here. The facts presented in this paper would seem to indicate that, although very likely some changes are needed, the basic idea behind it will have to be incorporated into generative theory.

NOTES

[1]For a discussion of these processes of linguistic change see King (1969).

[2]See Saciuk (1970) for an application of lexical strata to the phonology of Portuguese.

[3]For example, that the [+Native] label carries 'erroneous connotations of diachronic nature'. I made it clear that the lexical subdivision was based on rule applicability, and that lexical strata were a synchronic and not a diachronic device.

[4]I leave the discussion of Wanner's criticisms for another occasion.

[5]This is the part that I myself do not like too much. How is this to be handled in the lexicon in generative theory?

[6]See Saciuk (1969a:82-86).

[7]For Future and Preterite forms, and other apparent exceptions see Harris (1969:67-103) and Saciuk (1969a:81-90).

[8]Harris (1969:120) gives a much larger sample.

[9]Words like pristíno, caratúla, paralísis would not undergo the [+Nat] Vowel Lowering Rule because this rule applies only to lax high vowels.

REFERENCES

Alonso, Amado. 1930. Problemas de dialectología hispanoamericana. Biblioteca de Dialectología Hispanoamericana. 1.315-469.
Chomsky, Noam and Morris Halle. 1968. The sound pattern of English. New York, Harper and Row.
Foley, James A. 1965. Spanish morphology. Unpublished Ph. D. dissertation, Massachusetts Institute of Technology.
_____. 1967. Spanish plural formation. Language. 43.486-93.
Harris, James W. 1969. Spanish phonology. Cambridge, Mass., MIT Press.
King, Robert D. 1969. Historical linguistics and generative grammar. Englewood Cliffs, N. J., Prentice-Hall.
Kreidler, Charles W. 1972. Lexical strata and phonological features. Paper read at the annual meeting of the MLA.
Nessly, Larry. 1971. Anglicization in English phonology. In: Papers from the Seventh Regional Meeting of the Chicago Linguistic Society. 499-510.
Saciuk, Bohdan. 1969a. Lexical strata in generative phonology (with illustrations from Ibero-Romance). Unpublished Ph. D. dissertation, University of Illinois.
_____. 1969b. The stratal division of the lexicon. Papers in Linguistics. 1.464-532.
_____. 1970. Some basic rules of Portuguese phonology. In: Studies presented to Robert B. Lees by his students. Ed. by Jerrold Sadock and Anthony Vanek. Edmonton, Linguistic Research. 197-222.
Schane, Sanford A. 1972. How abstract is French phonology? In: Generative studies in Romance languages. Ed. by Jean Casagrande and Bohdan Saciuk. Rowley, Mass., Newbury House. 340-52.
Wanner, Dieter. 1972. The evidence for phonological rules in Romance. Unpublished paper.
Zamora Vicente, Alonso. 1967. Dialectología española. 2nd ed. Madrid, Gredos.

A LINK FOR PUSH AND DRAG CHAINS[1]

GREGORY K. BROWN

Indiana University

The historical development of a number of Romance languages and dialects provides some interesting examples of phenomena for which André Martinet coined the terms push chain and drag chain. These terms are meant to characterize covarying phonological shifts as exemplified by the following example from the Portuguese dialect of Algarve:[2]

FIGURE 1.

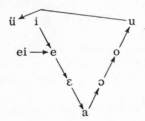

The changes depicted by the diagram could be viewed as resulting either from a push chain or a drag chain. Explanation by the former interpretation would indicate that /i/ lowered to /e/, /e/ to /ɛ/, /ɛ/ to /a/, after which /a/ raised to /ɔ/, /ɔ/ to /o/, /o/ to /u/, followed by the fronting of /u/ to front round /ü/. Explanations of such a phenomenon most usually assume that the phoneme which initiated the change gradually overstepped the bounds of its allophonic domain, thereby forcing the phoneme in its path in turn to extend itself beyond its own allophonic domain and encroach upon the phoneme in its path, etc., until, at some point, either a merger took place or a phoneme

38

not previously in the system was formed as the phoneme at the end of the line underwent some change to maintain its autonomy, such as /u/ becoming /ü/ in Figure 1.

On the other hand, analysis of the phonemenon as a drag chain would assume that first /u/ fronted to /ü/ and, in so doing, left a 'hole' (kind of a vacuum) into which /o/ subsequently gravitated as it found its allophonic domain on that side stretched to permit more variation. In turn, as it gravitated to the hole left by /u/, /ɔ/ then filled the resulting vacancy, and so forth, until finally, at the top of the front series, /i/ lowered to fill the hole left by /e/.

So far, for the languages in which chain shifts have been found to have occurred, for the most part there has been no evidence to favor one analysis over the other. Evidence to support a historical push or drag chain would consist of documentation of the effects of the various changes in a language such that, for a proposed shift A→B→C, A→B is found to have occurred historically prior to B→C in the case of a push chain, and B→C is found to be historically prior to A→B in the case of a drag chain. King (1969b) cites four cases of what he considers to be drag chains, only the first of which was based on an actual sequence of historical changes. But even this one, as he notes at the end of the paper, fails to qualify as an actual drag chain since the two rules involved were independent and later collapsed into one. And to my knowledge all other proposed cases of chain shifts fail to be accompanied by evidence as to whether a drag or push chain analysis should be favored.

In order to provide a rationale for making a decision, King (1969b) attempted to analyze chain shift phenomena within the framework of generative phonology, and as a result concluded (1) that push chains are non-occurring in natural language, and (2) that drag chains do occur and are analyzable as special cases of alpha-variable simplification. That is, given the addition of rule (1) to a grammar:

$$(1) \quad \begin{bmatrix} +\text{back} \\ +\text{high} \\ -\text{low} \\ +\text{round} \end{bmatrix} \rightarrow \begin{bmatrix} -\text{back} \\ +\text{high} \\ -\text{low} \\ +\text{round} \end{bmatrix}$$

which changes /u/ to [ü], this rule can subsequently be generalized to (2) to include the raising of /o/ to [u]:

$$(2) \quad \begin{bmatrix} +\text{back} \\ \alpha \text{ high} \\ -\text{low} \\ +\text{round} \end{bmatrix} \rightarrow \begin{bmatrix} -\alpha \text{back} \\ +\text{high} \\ -\text{low} \\ +\text{round} \end{bmatrix}$$

thereby accounting for the chain shift /u→ü, o→u/. Since it is not
the purpose of this paper to investigate King's comments on drag
chains, I will make no attempt to evaluate any strengths or weak-
nesses in his solution.

What this paper will concern itself with, however, is King's conclusion that push chains do not exist in natural language. His reasons
for such a conclusion are based on two assumptions held to be implicit in a push chain analysis as presented by Martinet:[3]

(1) the inception of sound change, or at least some sound
     changes, is gradual and imperceptible--a continuous
     process in which the allophonic norm of a phoneme
     assumes a new position in infinitesimal steps.[4]

(2) merger tends to be avoided in sound change.

The arguments against the gradualness hypothesis are well known
to linguists working within generative phonology, namely that sound
change is grammar change, a change in the speaker's competence,
and is not contingent on such factors as wax in the ears, moisture in
the mouth, etc. And the assumption that merger tends to be avoided
in sound change, to my knowledge, has not been substantiated by any
clear examples, for merger seems to happen about as many times as
it does not.[5] The logic follows, therefore, that if we discredit these
two assumptions, which are assumed to be implicit in push chains,
then push chains must also be discredited.

But the first question to be asked here is whether these two
assumptions are in fact implicit in a push chain argument. It is a
fact that recourse was made to these two principles by Martinet and
others working in an autonomous phonemic theory, one in which
sound change is not considered as change in the underlying system of
rules which account for a speaker's ability to evaluate and produce an
infinite set of utterances, but rather change in performance as determined by external factors such as those mentioned in the previous
paragraph. But simply because one theory makes these assumptions
does not mean that such assumptions are implicitly tied to the changes
they seek to explain. More exactly, they are part of the particular
theory which engendered them. And rejection of that theory does not
make the changes it sought to explain any more or less real, rather
it is the new theory which must attempt to re-evaluate and explain
the changes which have been observed, within its own framework.

But the existence of push chains cannot be determined by speculative argumentation. The most crucial matter to be considered is
whether or not a chain shift A→B→C can be documented as having
occurred or actually occurring in a given language, where A→B has

been observed to precede B→C. If such a case is found, then our thinking must be readjusted accordingly. I will now present what I feel to be the evidence needed to substantiate the existence of push chains in natural language.

My example is taken from the Portuguese dialect of Mirandese, more specifically Mirandese as spoken in the area of Sendim, located in the Tras-os-montes area on the border between León and Portugal. The first study of this dialect was published in 1901 by the man who discovered the dialect, José Leite de Vasconcellos, the first Portuguese dialectologist to investigate northern dialects systematically, and author of the basic work on Portuguese dialectology. In this extensive study, Vasconcellos characterized the oral tonic vowel system essentially as the following:

FIGURE 2.

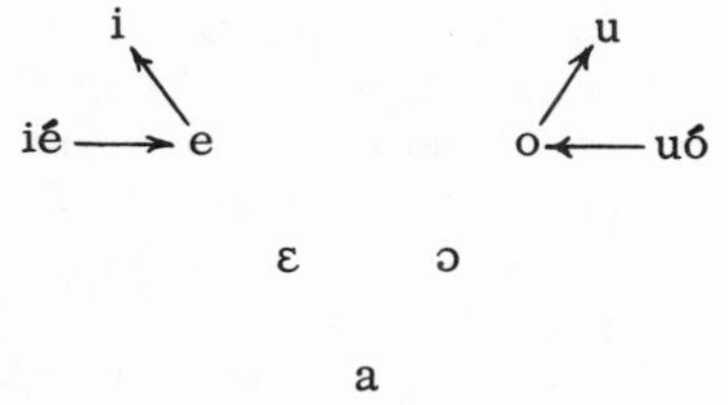

He remarked that the diphthongs [ié] and [uó] were at such a point of monophthongization that rarely were the diphthongs ever heard and it was not a case of merger with /é/ and /ó/ since these previously close midvowels were now being pronounced as the open vowels [ɛ] and [ɔ]. This in itself in no way constitutes evidence for a push chain interpretation since it could also be argued that the monophthongization of [ié] and [uó] was provided for by the lowering of the midvowels, thereby leaving vacancies into which the diphthongs gravitated as monophthongs.

But Vasconcellos further indicates that not only were the diphthongs being pronounced as close midvowels, but also that these resultant midvowels were optionally being realized as the corresponding high vowels [i] and [u]. Were this to be all the data available to us we would merely conclude that the monophthongized diphthongs underwent an optional rule of raising.

But there is still more. Over half a century later, María José de Moura Santos (1967) published a descriptive study of the Tras-os-montes dialects, including a detailed description of the vocalic system of Mirandese. Her characterization of the oral tonic vowel system of Sendinese was essentially as follows:

FIGURE 3.

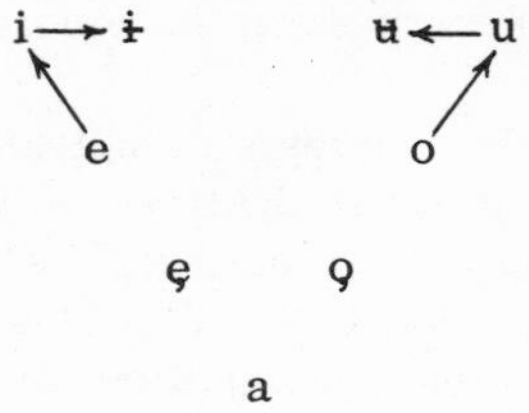

i—→ɨ   ʉ◄—u
 \   /
   \   /
     e   o

    ę   ǫ

         a

Her description indicates that the close midvowels /e/, /o/ are being
realized as [i] and [u] respectively (as Vasconcellos indicated to be
the trend in 1901) and that the high vowels /i/ and /u/ are being pronounced as unround central [ɨ] and round central [ʉ] respectively.

It should be pointed out here that Vasconcellos, in his study of
1901, made no mention whatsoever of any high central vowels such
as [ɨ] and [ʉ] although he did specifically indicate the optional raising
of /e/ and /o/ to [i] and [u]. Then later Moura Santos specifically
draws attention to the fact that while [i] and [u] are now the most
general pronunciations of /e/ and /o/, the most general pronunciation of former /i/ and /u/ is [ɨ] and [ʉ]. It is clear from a chronological point of view that the covarying shifts witnessed by Vasconcellos and Moura Santos are not instances of a drag chain, but rather
are an explicit example of a push chain, since the last vowel to be
realized differently is precisely the one which should have been the
first to change in a drag chain.

The point to be considered now is the following: if we disallow
push chains on the grounds that they presuppose (a) gradual sound
change and (b) a counter-merger mechanism, what must we say now
that an actual push chain has occurred? It is clear that it must be
accounted for in some way, and if we have disallowed the 'implicit
assumptions' presented, then perhaps it is the case that the assumptions and push chain phenomena are independent or in conflict with
each other. For either the data is wrong, or the assumptions are
wrong. And in the face of the data from Sendinese, I think the correct
posture to take is that the assumptions in question are irrelevant to
the occurrence of push chain phenomena, and so in some way the
latter must be accounted for. And generative phonology provides us
with a principled way of explaining the changes which have been observed. Now let us see how this came about.

The first change which took place in Sendinese, monophthongization, can be represented by the following rule, which was an
optional pronunciation at the time of Vasconcellos' study:

(3) MONOPHTHONGIZATION

$$\begin{bmatrix} -\text{cons} \\ -\text{voc} \\ +\text{high} \\ \alpha\text{back} \\ \alpha\text{round} \end{bmatrix} \rightarrow \emptyset \quad /— \begin{bmatrix} \acute{\text{V}} \\ -\text{high} \\ -\text{low} \\ \alpha\text{back} \\ \alpha\text{round} \end{bmatrix} \qquad \text{(OPTIONAL)}$$

(Glides delete before midvowels.)

The following rule was also in effect in the grammar, although
Vasconcellos makes clear that the rule was also optional:

(4) RAISING

$$\begin{bmatrix} \acute{\text{V}} \\ -\text{high} \\ -\text{low} \end{bmatrix} \longrightarrow [+\text{high}] \qquad \text{(OPTIONAL)}$$

(Close midvowels become high.)

Later when Moura Santos made her study, not only had Raising become essentially obligatory in Sendim, but the following rule had
also been added to the grammar:

(5) CENTRALIZATION

$$\begin{bmatrix} \acute{\text{V}} \\ +\text{high} \end{bmatrix} \longrightarrow \begin{bmatrix} +\text{central} \\ -\text{back} \end{bmatrix}$$

(High vowels become central: /i→ɨ, u→ʉ/)[6]

The crucial part of the analysis lies in the position of the Raising
and Centralization rules in the synchronic grammar at the time of the
innovation with respect to each other. It is evident that both the
Monophthongization and the Raising rules were added onto the end of
the grammar in the order given (whether simultaneously or chronologically). Thus all midvowels which result from monophthongization are optionally realized as the corresponding high vowels. But
if the Centralization rule is attached to the end of the grammar, which
would correspond to the chronological order in which it was added,
then the high vowels which result from Raising will also be centralized
when in fact only etymological high vowels undergo such a change.
Therefore, the point in the grammar where the Centralization rule
must be attached is actually before the Raising rule. This means

that the chronologically later rule is added to the synchronic grammar before the chronologically earlier rule. This is not a defect for it is not necessarily the case that chronology should be reflected in the synchronic grammar.

In order to see this more clearly, let us look at some proposed examples. King (1969) cites the case of Lachman's law in Classical Latin which involved the addition of a rule applying to underlying forms such as /agtum/ (from agō) and /regtum/ (from regō) with the effect of lengthening the checked vowel when followed by an obstruent cluster, the first segment of which was voiced. But the rule had to be attached in the synchronic grammar prior to the already existing rule devoicing syllable final obstruents when followed by a voiceless segment. Thus there were surface alternations of agō : āctum, regō : rēctum, as opposed to faciō : factum, which had an underlying voiceless consonant /faktum/. So it is clear that in order to produce the correct surface forms, the two rules must have been ordered in the synchronic grammar of Classical Latin in inverse historical order.

Possibly another example of the non-chronological ordering of rules in the synchronic grammar can be provided by observing the evolution of the French tonic back vowels in the area of Lorrain.[7] Fouché (1958) indicates that close /o/ had raised to [u] in all parts of France no later than the middle of the twelfth century. Thus this [u] was not affected by the palatalization of /u/ to [ü] which had already been occurring since the eighth century. However, in Lorrain, according to Fouché, the palatalization of /u/ did not begin to take affect until the thirteenth or even the fourteenth century, after /o/ had closed to [u], yet this [u] was not affected by the palatalization rule, for if it had been, there would have been no tonic /u/ in Lorrain.

In order to account for these changes, the following two rules can be posited to represent those added to the grammar:

(6) RAISING

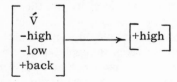

(ǫ raises to u)

(7) PALATALIZATION

$$\begin{bmatrix} \acute{V} \\ +high \\ +back \\ +round \end{bmatrix} \longrightarrow [-back]$$

(/u/ fronts to [ü])

The rules, as they appear here, are in the chronological sequence in which they were added to the grammar. The fact that the forms with [u], which resulted from etymological /o/, did not undergo palatalization suggests that the Raising rule was still in the grammar at the time the Palatalization rule was added to the grammar. (Derivational alternations in which the /o/ was not stressed did not undergo tonic raising.) Otherwise, in order to account for non-palatalization in precisely the forms of etymological /o/, we must assume that these forms were marked in some special way, for example [-palatalization], so as not to be fronted. But this is obviously a trick, and if we accept this solution, then there is no way to explain why just those forms from etymological /o/ did not become front, for we are left with no way to predict which forms should need such a feature, except for the fact that they do not palatalize. That is, the method of distinguishing the palatalizing forms from those which do not must be imposed externally upon each individual form, unpredictably, whereas by using two ordered rules, the forms are distinguished internally by the grammar in a general fashion.

It is evident then that the historical development of Sendinese is sufficient to compel us to consider more positively the existence of push chains, and the mechanism through which they operate, as exemplified by Lachman's law and French in Lorrain, as viable linguistic phenomena. Yet there are problems associated with a push chain interpretation. To illustrate this, let us refer back to the Portuguese dialect of Algarve as depicted in Figure 1. Accepting the account as a correct interpretation of the facts, we would need to write rules then, in order to characterize it as a push chain, for each vowel shift, that is, starting with /i/:

Diachronic	Synchronic
(1) i > e	(7) u > ü
(2) e > ɛ	(6) o > u
(3) ɛ > a	(5) ɔ > o
(4) a > ɔ	(4) a > ɔ
(5) ɔ > o	(3) ɛ > a
(6) o > u	(2) e > ɛ
(7) u > ü	(1) i > e

A push chain interpretation would mean that each of the rules in the left column, at the time of their inclusion in the synchronic grammar, must be inversely stacked as illustrated in the right column. Otherwise, each rule would feed the next until only [ü] remained.

Some may balk at the thought of such deep inverse stacking, but the results are not any more appealing if in a large shift such as this, where there is no evidence to indicate where the change began, we analyze it as a drag chain. King's rule for a similar change in the dialect of São Miguel of the Azores in which only the back vowels undergo changes is as follows:

(8)
$$\begin{bmatrix} +\text{back} \\ \alpha\text{high} \\ \beta\text{low} \\ \gamma\text{round} \end{bmatrix} \longrightarrow \begin{bmatrix} -\alpha\text{back} \\ -\beta\text{high} \\ -\gamma\text{low} \\ +\text{round} \end{bmatrix}$$

(u > ü, o > u, ɔ > o, a > ɔ)

King expressed that he felt the rule to be bizarre and pointed out the possibility of restructuring in between simplifications, and I agree that it need not be the case, nor is it probably ever the case, that at any specific time in the development of the language, all of the rules be present in the synchronic grammar. But this neither favors nor disfavors my claim that push chains exist. Restructuring could take place just as easily in the development of a push chain as it could in a drag chain, in which case only a few of the total rules which were added would be present in the synchronic grammar at any one time.

With regard to the assumption, supposedly implicit in a push chain interpretation, that merger tends to be avoided in sound change, we must now more critically evaluate it, since Sendinese presents evidence for the acceptance of push chains as occurring linguistic phenomena. King's disapproval of such an assumption stems from his seeing in it a further claim:

> that the speaker, or some mechanism internalized in the linguistic system of the speaker, possesses the capability of acting in specific ways to prevent potential merger. Anyone who believes claim (2) to be true must be able to provide evidence supporting the assumption of a mechanism which decides when merger is approaching and which offers an escape route. [8]

I tend to agree with this explanation, but what the assumption presupposes is not what is at issue here. I think it is still open to question whether a push chain implicitly makes a counter-merger claim. King's admission that merger seems to take place as often as it fails to take place implicitly supports the concept that at least in some cases merger is avoided. But I do not think that such an admission supports a counter-merger mechanism. In viewing chain shifts from the perspective of generative theory, it is not incompatible in the least to accept the addition, at some period, of an optional rule, which results in the realization of one segment identically to another. In fact, most historical changes are probably the result of the addition, at some period, of an optional rule. But the optionally identical realization of these two segments does not mean that the unchanged segment cannot subsequently undergo some type of change, in which case merger most definitely would be avoided. Nor does this mean that potential merger was the reason for the change, nor does it mean that the segment must change, for mergers do occur. In short, the fact that one segment may be optionally realized identically to another, does not mean that the latter must change in some way--it merely leaves open the possibility for such to happen, which is the solution utilized in Sendinese and possibly in French in Lorrain.

It is fruitful at this point to consider the implications of push chain phenomena in the light of recent developments concerning the ordering of rules. Koutsoudas, Sanders, and Noll (1971) maintain that the extrinsic ordering of rules in particular languages is unnecessary and that rules which are obligatory must apply to every form whenever their structural description is met. In some cases this involves a need for universal constraints. I will not review their arguments here except insofar as they pertain to the specific examples I have cited.

It should be apparent that the Raising and Centralization rules in Sendinese, and the Raising and Palatalization rules in Lorrain must be ordered respectively in a counter-feeding relation in order to produce the proper output. That is, if a rule A is applied before a rule B in a given derivation, 'B "counter-feeds" A if and only if the application of B would increase the number of forms to which A could apply if B were to apply before A.'[9] More specifically, if in Sendinese the Raising rule were to apply before the Centralization rule, the number of forms to which the latter could apply would be increased, resulting ultimately in the non-occurrence of [i] or [u] in the language, since the two rules would in fact have the combined effect of changing /e/ and /o/ to [ɨ] and [ʉ] respectively. Likewise, were the Raising rule in Lorrain to apply before the Palatalization rule, the number of forms to which the latter could apply would increase with the same resulting loss of /i/ and /u/.

In the counter-feeding example cited by Koutsoudas et al. (1971) of a Deaffrication rule and a Second Palatalization rule in Modern Polish and Old Church Slavic, it was possible to adjust the Deaffrication rule by the addition of a feature in order to sufficiently restrict

the rule's domain of application so that extrinsic ordering of the rules
was unnecessary, that is, they could apply whenever their structural
description was met, without affecting the forms already changed by
one or the other rule. However, there seems to be no way to change
any of the rules for Sendinese and Lorrain without adding some sort
of feature to the feature matrix of the forms which undergo raising
so that Centralization or Palatalization does not apply. But again,
this is a trick, and a very costly one, for it makes the assumption
that provision must be made at some level of abstraction for rules
which still have not applied. This seems to give an excessive amount
of power to the model, with no clear indication of how far one could
go in restricting the application of rules still future in the derivation.
Consequently, the facts of Sendinese and Lorrain seem to oppose the
conclusion arrived at by Koutsoudas et al. (1971:12):

> The hypothesis that there is no extrinsic ordering of phonologi-
> cal rules implies that similar explanations will be possible for
> facts accounted for by any other pair of rules extrinsically
> ordered in a counter-feeding relation. We know of no clear
> evidence that would contradict this implication.

I suggest that both Sendinese and French in Lorrain, as examined
here, seem to present just the type of contradictory evidence alluded
to.

What I have tried to show in this paper is that the two assumptions
felt to be implicit in a push chain interpretation and, as a result,
reasons to disallow such phenomena, are in fact independent of push
chains and irrelevant to their existence when viewed within generative
theory. Support for this conclusion is provided by an actually occurring push chain in the Portuguese dialect of Mirandese as spoken in
Sendim. One rather important aspect of a push chain interpretation
is the contradictory evidence it provides against the hypothesis that
extrinsic ordering of rules in a counter-feeding relation is non-
occurring in language.

NOTES

[1]I am indebted to David Fagan for bringing much of the data and
many of the ideas in this paper to my attention. I also thank R. Joe
Campbell and Mary Clayton Wang for their many comments and
suggestions.

[2]Both Lüdtke (1957) and Hammarström (1953) interpret the development of the vowels as drawn in the diagram, but since neither
linguist includes data to explicitly demonstrate the changes, I simply
include their findings as an illustrative example of an extreme case
of a chain shift.

[3]King (1969b), p. 6.

[4]This of course does not mean that the spread of a sound change across a geographical area is not gradual--in fact quite the opposite is true. A speaker may add a rule to his grammar after which an ever increasing number of speakers with which he comes in contact may also add the rule, but this does not mean the change itself is gradual. The speaker either has the rule in his grammar or he does not. (Cf. Ibid., p. 7.)

[5]Ibid., p. 7.

[6]The feature [central] is not one posited by Chomsky and Halle (1968). I use it here, however, because the generalization that both the back and front high vowels are centralized cannot be made, limiting oneself to just the features [high, low, back, round].

[7]Although no data is given, I assume Fouché to have found alternations which motivated him to make this distinction for the area of Lorrain.

[8]King (1969b), p. 8.

[9]Koutsoudas, Sanders, and Noll (1971), p. 2.

REFERENCES

Carvalho, José G. C. Herculano de. 1958. Fonologia Mirandesa. Coimbra.
Fouché, Pierre. 1958. Phonetique historique du français. Vol. II. Paris, C. Klincksieck.
Hammarström, Göran. 1953. Étude de phonétique auditive sur les parlers de l'Algarve. Uppsala, Almquist and Wiksells.
King, Robert D. 1969a. Historical linguistics and generative grammar. Englewood Cliffs, N. J., Prentice-Hall.
_____. 1969b. Push chains and drag chains. Glossa. 3.1-21.
Koutsoudas, Andreas, Gerald Sanders, and Craig Noll. 1971. On the application of phonological rules. Indiana University Linguistics Club. (Mimeograph.)
Lüdtke, Helmut. 1957. Beiträge zur Lantlehre portugiesischer Mundarten. In: Miscelánea homenaje a André Martinet. Ed. by Diego Catalán. Canarias, La Laguna. 95-112.
Moura Santos, María José de. 1964-65. Os falares fronteiriços de Tras-os-montes. Revista Portuguesa de filologia. Vol. XIII. Lisboa, Coimbra. 65-261.
_____. 1966-68. Os falares fronteiriços de Tran-os-montes. Revista Portuguesa de filologia. Vol. XIV. Lisboa, Coimbra. 213-415.
Vasconcellos, José Leite de. 1901. Estudos de philologia Mirandesa. Vol. I. Lisboa, Coimbra.

SOME EVIDENCE
FOR THE USE OF DIACHRONIC INFORMATION
IN NISSART PHONOLOGY

E. DEAN DETRICH

Michigan State University

1. 0 The language. Nissart is the Romance language spoken in the
city of Nice in the southeast corner of France. Despite the city's
proximity to the Italian border, and despite the fact that this area of
France was ruled by Italian princes for centuries, Nissart is more
properly considered a dialect of Provençal than of Italian. [1] It is
spoken by a small and diminishing number of people, most of whom
are over forty years of age. In order to give a general idea of
Nissart's position with reference to the other Romance languages,
suffice it to say that it is not understood by native speakers either
of French or of Italian, but a speaker of 'standard' Provençal (that
is, the Provençal spoken in the Arles region in the southern Rhône
valley) does understand Nissart, but with a certain degree of difficulty. Nissart has never been an official administrative language
and has no appreciable body of literature. Therefore it has no
standard orthography. The lack of historical data makes detailed
statements about the historical development of Nissart difficult, but
since it is a member of the Romance group certain general statements are possible. For the purposes of this study, a reference to
the Latin etymon usually will suffice.

2. 0 The problem. In constructing a model of the phonological
component of a transformational grammar of Nissart, there are
some difficulties in rule formulation which can be resolved adequately by taking diachronic data into account, but which can be
explained in a purely synchronic way only in a very ad hoc fashion.

50

The purpose of this paper is to justify the presence of certain consonantal segments at the systematic phonemic level of Nissart for
which there is little or no synchronic justification. Despite the problems created by such a procedure, this analysis represents a more
accurate picture of the reality of Nissart phonology than would a grammar that went to great lengths creating segments and rules whose only
justification is avoiding the obvious.

3. 0 The evidence.

3. 1 The first argument in support of the inclusion of these consonants in the systematic phonemics of this language centers around a
discussion of the derivation of a particular group of Nissart verb
infinitives. The infinitive form of the verb is made up of a base
morpheme plus a theme vowel plus the infinitive marker, /r/.
There are four verb conjugations in Nissart. The first conjugation
is characterized by the tense theme vowel /a/;[2] the second has the
tense theme vowel /i/; both the third and fourth conjugations have the
lax theme vowel /e/. The verbs we are interested in at this point
are of the third and fourth conjugation. At the systematic phonetic
level their infinitives end in [re]. In the case of the verb [r'ēndre]
'to render' the word final [re] is not difficult to explain. The underlying representation of [r'ēndre] is /#rend+e+r#/. The posttonic lax
theme vowel is deleted yielding #r'end+r#. The word final [e] is
added as a result of vowel epenthesis yielding #r'end+re#.

Rule 1 Vowel Epenthesis

$$\emptyset \rightarrow e \ / \begin{bmatrix} +\text{obstruant} \\ -\text{continuant} \end{bmatrix} \quad L \underline{\quad} \#$$

The rule for vowel epenthesis is stated in such a way that it could
not generate the word final [e] in the infinitive [kr'èyre] 'to believe'
if the verb stem ends in [y] as it appears. However, if we accept
the fact that the base morpheme of [kr'èyre] 'to believe' is the same
as the base morpheme of [kredibilit'a] 'cridibility' and of [kredit'ur]
'creditor', then we can posit an underlying representation of
/#kred+e+r#/ for [kr'èyre]. With this configuration we can again
bring the Vowel Epenthesis rule into play to explain the word final
[e]. The derivation of this particular infinitive is completed by an
independently motivated rule which rewrites a non-labial consonant
as [y] when it is preceded by a vowel and followed by [r].[3]
Although this derivation correctly generates the infinitive [kr'èyre],
the argument would be stronger if a stem final /d/ appeared somewhere in the verb paradigm, but it does not. Instead, the /d/ of

/kred/ is rewritten as [z], as we can see in the conjugation of the present indicative tense of this verb.

(1) Present Indicative of [kr'èyre]

[kr'ezi]	[krez'ẽ]
[kr'ezes]	[krez'ès]
[kr'eze]	[kr'ezu]

The rewriting of /d/ as [z] presents no particular problem and supports rather than detracts from the argument that the base morpheme of [kr'èyre] is /kred/.

The derivation of the verb [r'ire] 'to laugh' is similar to that of [kr'èyre] but requires an extra word of explanation. Again we have the word final [e], and again it would be convenient to insert it through Vowel Epenthesis. In this case also we can justify the positing of a stem final consonant on the basis of morphemic alternation. In this instance the derivational forms are [ridikül'us] 'ridiculous' and [ridik'ül] 'ridicule'. These alternations permit us to suppose an underlying representation of /#rid+e+r#/ for [r'ire]. Using the same rules as those which generated [kr'èyre] we get the string #r'iy+re# which in turn is rewritten as [r'ire] by a rule which deletes [y] when it occurs between [i] and a [+consonantal] segment. [4]

Unlike [kr'èyre], [r'ire] is a fourth conjugation verb. One of the characteristics of this conjugation is that in the paradigm a stem final stop consonant is deleted. [5]

(2) Present Indicative of [r'ire][6]

[r'iu]	[r'yẽ]
[r'ies]	[r'yès]
[r'i]	[r'iu]

The problem becomes more difficult still, however, upon examination of the fourth conjugation verbs [f'ayre] 'to make' and [d'ire] 'to say'. Each infinitive has the word final [e] which we have explained above as a result of Vowel Epenthesis. In the case of [f'ayre] we have a [y] which would seem to have been derived from a consonant as in [kr'èyre]. The same could also be true of [d'ire] with subsequent deletion of the [y] as was the case with [r'ire]. There is no evidence within either verb paradigm with which to justify the positing of a stem final consonant. Like other fourth conjugation verbs, [f'ayre] and [d'ire] exhibit no stem final stop consonants. Moreover in all other derived forms of the same base morpheme the needed stem final consonant does not exist, and for good reason. In Nissart phonology one never finds two contiguous stop consonants within a word. This is the result of an historical development whereby stop consonants were deleted when followed by another consonant. In this way the Latin prefix, 'extra-' became ['èstra] in Nissart; 'actor' became [at'ur]; 'factio' became [fas'yũ]; 'directus' became [dir'èt] etc. This is the very reason why we have no occurrences of stem final consonants of the base morphemes of [f'ayre] and of [d'ire]. In all the derived forms outside the verb paradigm, the base final consonant (which was /k/ in both cases) occurred before a consonant and was deleted. It is nevertheless desirable to retain these stem final consonants in the systematic phonemics of Nissart in order to correctly derive such forms as [f'ayre] and [d'ire], using rules already in the phonology of Nissart. The only other solution would be to posit an arbitrary rule to insert [e]'s at the end of both these infinitives and posit another arbitrary rule to insert a [y] before the [r] in [f'ayre]. [7]

If we choose to include these diachronically motivated consonants in the systematic phonemics of Nissart, we must also include the diachronic rule for preconsonantal stop consonant deletion as an ordered rule in the synchronic grammar of the language. This rule is formulated as follows:

Rule 2 Preconsonantal Consonant Deletion

$$C \rightarrow \emptyset \ / \ \begin{bmatrix} +\text{obstruent} \\ -\text{continuant} \end{bmatrix} \quad C$$

With this rule now at our disposal we can correctly derive [f'ayre] from /#fak+e+r#/; [fat'ur] 'mailman' from /#fak+t+ur#/; [d'ire] from /#dik+e+r#/ and [dit'a] 'dictation' from /#dik+ta#/.

3.2 The second strong argument in favor of the inclusion of preconsonantal stop consonants at the systematic phonemic level of Nissart stems from the way they influence the mapping of the underlying vowel system of Nissart onto its phonetic realization. Their presence or absence is in fact what determines the number of underlying vowel segments in the language.

On the surface it would appear that there are eight distinctive oral vowels in Nissart, that is, eight oral vowels which contrast phonemically. They are represented schematically with reference to their position of articulation in (3).

(3) [i] [ü]   [u]
     [e] [oe]   [o]
     [è]   [a]

The feature specification of these vowels is provided in (4).

(4)   i   e   è   a   o   u   ü   oe

	i	e	è	a	o	u	ü	oe
high	+	-	-	-	-	+	+	-
low	-	-	+	+	-	-	-	-
back	-	-	-	+	+	+	-	-
round	-	-	-	-	+	+	+	+

There is an additional phonetically distinct [+low] vowel, [ò], which is consistently pronounced either as a positional variant of [o] or is in free variation with [o]. A similar relationship exists between the vowels [e] and [è], but in this case there are several clear instances where these vowels appear to contrast phonemically. However, if the systematic phonemic representation of the words which show this contrast is correctly formulated, we can demonstrate that what appears on the surface to be a phonemic contrast between [e] and [è] is actually the realization of positional variants of the same underlying vowel segment. We shall suppose that this underlying segment is /e/ which is rewritten as [è] in certain environments. This is the case when /e/ is followed by a liquid and under certain conditions when it is followed by a glide, but of more interest to us are the combinations of consonants before which /e/ is rewritten as [è].
Let us examine the following data:

(5) [fr'eska] 'fresh'   [m'èstre] 'master'
     ['eska] 'bait'   [fen'èstra] 'window'
     [p'eska] 'fish'   [kamp'èstre] 'country'

In these data the underlying /e/ retains the specification [-low] before the string [sk] but is realized as [+low] when followed by [str]. The critical environment here is obviously the two [+consonantal] segments which follow the [s]. Rule 3 is designed to account for the vowel lowering in [m'èstre], [fen'èstra], and [kamp'èstre].

Rule 3 Vowel Lowering

$$e \rightarrow [+\text{low}] / \underline{\quad} \begin{bmatrix} +\text{consonantal} \\ +\text{continuant} \end{bmatrix} [+\text{obstruent}] [+\text{consonantal}]$$

With slight modification Rule 3 will also correctly derive the occurrences of [è] in the following list of data which includes the troublesome apparent phonemic contrasts discussed earlier.

(6) Phonetics	Gloss	Phonetics	Gloss
[s'èt]	'seven'	[s'et]	'thirst'
[d'èt]	'debt'	[d'et]	'finger'
[f'ès]	'you do'	[f'es]	'time'
[asp'èt]	'aspect'		
[dir'èt]	'direct'		
[kur'èt]	'correct'		

In order to correctly generate all the words in (6) we must do two things. First we must accept the obvious. At the systematic phonemic level the words in the left-hand column of (6) have two [+consonantal] segments after the /e/. Next we must modify Rule 3 slightly to make the occurrence of [s] before the two [+consonantal] segments optional.

Rule 4

$$e \rightarrow [+ \text{low}] \; / \; \underline{\hspace{1cm}} \; \left(\begin{bmatrix} +\text{consonantal} \\ +\text{continuant} \end{bmatrix} \right) \begin{bmatrix} +\text{obstruant} \\ -\text{continuant} \end{bmatrix} \; [+\text{consonantal}]$$

The rules are ordered so that Rule 4 will rewrite /e/ as [è] and then the rule for Preconsonantal Consonant Deletion will apply, yielding the correct pronunciation, as we can see in (7).

(7) Phonemics		Rule 3		Cons. Delet.		Phonetics	Gloss
/#sept#/	→	#s'èpt#	→	#s'èt#	→	[s'èt]	'seven'
/#set#/	→	___		___		[s'et]	'thirst'
/#debt#/	→	#d'èbt#	→	#d'èt#	→	[d'èt]	'debt'
/#det#/	→	___		___		[d'et]	'finger'
/#fets#/	→	#f'èts#	→	#f'ès#	→	[f'ès]	'you do'
/#fes#/	→	___		___		[f'es]	'time'
/#kurekt#/	→	#kur'èkt#	→	#kur'èt#	→	[kur'èt]	'correct'
/#aspekt#/	→	#asp'èkt#	→	#asp'èt#	→	[asp'èt]	'aspect'
/#direkt#/	→	#dir'èkt#	→	#dir'èt#	→	[dir'èt]	'direct'

Clearly, without positing these underlying preconsonantal consonants, for which there is ample diachronic justification but no synchronic justification, the only way to explain the contrast between [sèt] and [set], between [fès] and [fes], and between [dèt] and [det] would be to add /è/ to the list of systematic phonemic vowel segments of Nissart. This would be an ad hoc solution whose only function would be to avoid a better solution, the one outlined above.

3.3 Further support for the positing of these preconsonantal consonants in the systematic phonemics of Nissart can be provided by studying the problem of stress placement in the verb paradigm. How can we best account for the difference in stress placement in the following very forms?

(8) Singular   Gloss   Plural
     [k'ãntes]   'you sing'   [kãnt'as]
     [r'ēndes]   'you render'   [rēnd'ès]
     [fin'ises]   'you finish'   [finis'ès]
     [d'eves]   'you must'   [dev'ès]

First, it has already been claimed that there is a single underlying vowel from which [e] and [è] are derived. If the [è] in the verb forms [rēnd'ès], [finis'ès], and [dev'ès] is to be derived from an underlying /e/, that /e/ must be in an environment requiring Rule 4 to apply, that is, the /e/ should be followed by two [+consonantal] segments. There is diachronic justification for positing /ts/ as a second person plural marker in Nissart. With such an ending we can adequately account for /e/ being rewritten as [è] in the second plural of verbs, and we are able to place stress correctly as well.

The Main Stress rule for Nissart is a somewhat complicated affair which would require a presentation longer than the present paper to be fully described. Such a discussion would involve a complete presentation of the tense and lax vowel systems, which is not directly pertinent to the question at hand. Suffice it to say that if the second person plural marker in the Missart verb paradigm were /s/ rather than /ts/, then at the point in the derivation of [r'ēndes] and [rēnd'ès] where the Main Stress rule applies, the realization of these two verb forms would be nearly identical (#rend+es# in the singular and #rend+e+s# in the plural), and in both cases stress would be placed on the stem vowel, leaving an incorrect second person plural, *[r'end+e+s]. However, with a second person plural marker in /ts/ the Main Stress rule, whose justification is entirely independent of this discussion, correctly places stress on the theme vowel. In (9) we have a representative derivation.

(9) Systematic Phonemics   /#rend+e+ts#/
     Main Stress   #rend+'e+ts#
     Vowel Lowering   #rend+'è+ts#
     Consonant Deletion   #rend+'è+s#
     Systematic Phonetics   [rēnd'ès]

The only real alternative to this analysis is to mark the second person plural of all polysyllabic verbs as exceptions to the Main Stress rule, which is tantamount to having one Main Stress rule for the second person plural of verbs and another Main Stress rule for

all the other words in the language. The only argument against this
solution is that nowhere in modern Nissart is there a pronunciation
[ts] for a second person plural verb form.

4.0 Conclusion. There are many questions left unanswered in
this paper. There has been no discussion of whether all preconsonantal stop consonants which have been deleted in the historical development of Nissart should be included in the systematic phonemics
of this language. For example, should the underlying systematic
phonemic representation of [at'ur] 'actor' be /#akt+ur#/ or should it
be /#at+ur#/? In this instance there is no primary or secondary
synchronic justification for including the /k/ although we know that
it has as much diachronic justification as the underlying /k/ of
/#direkt#/. If we include an underlying /k/ in /#akt+ur#/, our
systematic phonemic representation is overspecific. At the same
time, no problem is created. The rule for Preconsonantal Consonant
Deletion would eliminate the /k/ in any case. There is another more
difficult problem of oversimplification. Since the /t/ of the second
person plural marker /ts/ is never pronounced in modern Nissart, it
is not necessary to fully specify it as a /t/ in the systematic phonemics. For the Main Stress rule, the Vowel Lowering rule and
Preconsonantal Consonant Deletion rule to apply to the second person
plural of verbs, we only need a person number marker made up of
the segments:

$$/ \begin{bmatrix} +\text{obstruant} \\ -\text{continuant} \end{bmatrix} s/$$

Should we prefer this formation to the formulation /ts/?

However important these questions may be, the goal of this paper
has not been to answer them, but rather to demonstrate that they must
be answered. A grammar of Nissart phonology which includes an
extra vowel segment at the systematic phonemic level, which inserts
the glide [y] in verb forms in an arbitrary fashion and which puts
special constraints on the placement of stress of particular verb
forms can be descriptively adequate. But if our goal is explanatory
adequacy, we must accept the fact that there are certain consonants,
or at least certain feature specifications of consonants necessary, in
the systematic phonemics of Nissart, which never appear in the
systematic phonetics of this language.

NOTES

[1]One of the main reasons behind Bailet's book, <u>Joseph-Rosalinde Rancher et le dialecte niçard</u> (1956), is to demonstrate that Nissart is a dialect of Provençal rather than Italian. 'Lorsque le dialecte de Nice se rapproche de l'italien, c'est que le Provençal dans l'ensemble s'en rapproche aussi . . . Lorsque le niçard diffère du provençal rhodanien, il a un traitement à part, commun souvent au provençal maritime, diffèrent aussi de l'italien . . . Si dans certains cas l'italien a influencé le dialecte de Nice (Ex.: question des pro-parosytons) cela n'amène pas à dire que le niçard soit d'origine italienne.'

[2]Since the distinction between tense and lax vowels is not a major concern in this paper, distinctive symbols for tense and lax vowels have not been used in transcriptions.

[3]Note the following alternations as a brief justification of the rule rewriting non-labial consonants as [y] between a vowel and [r]:

[petrifik'a]	'to petrify'	[p'èyre]	'Peter'
[patrim'òni]	'to patrimony'	[p'ayre]	'father'
[matrim'òni]	'matrimony'	[m'ayre]	'mother'

Each of the alternating pairs has a common base morpheme contain-ing /t/ before /r/ in the systematic phonemics. In all the right-hand examples, the /t/ is rewritten as [y], but only after the rule for Vowel Epenthesis has inserted a word final [e].

[4]There is independent motivation for this rule in that a similar rule is necessary in order to delete the glide [w] when it occurs be-tween [u] and a [+consonantal] segment. This rule is formulated as follows:

$$G \rightarrow \emptyset \ / \ \begin{bmatrix} V \\ +\text{high} \\ \alpha\text{round} \\ \beta\text{back} \end{bmatrix} \begin{bmatrix} \underline{\quad} \\ \alpha\text{round} \\ \beta\text{back} \end{bmatrix} \quad [+\text{consonantal}]$$

[5]See Schane (1968), p. 114.

[6]Although there is no stem final consonant in the verb paradigm of [r'ire], the /d/ of the morpheme /rid/ is realized as [z] in the derived forms [riz'ible] 'laughable' and [rizibilit'a] 'laughability'.

[7]The stem final /k/ in /fak/ is also necessary for the correct generation of the past participle of [f'ayre]. The underlying repre-sentation of this form is /#fak+e+t#/, with /t/ being the past partici-ple marker. The posttonic lax theme vowel /e/ is deleted, /t/ is rewritten as [c] when preceded by a [+high] segment, and /k/ is

deleted by Preconsonantal Consonant Deletion. If there is no /k/ in /fak/, there is no justification for rewriting /t/ as [c].

REFERENCES

Bailet, Christiane. 1956. Joseph-Rosalinde Rancher et le dialecte niçard. Série: Travaux et mémoire, no. 2. Aix-en-Provence, Publications des annales de la Faculté des Lettres.

Detrich, E. Dean. 1972. Nissart verb morphology: A transformational approach. Unpublished Ph. D. dissertation, The Pennsylvania State University.

Schane, Sanford A. 1968. French phonology and morphology. Research Monograph no. 45. Cambridge, MIT Press.

LONG VOWELS
AND UNDERLYING POSTVOCALIC r
IN CREOLE FRENCH

ALBERT VALDMAN

Indiana University

A fundamental problem in generative phonology is that of the motivation of abstract underlying forms. This problem raises many theoretical issues even in the analysis of languages exhibiting extensive
inflectional and derivational morphophonemic alternations and whose
well-documented historical development permits appeal to diachronic
rules which can be assumed to be reflected at the synchronic level.
The motivation of abstract underlying forms is particularly troublesome in the case of languages lacking inflectionally related forms
and whose historical development is not well charted. Such is indeed
the case for Creole French, [1] hereafter referred to as Creole, a
creolized language resulting from the convergence of Northern (Oïl)
varieties of French and West African languages, presumably in a
situation of multilingual contact. Given the multiplicity of its putative
source languages, it is difficult to specify with confidence the termi-
nus a quo of Creole. In this paper, I will attempt to show that the
postulation of abstract underlying forms on the basis of isolated
derivationally related forms and appeal to uncertain diachronic relationships results in erroneous analyses that obscure structural
facts. Indeed, the misanalysis I will attempt to refute is the result
of the view, espoused by many creolists, that, in its phonological
and lexical systems at least, Creole derives directly from Standard
French (SF). The specific phonological problem discussed here is
that of the relationship between the so-called 'long' vowels and postvocalic r on the one hand, and between long and nasal vowels on the
other.

Long vowels. The oral vowel system of Creole is composed of seven units characterized by the following distinctive feature matrix:[2]

(1)		i	u	e	ɛ	a	ɔ	o
high		+	+	+	−	−	−	+
mid		−	−	+	+	−	+	+
front		+	−	+	+	+	−	−
round		−	+	−	−	−	+	+

Supporting contrastive data is given in (2).

(2)	i/e	[si]	'if'	[se]	'it is'
	e/ɛ	[pe]	'hush'	[pɛ]	'priest'
	ɛ/a	[pɛ]	'priest'	[pa]	'not'
	i/u	[si]	'if'	[su]	'under'
	u/o	[pu]	'for'	[po]	'skin'
	o/ɔ	[bo]	'kiss'	[bɔ]	'edge'

In Lesser Antilles varieties of Creole, notably in Dominican and Saint-Lucian, there are in addition contrasts between short and long low-mid ([−high, +mid]) vowels:

(3)	[nɛf]	neuf	'nine'	[nɛ:f]	nerf	'nerve'
	[sɔt]	sot	'stupid'	[sɔ:t]	sort	'to go out'
	[pɔt]	pot	'pot'	[lapɔ:t]	porte	'door'

In these varieties of Creole there are also contrasts between long and short a in which the longer vowel may also have a backer articulation or vary freely with the short back vowel:[3]

(4)	[pak]	Pâques	'Easter'	[pa:k]	parc	'enclosure'
				or [pɑ:k] or [pɑk]		
	[lam]	lame	'wave'	[la:m]	larme	'tear'
				or [lɑ:m] or [lɑm]		

Finally, in Dominican and Saint-Lucian [a] and [ɑ] may contrast in utterance-final free syllables:

(5)	[pa]	pas	'not'	[pɑ]	par	'through'
	[la]	la	'there'	[lɑ]	lard	'lard'

On the basis of their correspondence to vowel + r combinations of French cognates, Douglas Taylor (1947) was led to interpret the 'long' vowels as sequences vowel + r, so that [nɛ:f] was analyzed as /nerf/, [lapɔ:t] as /laport/, and [pa:k] as /park/.

Blocking of assimilation of nasality. While phonetically long vowels are absent in Haitian Creole, one finds vowels that have a peculiar behavior in the environment of nasal consonants.[4] To place these facts in proper perspective, it is necessary first to characterize vowel nasalization in that variety of Creole.

At first sight the nasal vowel system of Creole differs from that of SF only by the absence of front rounded [œ̃] and by the presence of the high nasals [ĩ] and [ũ] about whose phonological status there is considerable debate among creolists.[5] But the differences are more profound. First, nasal vowels are differently distributed in the two languages. In SF, nasal vowels do not occur before utterance-final nasal consonants, and it is this feature of their distribution that makes it possible to interpret them as underlying sequences of vowel plus nasal consonant. In Creole, on the other hand, the three nasal vowels that have SF equivalents--[ẽ], [ʌ̃], [õ]--occur freely before nasal consonants, see (6).[6]

(6)

Final position				Before final nasal consonant			
[ve]	'wish'					[ven]	'our wish'
		[vẽ]	'twenty'	[vẽn]	'vein'		
[vɛ]	'glass'					[vɛn]	'our glass'
[mo]	'word'					[mon]	'our word'
		[nõ]	'name'	[mõn]	'world'		
[mɔ]	'dead'					[mɔn]	'hill'
[sa]	'that'	[sʌ̃]	'blood'	[šʌ̃m]	'room'	[šam]	'spell'

The nasal quality of Creole has been noted by various analysts who have attempted to account for it by positing powerful nasal assimilation rules operating in the environment of nasal consonants. Thus Carrington (1967) states that any vowel may be optionally nasalized when it precedes a nasal consonant.[7] For Hall (1950) nasal assimilation occurs in the vicinity of a nasal consonant with shift to casual speech. Jourdain (1956) proposes an obligatory assimilation of vowels by the effect of any neighboring nasal consonant to which only a small set of morphemes are exempt. Tinelli (1970) and d'Ans (1968) propose nasal assimilation rules that are more narrowly constrained. Tinelli posits a regressive nasal assimilation rule that operates only across morpheme boundaries:[8]

(7) pu li 'for him'   vs.   pũ mwẽ 'for me'

For d'Ans vowels are nasalized if (i) they are followed by an utterance-final nasal consonant or (ii) preceded by a nasal consonant and followed by a voiced obstruent, that is:

(8) (i) V → [+nasal] / ___ $\begin{bmatrix} +cons \\ +nasal \end{bmatrix}$ #   pan→pãn 'to hang'

   (ii) V → [+nasal] / $\begin{bmatrix} +cons \\ +nasal \end{bmatrix}$ ___ $\begin{bmatrix} +cons \\ +obs \\ +voice \end{bmatrix}$ remɛd→remẽd
   'medicine'

It is clear that some of the items appearing in (6), namely, [ven] 'our wish', [vɛn] 'our glass', [mon] 'our word', [mɔn] 'hill', and [šam] 'spell', constitute counter-examples to all the nasal assimilation rules proposed except that posited by Tinelli (7). The blocking of nasal assimilation in [ven], [vɛn], and [mon] may be accounted for by the existence of a morpheme boundary, for all three forms contain the truncated alternant of the possessive determiner [nũ] 'our, inclusive'. But it cannot be explained in the other two forms which are composed of a single morpheme. 9

Underlying r̠ solution. D'Ans claims that vowels which constitute exceptions to the first of his two nasal assimilation rules (8. i) are in Haitian Creole followed in fact by a weakly articulated centro-palatal glide which he represents by [ᵊ]: [mɔᵊn] 'hill', [šaᵊm] 'spell' (1968: 53, 73)--it will be recalled that Taylor (1967) notes these items with long vowels. D'Ans then suggests that the glide blocks nasal assimilation. The assignment of this glide to /r/ is fairly well motivated since that phoneme is realized in other environments as a weakly articulated palato-velar continuant ([ɣat] 'rat', [diɣ i] 'rice'), hardly distinguishable from [w] before a rounded vowel ([ɣʷuž] 'red', [p ɣ ʷɔmne] 'to take a walk'). In addition, since by proposing the progressive assimilation rule in (8. ii) d'Ans claims that vowels are not subject to nasalization when they occur after a nasal consonant and before a consonant other than a voiced obstruent, the centro-palatal glide cannot be a voiced obstruent, a condition met by /r/. According to d'Ans the forms in (6) ending with a nasal consonant would be reanalyzed as:

(9) [vẽn] /ven/   'vein' vs. [vɛᵊn] /ver+n/ 'our glass'
                            vs. [ven]   /ve+n/   'our wish'
    [mõn] /mon/   'world' vs. [mɔᵊn] /morn/   'hill'
                            vs. [mon]   /mo+n/   'our word'
    [šᾶm] /šam/   'room' vs. [šaᵊm] /šarm/   'spell'

Postvocalic /r/, termed 'r structurel représenté par zéro sur le plan phonologique' (1968:57), posited to account for the blocking of nasalization on the basis of its identification with a glide that d'Ans alone among creolists is able to perceive, is now available to handle contrasts between 'long' and short low-mid and low vowels:

(10) [nɛf] /nef/ 'nine' vs. [nɛᵊf] /nerf/ 'nerve'
     [sɔt] /sot/ 'stupid' vs. [sɔᵊt] /sort/ 'to go out'
     [pak] /pak/ 'Easter/ vs. [paᵊk] /park/ 'enclosure'

It will be noted that underlying postvocalic r always follows a low-mid or low vowel. Several creolists (d'Ans 1968, Tinelli 1970) seem to think that Creole, like SF, is characterized by an inherent drive toward the complementary distribution of high-mid and low-mid vowels: the high-mid member occurring in free syllables and the low-mid member in checked syllables; this state of affairs is termed la loi de position. Contrasts between high and low-mid vowels in utterance-final free syllables, such as [pe] 'hush' vs. [pɛ] 'priest' constitute violations of this inherent complementation. But if in these contrasts it is assumed that low-mid vowels are checked by an underlying postvocalic r, complementation is preserved and, in addition, the oral vowel inventory reduced.

To recapitulate, utterance-final vowels exhibit two sets of surface phonetic features that may be related if an underlying r is posited. First, in some Lesser Antilles varieties of Creole length is contrastive before low-mid and low vowels; in Haitian Creole length corresponds to a centro-palatal glide [ᵊ], although the accuracy of this observation is questionable. Second, when they occur before a nasal consonant in some morphemes low-mid and low vowels block regressive assimilation of nasality. In addition, the postulation of an underlying postvocalic r permits a reduction of the oral vowel inventory from eight to five units:

(11)
i	u		i		u
e	o	→	e		o
ɛ	ɔ				
a	α		a		

This solution requires only an independently motivated nasal assimilation rule and rules specifying that [+mid] mowels are [+high] when they occur in a checked syllable but [-high] when they occur in a free syllable and that low ([-mid, -high]) vowels are [+front] in a free syllable but [-front] in a checked syllable. Dominican and Saint-Lucian Creole would also require a rule lenghtening all vowels in the environment rC. Finally, the underlying r solution has the added advantage of relating Creole morphemes containing 'long' (including nasal assimilation-blocking vowels) and syllable-final low-mid or low vowels to their presumed SF etymon.

Objections to the underlying postvocalic r̠ solution. The postulation of an underlying postvocalic r̠ obscures many important facts
about the phonological structure of Creole and is to be rejected on the
basis of the following six sets of considerations.

(1) There are no alternations involving forms containing long
vowels or non-nasal vowels followed by a final nasal consonant on the
one hand, and forms containing a phonetically manifest r̠, on the other.
In other words, the postulated underlying r̠ would undergo absolute
deletion. There are a handful of derivationally related forms containing alternations r̠ and zero: [tɛ] 'earth' ~ [ʌ̃tɛmʌ̃] 'burial' ~ [ʌ̃teɣ e]
'to bury', [žumʌ̃] 'profanity' ~ [žu ɣe] 'to swear': [šaž] 'load' ~ [šažmʌ̃]
'load' [ša ɣɛt] 'cart'. In view of the uncertain semantic relationship
between members of these derivational sets and the marginal nature
of the alternation, it is doubtful that Creole speakers relate them, and
it would be difficult to prove that for the speakers of the language
underlying r̠ had any psychological reality.

(2) Within the framework of an interpretation of the Creole vowel
system based on the postulation of an underlying postvocalic r̠, the
view that emerges is that of an unstable four-tongue height system
evolving toward a three-tongue height system by means of the complementary distribution of high-mid and low-mid vowels. Descriptive
facts suggest in fact a contrary view. Not only, as is indicated in
(2), do high-mid and low-mid vowels contrast in final free syllables,
but apocope of the final vowel of verb forms particularly characteristic of Haitian Creole, results in many contrasts between these two
sets of vowels in checked syllables:

(12)

[mɛt]	maître	'master'	vs.	[met] ~ [mete]	mettre	'to put'
[paɣ ɛt]	paraître	'to appear'	vs.	[ɣet] ~ [ɣete]	rester	'to remain'
[sɔt]	sot, sotte	'stupid'	vs.	[sot] ~ [soti]	sortir	'to leave'
[lapɔt]	porte	'door'	vs.	[pot] ~ [pote]	apporter	'to bring'

Nor is there complementary distribution between high-mid and low-
mid vowels in non-final syllables. Numerous instances are found,
particularly, of low-mid vowels in internal free syllables which do
not correspond to SF sequences mid-vowel plus r̠: [bɛbɛ] 'mute',
[bɔkɔ] 'sorcerer, voodo priest', [gɣʷɔsɛ] 'size' (compare to [gɣʷo]
'large'), [vɔlɛ] 'thief'.

(3) The postulation of an underlying postvocalic r̠ entails assuming
a double origin for nasal vowels in Creole. When they occur in free
syllables, independently of a nasal consonant, they are derivable
from underlying nasal vowels, i.e. vowels marked [+nasal] in the
lexicon. In the context of a nasal consonant it is impossible to

distinguish between underlying nasal vowels and those generated by
nasal assimilation rules such as (8). For the underlying postvocalic
r solution to hold, it must be demonstrated that there are no oral
vowels in the environments meeting the structural description of
rules (8). Such is not the case, however, for there are counter-
examples to these rules too numerous to be handled by a list of exceptions, e.g. [emab] 'nice', [somɛj] 'sleep', [nɛg] 'guy', [menaž]
'concubine', [limonad] 'lemon juice'.

Furthermore, analyses of vowel nasalization in Creole in terms of
an underlying set of nasal vowels and another introduced by assimilation rules do not reveal the real descriptive problems in this aspect
of the phonology of Creole. First, opposed to the nasalized vowels of
SF, those of Creole appear to represent two distinct types from a
perceptual point of view. When they occur in free syllables the vowels
[ẽ], [õ], and [ɑ̃] are as fully nasalized as their SF corresponding
vowels and it may be assumed that they share their articulatory and
acoustic characteristics (Delattre 1965, 1968). But when they occur
in the environment of a nasal consonant, Creole nasal vowels, including [ĩ] and [ũ], have a more diffuse and less perceptible nasality.[10]
It is tempting to posit that this latter type of nasality is derivable by
transformational rules such as (8) applied to underlying oral vowels.
But, unfortunately, it is not the case that vowels with diffuse nasality
occur only in the environment of a nasal consonant. High nasal vowels
occur in free syllables, e.g. [nũ] '1st pl. inclusive pronoun'--al-
though such cases are quite rare. On the other hand, non-nasal high
vowels occur before a nasal consonant, e.g. [mun] 'person', [mašin]
'machine'. Second, there appears to be considerable free variation
in the appearance of nasal and oral vowels in the context of a nasal
consonant: [demõ] ~ [dẽmõ] 'malevolent supernatural being', [samdi]
~ [sɑ̃mdi] 'Saturday'. This type of alternation cannot be accounted
for in terms of style shift, as Hall (1947, 1953) advanced. There are
also alternations between nasal and oral vowels in derivationally related sets of words with obvious French etyma containing an oral
vowel: [amu] 'self-esteem, pride, vanity' vs. [fɛlɑ̃mu] 'to make
love', [amtije] 'type of climbing plant' vs. [zɑ̃mi] 'friend'; [tutɔm]
'each one' vs. [nõm] 'man'. These facts, which require detailed
empirical study, are best accounted for, not by analyzing nasalization as automatic or non-distinctive in the environment of a nasal
consonant, but by assuming that it must be specified in the lexicon
for every morpheme. Thus, whereas [mõn] 'world' would be listed
as mõn, forms in which nasalization is blocked would be specified
with an oral vowel, viz. [mɔn] ~ [mɔ:n] 'hill' would be entered as
mõn.

(4) All varieties of Creole exhibit alternations in the form of the
postposed definite determiner conditioned by the nature of the final

segments of the immediately preceding element of the noun phrase.
In Haitian Creole, where the system of alternation is the most complex, there are five variant forms [a], [ʎ], [la], [lʎ], and [nʎ] (13).

(13) fig la　　　　'the banana'
      šẽn nʎ⎫
      šẽn lʎ⎬　'the chain'
      papa a　　　'the father'
      šẽ ʎ　　　　'the dog'
      pɛ a　　　　'the priest'
      bɔ a　　　　'the edge'

The truncated forms [a] and [ʎ] occur after vowels while the three
full forms occur after consonants. If forms such as [pɛ] 'priest' or
[bɔ] 'edge' contained a final underlying r, we would expect them to be
followed by the [la] alternant, i.e. per-la [pɛla] and bor-la [bɔla].
Instead, as shown in (13), these forms are followed by the [a] alternant of the post-posed definite determiner.

(5) Another shortcoming of the postulation of an underlying postvocalic r is that it would introduce the only type of productive final
consonant cluster in the language: [mɔn] morn 'hill', [nɛf] nerf
'nerve', [šam] šarm 'spell'.[11] Elsewhere, where etymologically
related Standard French forms have final consonant clusters, Creole
forms end in a single consonant. Compare, for example, [mɛt]
maître 'master', [šʎm] chambre 'room', [bab] barbe 'beard', [žis]
juste 'just'.

(6) Finally, the reduction of the oral inventory obtained by interpreting low-mid vowels as sequences of vowel + r is illusory. The
features [high] and [mid], needed to specify the eight-vowel system,
are also required to characterize the reduced five-vowel system:

(14) | | i | e | a | o | u |
     |-------|---|---|---|---|---|
     | high | + | + | − | + | + |
     | mid | − | + | − | + | − |
     | front | + | + | + | − | − |
     | round | − | − | − | + | + |

NOTES

*I am indebted to Yves Dejean for most of the crucial Haitian
Creole examples contained in this paper as well as for his judicious
criticism of Valdman (1968), which forced me to abandon an analysis
of the oral vowel system of Creole in terms of contrastive underlying
short and long low and mid vowels in favor of the present analysis.

[1]The term Creole French here subsumes Caribbean varieties for which fairly reliable and systematic descriptions are available: Dominican (Taylor 1947), Guyanese (Saint-Jacques-Fauquenoy 1972), Haitian (Hall 1953, d'Ans 1968, Valdman 1970, Tinelli 1972, 1973), Saint-Lucian (Carrington 1967, Valdman and Carrington 1968). Except for those relevant for the discussion of phonetically long vowels, examples cited are from Haitian Creole. Specifically excluded from our study are Indian Ocean dialects of Creole which appear to have a phonetically manifest postvocalic r̲ (Moorghen 1972).

With regard to the genesis of Creole note that by the choice of the term 'convergence' we are rejecting implicitly the theory according to which Creole is a mixed language composed of a Northern French-based lexicon and phonology and a grammatical system derived from West African languages.

[2]Front rounded vowels ([y], [ǿ], [œ]) need to be posited for certain dialects to account for such contrasts as [plim] 'feather' vs. [plim] or [plym] 'pen', [pɛ] 'priest' or 'pair' vs. [pɛ] or [pœ] 'fear', and [de] 'thimble' vs. [de] or [dǿ] 'two'. In Haiti, because the variant containing the front rounded vowel is often attested in the speech of French-Creole bilingual members of the elite or monolingual Creole speakers who come in frequent contact with them, it has been proposed that the front rounded vowels constitute a sub-system borrowed from French. However, variants with front rounded vowels are also attested among rural monolingual speakers (Hyppolite 1950). In addition, Taylor (1947:173) reports a high back unrounded vowel (sometimes centralized in the speech of the younger generation) which contrasts with [i]: [šïk] 'chigoes (parasites)' vs. [tik] 'ticks (parasites)' and [sïme] 'sowed' vs. [fime] 'smoke'. The front rounded vowels can be accommodated by the set of distinctive features proposed:

	[y]	[ǿ]	[œ]
high	+	+	-
mid	-	+	+
front	+	+	+
round	+	+	+

[3]Taylor (1947) points out, however, that this distinction is characteristic of the speech of older speakers. In the course of fieldwork in Saint-Lucia many of our younger informants also distinguished their speech from that of older persons.

[4]A preliminary investigation of the perception of vowel length on the part of speakers of Haitian Creole and its acoustic correlates reveals that there is no consistent difference between short and 'putative' long vowels. A bilingual informant born in Gonaïves and

educated in Port-au-Prince was asked to produce four renditions of the putative contrasts [pɔt] 'pot' vs. [pɔ:t 'door', [pak] 'Easter' vs. [pa:k] 'enclosure', [pɛ] 'hush' vs. [pɛ:] 'priest', and [sɔt] 'stupid vs. [sɔ:t] 'to have just'. These utterances were then presented to the same informant in random order, and he was asked to identify them. He was only able to identify correctly fourteen of twenty-three items recorded, slightly better than chance. Spectrograms were made of the utterances and the duration of the vowels measured; there was no significant difference in length between members of the various pairs. (Grateful acknowledgment is made to Dr. Marvin Carmody who administered the perception test and collected the spectrographic data.)

5These vowels generally occur preceding a nasal consonant, e.g. [kačĩmbo] 'earthenware pipe', [bũnda] 'arse'. Except for Tinelli (1973) who cites numerous instances of [ĩ] and [ũ] following but not preceding a nasal consonant ([mĩ] 'ripe', [mũri] 'to die'), creolists have noted only two morphemes that contain a nasalized high vowel: [j̃ũ] 'indefinite determiner' (occurring also in the variants [ũ] and [õ]) and [nũ] 'first person plural inclusive pronoun'. There are other instances of [ũ] occurring outside of the context of a nasal consonant but in all cases there is a variant containing a brief nasal closure homorganic to the following oral consonant: [ũgã] or [ũ^{n}gã] 'voodoo priest', [ũfɔ] or [ũ^{m}fɔ] 'voodoo temple. A point at issue is whether, before a nasal consonant, the high vowels occur at all without perceptible nasalization, e.g. /kuzin/ 'cousin', /larim/ 'mucus', /mun/ 'person'. Tinelli claims that they do not and accounts for the difference of opinion among creolists by the particular phonetic nature of nasalization accompanying high vowels: 'the nasality of [ĩ] can easily be missed on first hearing, especially if one's native language does not have any high nasal vowel phoneme' (1973:8). Tinelli also adds that the nasalization is clearly audible when the alleged nasal high vowel occurs before the definite determiner la which is nasalized in that environment: [pitimĩ] 'millet' vs. [pitimĩʎ̃] 'the millet'. Clearly, only instrumental evidence can resolve the controversy.

6Hall (1953:18) was first to note Haitian Creole nasal vowels with a set of IPA symbols different from those used traditionally to represent the nasal vowels of French, namely [ẽ ə̃ õ], instead of [ɛ̃ ɑ̃ ɔ̃], respectively. This choice of symbols would seem to indicate that Haitian Creole nasal vowels are higher and more central than their French equivalents. This appears only partially correct on the basis of preliminary acoustic evidence we have gathered.

Spectrograms were made of the five nasal vowels posited by most phonological analyses of Haitian Creole. The vowels were produced by the speaker described in note 4 of this article, first in isolation, but with reference to a key word, and then in a variety of word-length utterances illustrating the typical environments in which the vowels occur. The first and second formant (F_1 and F_2) values obtained appear in Table 1. These values represent the average of the number of vowel tokens (appearing in parentheses) and they are compared to values for Standard French nasal vowels given by Delattre (1965) and obtained from one of our Parisian informants--no doubt, the values given by Delattre are more reliable than ours but only ours are relevant in this discussion since they were obtained under the same experimental conditions as the Creole data:

TABLE 1.

Haitian Creole			Standard French				
				Our values		Delattre values	
	F_1	F_2		F_1	F_2	F_1	F_2
ĩ (3)	450	2200					
ẽ (9)	700	2200	ɛ̃	600	1500	550	1800
ʌ̃ (7)	950	1400	ã	500	1100	550	1000
ɔ̃ (8)	700	1100	ɔ̃	450	900	550	750
			œ̃	550	1400	550	1400
ũ (4)	500	900					

On a two-dimensional logarithmic plot in which F_1 values are plotted on the ordinate with values increasing from top to bottom and F_2 values plotted on the abcissa with values increasing from right to left (so that vowels form a display comparable to that of the articulatory quadrilateral), Haitian Creole nasal vowels are much lower than their Standard French equivalents. In the case of [ẽ], [ʌ̃], and [ɔ̃] they are also more fronted and, in the case of [ʌ̃] and [ɔ̃], more central. In addition to a front rounded series ([ỹ], [ø̃], [œ̃]), d'Ans (1968:64) recognizes two low vowels equivalent to Hall's [ɔ̃].

[7]Saint-Jacques-Fauquenoy notes a similar phenomenon in Guyanese Creole: 'à une nasalité pertinente . . . s'ajoute une nasalité contextuelle qui n'est pas distinctive . . . Nous dirons donc que l'opposition /e/ - /ẽ/ est neutralisée dans les cas où /e/ est suivi d'une consonne nasale' (1972:43).

[8]But Tinelli posits a morpheme structure condition by which all vowels are nasal before a nasal consonant. In effect, this has the same result as the nasalization rule posited by Jourdain, d'Ans, and Saint-Jacques-Fauquenoy.

[9]Tinelli grants the existence of such contrasts--he cites [pan] 'breakdown' vs. [sispʌ̃n] 'to hand') but claims that they are attested only in the speech of bilinguals and that in /pan/ the vowel is slightly nasalized. For him, oral vowels occurring before nasal consonants are gallicisms absent from the speech of monolinguals. Indeed,

existing phonological descriptions of Haitian Creole based as they are on the speech of bilinguals or on that of monolingual speakers observed in an urban setting fail to reflect the speech of the primary speakers of the language, the monolingual rural masses of Haiti.

[10]Some creolists (Hall 1950, Valdman 1968, Tinelli 1973) have commented on perceptual differences between two types of nasal vowels in Creole. Tinelli accounts for the difference in terms of 'the relative opening of the nasal cavity related to the relative lowering of the velum' (1973:3). We would account for this phonetic difference in terms of the two types of nasalization posited by Pierre Delattre (1968). Delattre distinguishes two types of nasal vowels: those characterized by 'cancellation' (annulation) and those characterized by 'damping' (amortissement). Nasal vowels of the former type are characterized by a first formant of reduced intensity due to the counter-resonance produced by a cavity formed behind the velum. This velic cavity partially cancels the effect of the pharyngal (back mouth) cavity. Nasal vowels characterized by cancellation often have velic and pharyngal cavities of equal volume, a situation which is typical of the relatively low nasal vowels of French. The second type of nasal vowels are characterized by the spread of the first formant over a greater number of harmonics, and they are produced by the lowering of the velum without the formation of the velic cavity. Delattre points out that nasal vowels produced by cancellation produce an impression of greater nasalization than those resulting from damping. Also, the higher a nasal vowel, the less distinctive its nasalization, or, to put it differently, high nasal vowels tend to be produced by damping and low nasal vowels by cancellation. We have studied spectrograms of nasal vowels pronounced by a bilingual informant from the Cape Haitian region. These appear to confirm Delattre's theory: nasal vowels such as those of [põ] and [pɛ̃s] occurring in free syllables or in syllables checked by an oral consonant exhibit a weakened first formant; nasal vowels occurring in the context of a nasal consonant and the high vowels [ĩ] and [ũ] have a diffuse first formant.

[11]However, there are a few morphemes (mostly proper nouns) that end in two-consonant clusters of the type stop + [s]: [viks] 'Vicks', [maks] 'Max', [fiks] 'fixed', [rɛps] 'rep, a type of cloth'.

REFERENCES

d'Ans, M.-A. 1968. Le créole français d'Haïti: Etude des unités d'articulation, d'expansion et de communication. The Hague, Mouton.
Carrington, L. D. 1967. Saint-Lucian Creole: A descriptive analysis of its phonology and morphosyntax. Unpublished dissertation, University of the West Indies (Jamaica).

Delattre, Pierre. 1965. La nasalité vocalique en français. French
Review. 39.92-109.
_____. 1968. Divergences entre nasalités vocalique et consonanti-
que, Word 24.64-72. Studies presented to André Martinet, part
II, Indo-European Linguistics.
Hall, R. A., Jr. 1950. Nasalization in Haitian Creole. Modern
Language Notes. 65.474-78.
_____. 1953. Haitian Creole: Grammar, texts, vocabulary.
American Anthropologist 55, Memoir 74. Washington, D.C.,
American Anthropological Association.
Hyppolite, Michelson. 1950. Les origines des variations du créole
haïtien. Port-au-Prince, Imprimerie de l'Etat.
Jourdain, Elodie. 1956. Du français aux parlers créoles. Paris,
Klincksieck.
Lightner, T. M. 1971. Generative phonology. In: A survey of lin-
guistic science. Ed. by W. O. Dingwall. College Park, Md.,
University of Maryland, Department of Linguistics. 493-575.
Moorghen, P.-M. J. 1972. Etude structurale du créole de l'Ile
Maurice. Unpublished dissertation, University of Nice.
Saint-Jacques-Fauquenoy, Marguerite. 1972. Analyse structurale
du créole guyanais. Paris, Klincksieck.
Schane, S. A. 1972. How abstract is French phonology? In:
Generative studies in Romance languages. Ed. by J. Casagrande
and B. Saciuk. Rowley, Mass., Newbury Press. 340-53.
Taylor, Douglas. 1947. Phonemes of Caribbean Creole. Word.
3.173-79.
_____. 1968. Le créole de la Dominique. In: Le language. Ed. by
A. Martinet. Paris, Gallimard (Encyclopédie de la Pleïade).
1022-49.
Tinelli, Henri. 1970. Generative phonology of Haitian Creole.
Unpublished dissertation, University of Michigan.
_____. 1972. Elision rules, syllabic consonants, and vowel har-
mony in Haitian Creole. Unpublished manuscript.
_____. 1973. Generative and creolization processes: Nasality in
Haitian. Unpublished manuscript.
Valdman, Albert. 1968. Nasalization in Creole French. In: Proceedings of the Sixth International Congress of Phonetic Sciences
held at Prague 7-13 September 1967. Ed. by H. Hála et al.
Prague, Acad. Pub. House of the Czech. Acad. of Sciences.
967-70.
_____. 1970. Basic course in Haitian Creole. Bloomington,
Indiana University Research Center for the Language Sciences
and The Hague, Mouton.
Valdman, Albert and L. D. Carrington. 1969. Saint-Lucian Creole
basic course. Unpublished manuscript.

HOW CAN WE INCLUDE CONSIDERATIONS OF STYLE IN A PHONOLOGICAL DESCRIPTION? THE FRENCH E MUET[1] (AGAIN)

NICOLE Z. DOMINGUE

Indiana University, South Bend

The purpose of this paper is to show that it is possible to include considerations of stylistic variation into a grammatical description. Why should we want to do such a thing? Because observation of the linguistic reality forces us to admit that stylistic variation is a part of the competence of the native speaker. Though we agree that this type of variation should be treated on the lowest level of the description, it must be a part of that description since it is learned during the process of language acquisition. A sentence such as 'This new concept in linguistic science ain't gonna lead us nowhere.' can be accepted only as representing a humorous switching of styles. In French, a sentence such as

(1) Monsieur, tu es gentil.

where the second person singular [- formal] is used to speak to a person addressed as 'Sir', can be heard only in the speech of children, who have yet to learn the niceties of stylistic complexity.

There are two ways to account for stylistic variation. One way is to set up levels of style and provide a description representing each of these levels. Beside the great amount of redundancy produced by these 'multi-descriptions', the criteria used to define the levels must be arbitrarily chosen out of an extra-linguistic vocabulary. I am referring to terms like 'formal', 'informal', 'frozen', etc. Moreover, these terms hide the fact that stylistic variation is a continuum rather than a series of discrete levels.

The other way of considering variation is to deal with the data without looking for extra-linguistic categories to classify it. The mutual co-occurrence relationships of the features of stylistic variation can be used as a basis for a classification.

As an example of this procedure, I would like to show that the variation in the use of the French ǝ can be most usefully handled in this manner.

The French central vowel ǝ appears in underlying lexical representations as established for instance by Schane (1968). A late phonological rule deletes it when it appears before a vowel. Such a rule is described by Schane (1968) as a part of his truncation rule, or by an alternate rule which he argues for in his paper 'There is no French truncation rule' (p. 89, this volume):

    (2) #la#grãdǝ#ilǝ# ⟶ #la#grãdǿ#ilǝ#

but

    (3) #la#grãdǝ#mɛzõ#

As Schane also points out, ǝ is not deleted before glides:

    (4) #lǝ#jogi#
          #lǝ#warf#
          #lǝ#hero#

As an exception to the vowel deletion rule, the ǝ fails to be deleted in front of the vowel of onze:

    (5) #lǝ#õz#e#lǝ#duzǝ#

The underlying representations and the vowel deletion rule posited by Schane are sufficient to describe the surface strings of the phonological component, but they do not account for the systematic deletion of ǝ which may occur in other environments. These further rules of ǝ deletion are the object of this presentation.

Previous studies have been interested mainly in setting up the conditions which warrant the obligatory occurrences of ǝ. Possible articulatory sequences and/or systemic permissibility are the basis of such statements. The treatment presented here, however, considers the conditions under which ǝ can be deleted.[2] These conditions are also stated in phonological terms, but they are systematically correlated to style in a crucial way.

Stylistic considerations cannot be ignored by the student of the French ə. Such considerations account for some of the exceptions to M. Grammont's <u>loi des trois consonnes</u>. Likewise, later studies consist of establishing a main rule which describes a type of speech representative of the informal style of educated speakers; indications of variations are also mentioned, but as exceptions or stylistic particularities. Robert A. Hall (1946) chose to describe stylistic variation by setting up three stylistic categories based on the number and the type of ə occurrences. These categories, however, cut arbitrarily through the linguistic data, without allowing for 'in-between' varieties. Hall was also unable to integrate his observations into one system, and therefore his description consists of three juxtaposed phonological descriptions. Ernst Pulgram (1961) endorsed the idea that extralinguistic considerations should legitimately be included in a synchronic description and set out to do just that. Unfortunately, his very enlightening paper does not reflect appropriately his theoretical standpoint for lack of a suitable technical device.

This study intends to observe the range of optionality of ə deletion and to give a systematic classification of these observations. The classification is then used as a criterion for the characterization of styles. To achieve this aim, it is necessary to devise not one rule, but a whole set of phonetic rules, each of which accounts for one special case of deletion. These rules are then ordered implicationally: if rule (2) is operating, so is rule (1); if rule (3) is in operation, so are rule (2) and rule (1), etc. The device which makes this ordering possible is the implicational scale[3] which represents the kind of co-occurrence relations just described.

The data for this study have been collected from twenty-five native speakers chosen from different age groups but within the bounds of Standard French.[4] Though speakers show some fluctuation in their judgments, an unusual amount of agreement was found in deciding which are appropriate or inappropriate[5] combinations. When a question arose as to which order to follow, my own speech was taken as a model.[6]

The rules.

Rule A:[7] ə ⟶ null / ___ ##

This deletes phrase final ə:

(6) #la#grãd#ilə̸##
          +A

      #ɛl#ɛ#žoliə̸##
          +A

Rule B: $\vartheta \longrightarrow$ null/ VC ___ (#) C_1

where C is a [-vocalic] segment. This deletes the $\underline{\vartheta}$ which stands between two single consonants in a non-initial syllable:

(7) #sa#pətit$\not\!\!\vartheta$#kamarad$\not\!\!\vartheta$#viɛ̃#lə#sam$\not\!\!\vartheta$di##
         +B   +B   +B

Note that the environment to the right of the deletion may contain more
than one consonant:

(8) #pətit$\not\!\!\vartheta$#fripuj$\not\!\!\vartheta$##
     +B   +A

    #pətit$\not\!\!\vartheta$#klɛptoman$\not\!\!\vartheta$##
     +B   +A

    #pətit$\not\!\!\vartheta$#splãdœr##
     +B

A case could be made, however, for an environment which would be
somewhat more constraining, as a cluster of stops would be:

(9) #yn$\not\!\!\vartheta$#pətit$\not\!\!\vartheta$#ptoz$\not\!\!\vartheta$ ##
     +B   +B   +A

    #yn$\not\!\!\vartheta$#ptoz$\not\!\!\vartheta$##
     +B   +A

    #yn$\not\!\!\vartheta$#gzenofob#ãraže$\not\!\!\vartheta$##
     +B   +A

Aside from the fact that this type of initial clusters is rare in French,
it does not have the same constraining power when preceded by a non-
stop consonant: un$\not\!e$ ptôs$\not\!e$, c'est un$\not\!e$ x$\not\!e$nophobe enrag$\not\!e\not\!e$. For reasons
of simplicity a special rule has not been established here to take these
cases into account, but there is no theoretical reason why that could
not be done if a need for it were felt. [8]
There are, however, two conditions on rule B:

Condition 1: C_1 must not be a cluster of liquid + palatal glide
($\underline{rj}$ or $\underline{lj}$). This condition is justified by the following observations:

(10) #nuz#abitə́rõ## but #nuz#abitərjõ##
      +B   -B

      #la#šapəliɛrə́#n#a#ply#də#šapə́lyrə́##
      -B +B   +B +A

      #nə#ditə#rjɛ̃##
      -B

Condition 2: C_1 is not an <u>h</u> (<u>h aspiré</u>). The rule which deletes this consonant or changes it into a glottal stop must then be ordered after the set of ə rules. This particular constraint is evident in:

(11) #ynə́#pətitə́#tašə́## but #ynə́#pətitə#hašə́##
      +B   +B   +B   -B   +A

      #s#ɛt#ynə́#bote## but #s#ɛt#ynə#hõtə́##
      +B   -B   +A

Rule C: ə⟶ null/ V#C ___ (#) C_1

ə is deleted in initial syllables:

(12) #sa#pə́titə́#kamaradə́#nə#viɛ̃#kə́#lə#samə́di##
      +C +B   +B   +C   +B

Notice that ə in <u>nə</u> and <u>lə</u> is retained since it is preceded by a consonant cluster resulting from the deletion of ə in the preceding words. This leads to the conclusion that the rules apply from left to right, a fact which was pointed out in other studies concerned with the deletion of ə in sequences such as: <u>je né te lé redémandé pas</u> and <u>je né te rédemandé plus,</u> with the exception of the 'frozen groups' (<u>groupes figés</u>).[9] Here also, C_1 can be a consonant cluster:

(13) #ɛlə́#s#ɛ#rə́frwadiə́##
      +B   +C   +A

      #il#va#še#lə́#psikiatrə́##
            +C   +A

      #pa#də́#skãdalə́##
      +C   +A

As in rule B, the restrictions on C_1 are also valid:

Condition 1:

(14) #lə#rəljœr#nɛ#pa#rǿlyizã#
      -C   +C

     #il#s#ocypɛ#dǿ#rãtǿ#mɛz#il#nə#s+ocypǿ#ply#də#rjɛ̃##
           +C   +B   +B   -C

Condition 2:

(15) #il#va#dǿdã## but #il#va#dəhor##
        +C   -C

     #nə#fɛ#pa#lǿ#malɛ̃## but #nəfɛ#pa#lə#hero##
            +C   -C

Rule D: ə⟶ null/ ##C ___ (#) C_1

ə is deleted in phrase initial position:

(16) ##sǿ#tablo#ɛt#afrö#mɛ#sɛtǿ#skyltyrǿ#ɛt#etonãtǿ##
     +D   +B   +B   +A

Deletion occurs also when ə is followed by more than one consonant:

(17) ##lǿ#skribujar#s#ɛt#ãkorǿ#trõpe##
     +D   +B

     ##sǿ#trakase#nǿ#sɛr#a#rjɛ̃##
     +D   +C

Condition 1 must be altered to include only the group rj:

(18) ##dǿmãdǿlyi## but ##də#rjɛ̃##
     +D   -D

Condition 2 is also operating:

(19) ##sǿ#vilaž#ɛ#šarmã## but ##sə#hamo#ɛ#šarmã##
     +D   -D

Rule E: ə⟶ null/ VrC ___ #C_1

ə is deleted following a cluster of r + consonant:

(20) #fɛrmǿ#la#portǿ##
      +E   +A

Notice that in this rule the word boundary is not optional: the ə must not be deleted inside a word, as can be seen in fermement. C_1 can be a consonant cluster:

(21) #il#nə#parlǿ#pa## and #il#nə#parlǿ#ply##
      +E   +E

Condition 1 again holds only for rj:

(22) #il#nə#m#aportǿ#ply#rjɛ̃## but #il#nə#m#aportə#rjɛ̃##
      +E   -E

The cluster lj does not seem to play a role in the rule: quatorzǿ loups and quatorzǿ lions. The sequence la garǿ de Lyon cannot be used as evidence since we also have la garǿ de Vincennǿs or la garǿ de Bordeaux; it seems that la garǿ de is a 'frozen group'.

Condition 2 is still necessary:

(23) katorzǿ#vajã#hero## but #katorzə#hero##
      +E   -E

Rule F: ə ⟶ null/ Vr # C ___ (#) C_1

ə is deleted in initial syllables and following the same cluster as in rule D:

(24) #ɛl#adorǿ#sǿ#šapo#e#lǿ#portǿ#tu#le#zur#
      +B +F   +C   +E

When C_1 is a cluster we obtain:

(25) #lǿ#dezir#dǿ#plɛrǿ##
      +D   +F   +A

      #ɛl#adorǿ#sǿ#grədɛ̃##
       +B +F

      #pur#kǿ#sǿla#sãblə#naturɛl##
       +F +C

Condition 1 holds for the group rj:

(26) #pur#kǿ#rišar#vjɛnǿ## but #pur#kə#rjɛ̃#nǿ#sə#pasǿ##
        +F   +A   -F   +C   +A

Condition 2 is still present:

(27) #pasǿ#par#lǿ#vilažǿ## but #pasǿ#par#lə#hamo##
        +B   +F   +A   +B   -F

      #pur#sǿ#garsõ## but #pur#sə#hero##
        +F   -F

Rule G: ə⟶ null/ sC ___ # C₁

ə is deleted after a cluster of s + consonant:

(28) #il#nə#mǿ#rɛstǿ#k#ynǿ#pomǿ##
        +C   +G   +B   +A

As in Rule E, the word boundary is compulsory, since no deletion occurs inside the word: lestement, justement.

C₁ can be a consonant cluster:

(29) #unǿ#vastǿ#plɛnǿ##
        +B   +G   +A

      #rɛst#trăkilǿ##
        +G   +A

Condition 1 is valid only for the group rj:

(30) #il#nə#rɛstǿ#ply#rjɛ̃## but #il#nə#rɛstə#rjɛ̃##
                        +G   -G

Condition 2:

(31) #il#rɛstǿ#laho## but #il#rəstə#ho#pɛrše##
        +G   -G

Rules C and E appear to be generalizations of Rule B. Likewise, Rule F is a generalization of Rule E. It is possible to generalize further the rules described above by removing Conditions 1 and 2. In this way it can be shown that the environment for possible ə

deletion is expanded. More ə can be deleted, but not without a
simplification of the preceding clusters:

(32) #ynə̸#fjɛvṭə̸ #də#šə̸val##
      +B   +B   +C

      #œ̃n#akṭə̸#d#agrɛsjõ##
            +B

      #œ̃#pœpḷə̸#kuražö##
            +B

This cluster simplification is not treated here. After such simplifications, the rules of ə deletion described above operate again.

The ordering of the rules. The rules can be ordered significantly
in co-occurrence relationships by observing how they appear in a
common environment. Let us consider first an environment from
which Rule A is absent:

(33) #pətitə#kamaradə##
      -C -B   -A

In this environment, none of the other rules appear, lest unappropri-
ate sequences occur:

   *#pətitə̸#kamaradə##
     -C +B   -A

   *#pə̸titə#kamaradə##
     +C -B   -A

   *#žə̸#vwa#ma#kamaradə##
     +D   -A

   *#fɛrmə̸#la#portə##
     +E   -A

   *#pur#kə̸#ty#vjɛnə##
     +F   -A

   *#rɛstə̸#dã#ta#šãbrə##
     +G   -A

This shows that Rule A has to be present before any other rule can operate; Rule A is the first rule on the implicational scale since the presence of any other rule implies its occurrence.

To determine which rule immediately follows Rule A on the scale, we can establish co-occurrence matrices in which the possible combinations of two features are examined for appropriateness:

(34a) #pətitə#kamarad∮##
      −C −B   +A

(34b) #pətit∮#kamarad∮##
      −C +B   +A

(34c) *#p∮titə#kamarad∮##
      +C −B   +A

(34d) #p∮tit∮#kamarad∮##
      +C +B   +A

Since combination (34c) is not acceptable, we conclude that Rule B must be present if Rule C is to occur. The same observation can be made about Rules D, E, and F; the absence of Rule B prevents their occurrences:

(35) *#r∮garde#ma#žœenə#kamarad∮##
     +D   −B   +A

      *#ma#kamaradə#fɛrm∮#la#port∮##
              −B +E   +A

      *#pur#k∮#ma#kamaradə#vjɛn∮##
        +F   −B +A

Rule B then must follow Rule A on the scale. The same procedure is applied to determine the co-occurrence relations which exist between each set of two rules. When Rule C and Rule D are considered, the precedence of Rule C is established:

(36a) #žə#vwa#ma#pətit∮#kamarad∮##
     −D   −C +B   +A

(36b) #žə#vwa#ma#p∮tit∮#kamarad∮##
     −D   +C +B   +A

(36c) *#žǿ#vwa#ma#pətitǿ#kamaradǿ##
    +D   -C +B   +A

(36d) #žǿ#vwa#ma#pǿtitǿ#kamaradǿ##
    +D   +C +B   +A

Let us now examine the relations between Rules C and E:

(37a) #ma#pətitǿ#kamaradǿ#fɛrmə#la#portǿ##
      -C +B   +B   -E   +A

(37b) *#ma#pǿtitǿ#kamaradǿ#fɛrmə#la#portǿ##
      +C +B   +B -E   +A

(37c) #ma#pətitǿ#kamaradǿ#fɛrmǿ#la#portǿ##
      -C +B   +B +E   +A

(37d) #ma#pǿtitǿ#kamaradǿ#fɛrmǿ#la#portǿ##
      +C +B   +B +E   +A

(37b) is not appropriate, because Rule C does not occur when Rule E is absent. This shows that Rule E precedes Rule C on the scale. By setting up similar four-way matrices between the remaining rules, Rule E is shown to be followed by Rules C, D, and F in that order. As an additional example, let us consider the two crucial combinations of Rules D and F:

(38a) #žǿ#vwa#kǿ#ma#kamarad#adorǿ#sə#šapo##
    +D   +C   +B -F

(38b) *#žə#vwa#kǿ#ma#kamarad#adorǿ#sǿ#šapo##
    -D   +C   +B +F

Rule D must be present if Rule F is to operate.

Rule G patterns after Rules C and D, but no significant order can be established between Rules F and G since only two combinations are found:[10]

(39a) #pur#kə#ty#rɛstə#la##   (39d) #pur#kǿ#ty#rɛstǿ#la##
      -F   -G   +F   +G

The two rules are ordered similarly in relation to the other rules and consequently must appear at the same point on the scale.

The co-occurrence relationships pointed out by the series of matrices can be summarized in a table:

(40) Rule A   − + + + + +
      Rule B   − − + + + +
      Rule E   − − − + + +
      Rule C   − − − − + +
      Rule D   − − − − − + +
      Rule F/G − − − − − − +

This table shows that when Rule A does not occur, none of the other
rules can occur. Likewise, the absence of Rule B implies the absence
of Rules E, C, D, and F/G. Conversely, if Rule F/G is marked as
occurring, all rules above it must be marked positively. And if Rule
D is present, all rules above it are present. A linear scale can represent the relations of co-occurrence between the rules of ə deletion:

(41)
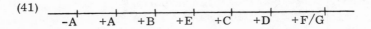

The mention of only one rule is necessary to characterize any type of
speech: if, for instance, +E is indicated as occurring, it implies
automatically that Rules A and B apply as well, and that none of the
other rules does. The scale represents a set of constraints on a
derivation, which filters out inappropriate combinations of ə deletion.

   Stylistic categories. The types of speech distinguished by the
presence of any one rule in the description can serve as a basis for
the characterization of stylistic categories. The very small number
of informants used in this study precluded the possibility of establishing a stylistic classification of any statistic value. Such a classification was not however the aim of this paper; rather, my purpose was
to propose a systematic organization of phonetic rules. Nevertheless,
a tentative indication of the way styles could be classified is given below.

   The style characterized by the absence of Rule A is found in traditional songs:

   En passant par la Lorraine . . .
   Au clair de la lune . . .

The style characterized by the presence of Rule A and the absence
of Rule B is the style of poetry:

   Par la Naturé, --heureux comme avec une femmé (Rimbaud)
   Heureux qui commé Ulyssé a fait un beau voyagé (Du Bellay)

The presence of Rule B indicates oratorical style:

A travers une̸ brousse̸ deve̸nue̸ pauvre̸, les larges brèche̸s
ouvertes par les mineurs sont très apparente̸s (Balandier)

and

Bien que ce̸la lui en coute̸, Montaigne̸ part soudaine̸ment pour
Paris et y demeure̸ pendant deux se̸maine̸s (Dassonville).

The style distinguished by Rule E is the style of the narrative:

Le résultat obtenu, il referme̸ les yeux et se̸ rendort pour
encore̸ une̸ petite̸ heure̸. Cette̸ dose̸ supplémentaire̸ de
sommeil, il la re̸ssent comme̸ nécessaire̸ (adapted from
Queneau).

Rule C characterizes the careful style in the speech of educated
speakers (preferably middle-aged):

Je sais qu'il vient pour que je̸ lui donne̸ à dîner, mais je̸ me
démande̸ pourquoi il ne parle̸ pas plus claire̸ment.

Rule D distinguishes the informal style of the same speakers, or
the careful speech of younger speakers:

Le̸ mur de pierre̸ qui entoure̸ le parc est très abimé et il ne
reste pas grand chose̸ des grille̸s.

Rule F/G is characteristic of a style still more informal or more
rapid:

Je̸ sais bien qu'il n'en reste̸ pas grand chose̸, il faudra finir
par le̸ démolir complète̸ment.

In this study, I have tried to show that an implicational ordering
of phonetic rules could be justified on two points: (1) It permits the
description of variation without calling for extra-linguistic criteria,
thus including the facts of variation in the grammar. Variation resulting from ǝ deletion should, in a complete study, be related to
variation resulting from optionally deleted liaisons, alternate grammatical constructions, and vocabulary choices. As an example of the
interrelation of ǝ deletion and liaison, the expression vénez-ici seems
inappropriate: when ǝ is deleted there is probably no liaison as in
véne̸z-ici. The relevance of grammatical facts appears in the observation that Rule E usually does not occur in questions like que voulez-
vous? *que̸ voulez-vous? would probably be replaced by qu'est-ce̸

que vous voulez? or qu'est-cé qué vous voulez? Vocabulary choice
is also related to ə deletion: il est nécessaire de reprendre couragé
and il faut réprendre couragé.

(2) A linguistic classification of variation can be used as the basis
for a non-arbitrary classification of styles. Extra-linguistic factors
such as age, education, socio-economic levels, speed of speech are
difficult to reduce into common distinctive units and produce arbitrary
categories. Also the complex interrelation of these extra-linguistic
factors might not always be consistent through the levels of style; for
instance age could be a determining factor for one level while speed
of speech would distinguish another level. With the procedure used
here, the stylistic categories are based on a linguistic classification
which is internally justified.

NOTES

[1]The traditional term has been retained here even though it does
not describe the sound very adequately. For ease of presentation it
will appear as ə from now on.

[2]Some words must be marked in the lexicon for not undergoing the
set of rules, for example peser, querelle, bedeau, merise. A syntactic environment equally prevents the rules from applying: the object pronoun le [lə] is not reduced when it comes after the verb as in
prends le, fais le tout dé suité.

[3]For a description of the procedure involved see DeCamp (1968).

[4]In effect, this means French as spoken without regional characteristics.

[5]The use of the asterisk will mark inappropriate sentences.

[6]I feel justified to do so since I believe that the co-occurrence
relations of the rules are learned by children as part of the language
system, hence that they are a systematization of a native speaker's
competence.

[7]The order in which the rules are listed is arbitrary and insignifi-
cant as yet.

[8]This is far from being a unique case in this presentation. As was
mentioned earlier, a special rule can be established for every particular environment. Only a few rules among many have been chosen to
illustrate the point of view expressed here.

[9]For a treatment of frozen groups, see Delattre (1951:348-49).
There is, however, a certain amount of disagreement among native
speakers as to the preferred pronunciation of groups like je mé
demandé or jé me démandé. Another type of sequences seems to
fall also in the category of frozen groups, the number of syllables
being the probable factor of the 'freeze':

garde feu / gardé malade
porte feuillé / porté monnaié

[10]The ordering of Rule G gave rise to a certain amount of disagreement among the speakers interviewed. Some would have placed it between D and F, others in co-occurrence with F.

REFERENCES

Bailey, Charles-James N. 1969. The integration of linguistic theory: Internal reconstruction and the comparative method in descriptive linguistics. In: Linguistic change and generative theory. Ed. by Robert P. Stockwell and Ronald K. S. Macaulay. Bloomington, Indiana University Press, 1972.

Barker, James L. 1925. Neutral vowels in French and English. Modern Philology. 22.273-81.

DeCamp, David. 1968. Toward a generative analysis of a post-Creole speech continuum. In: Pidginization and creolization of languages. Ed. by Dell Hymes. Cambridge, Cambridge University Press, 1971.

Delattre, Pierre. 1951. Le jeu de l'e instable interieur en français. French Review. 24.341-51.

Domingue, Nicole Z. 1971. Bhojpuri and Creole in Mauritius: A study in synchronic variation and language change. Unpublished Ph.D. dissertation, University of Texas at Austin.

Grammont, Maurice. 1894. La loi des trois consonnes. Mémoires de la Société de Linguistique de Paris. 8.53-90.

Haden, Ernest. 1965. Mute e in French. Lingua. 13.166-76.

Hall, Robert A., Jr. 1946. Colloquial French phonology. Studies in Linguistics. 4(3-4).70-90.

Leray, F. 1930. La loi des trois consonnes. Revue de philologie française et de litérature. 42.161-84.

Malecot, André. 1956. The elision of French mute e within complex consonantal clusters. Lingua. 5.45-60.

Martinet, André. 1949. About structural sketches. Word. 5.13-35.

Pulgram, Ernst. 1961. French /ə/: Statics and dynamics of linguistic subcodes. Lingua. 10.305-25.

Schane, Sanford A. 1968. French phonology and morphology. Research Monograph No. 45. Cambridge, Mass., MIT Press.

_____. 1973. There is no French truncation rule. In: Linguistic studies in Romance languages. Ed. by R. Joe Campbell, Mark G. Goldin, and Mary C. Wang. Washington, D.C., Georgetown University Press.

Weinreich, Harald. 1958. Phonologischen Studien zur romanischen Sprachgeschichte. Munster.

THERE IS NO FRENCH TRUNCATION RULE

SANFORD A. SCHANE

University of California, San Diego

1. In French the phonological adjustments between words are referred to as 'elision' and 'liaison'. Most grammars have treated
these as separate phenomena, where 'elision' is the deletion of a
final vowel before a word beginning with a vowel and 'absence of
liaison' is the deletion of a consonant. Since in both cases we are
dealing with the deletion of a segment in final position, in Schane
(1968:1-7) I argued that these were manifestations of a single process,
what I called 'truncation'.

Since it is possible for a word to terminate in a consonant, vowel,
liquid, or glide, and for the next word to begin with any one of these
four classes of sounds, there are sixteen possibilities.

(1)	#C	#V	#L	#G
C #	peti(t) camarade	petit ami	peti(t) rabbin	petit oiseau
V #	admirable camarade	admirabl(e) ami	admirable rabbin	admirabl(e) oiseau
L#	cher camarade	cher ami	cher rabbin	cher oiseau
G#	pareil camarade	pareil ami	pareil rabbin	pareil oiseau

From these data we see that:

(2) In word final position;
- (a) Consonants are truncated before consonants and liquids.
- (b) Vowels are truncated before vowels and glides.
- (c) Liquids and glides are never truncated.

89

At that time, I was making use of the Jakobsonian distinctive features so the four classes of segments are differentiated by means of the features [consonantal] and [vocalic].

(3)

	Consonant	Liquid	Vowel	Glide
Consonantal	+	+	-	-
Vocalic	-	+	+	-

The following rule, known as the 'truncation rule', formalized the statements in (2).

(4) $\begin{bmatrix} \alpha \text{cons} \\ -\alpha \text{voc} \end{bmatrix} \rightarrow \emptyset /$ ___ [-segment] [α cons]

The truncation rule applies between morphemes as well as between words so that the rule refers to either type of boundary.

Because final consonants are deleted also at the end of the phonological phrase (e.g. il est peti(t)), there is an additional rule, which I called 'final consonant deletion'.

(5) $\begin{bmatrix} +\text{cons} \\ -\text{voc} \end{bmatrix} \rightarrow \emptyset /$ ___ # $\begin{cases} \% \text{ (where \% is a phrase boundary)} \\ X \text{ (the conditions for X are discussed} \\ \quad \text{later)} \end{cases}$

Now the truncation rule is the more interesting of the two rules. As already noted it allows elision and absence of liaison to be formulated as a single process. It was one of the earliest examples of the variable notation used with major class features. It made the interesting claim that:

> . . . in French, vowels and consonants form a class of segments which can be truncated whenever the following segment agrees in consonantality, and that this class is opposed to the class of liquids and glides, which does not undergo truncation. Without the alpha notation it would not be possible to characterize the vowels and true consonants as a natural class opposed to the class of liquids and glides, and instead of a single general rule for truncation we would have to postulate two distinct rules: one for the deletion of vowels and another for consonants (1968:4).

Finally, the elegance and conciseness of the truncation rule lent support to the major class features [consonantal] and [vocalic] and the way in which they characterized a division into vowels, true consonants, liquids, and glides.

Chomsky and Halle (1968:353–55) cite the French truncation rule as an important example of the use of variables in phonological rules. Citing data from J.-C. Milner (1967) they state that the truncation rule properly accommodates native forms but is inadequate for certain foreign words, where vowels are truncated before vowels but not before glides (e.g. le yod, le watt). For this reason, Chomsky and Halle propose two different truncation rules, one for native words and one for foreign words. They state the rules using their proposed major class features [consonantal], [syllabic], and [sonorant].

(6) (a) $\begin{bmatrix} \alpha\text{cons} \\ -\alpha\text{syll} \end{bmatrix} \rightarrow \emptyset \ / \ \underline{\quad} \ [\text{-seg}] \ \begin{bmatrix} \alpha\text{cons} \\ -\text{foreign} \end{bmatrix}$

(b) $\begin{bmatrix} \alpha\text{cons} \\ -\alpha\text{syll} \end{bmatrix} \rightarrow \emptyset \ / \ \underline{\quad} \ [\text{-seg}) \ \begin{bmatrix} -\alpha\text{syll} \\ +\text{foreign} \end{bmatrix}$

Chomsky and Halle accept that elision and absence of liaison are to be handled by a single rule and they furthermore assume that the rule must be stateable in any proposed feature system. They conclude their discussion of the French truncation rule by saying: 'This example is, thus, of the greatest importance for our feature framework' (355). [1]

Arnold Zwicky (1970) has proposed a notation whereby 'the complement C' of any class C of phonological segments [is] to be specified with the same number of feature markings as C itself' (262). He states: 'Although it is difficult to find cases where this new notation would permit putative regularities to be expressed more simply than standard frameworks, there is at least one such case, the French truncation rule' (263).

(7) $\begin{bmatrix} \alpha\text{voc} \\ -\alpha\text{cons} \end{bmatrix} \rightarrow \emptyset \ / \ \underline{\quad} \ [\text{-seg}] \quad \alpha \begin{bmatrix} -\text{cons} \\ \begin{pmatrix} +\text{voc} \\ +\text{foreign} \end{pmatrix} \end{bmatrix}$

Here again the French truncation rule is being used to justify a theoretical construct.

2. The French truncation rule as stated in (4) notationally abbreviates the two rules (8a) and (8b).

(8) (a) $\begin{bmatrix} -\text{cons} \\ +\text{voc} \end{bmatrix} \rightarrow \emptyset \ / \ \underline{\quad} \ [\text{-seg}] \ [\text{-cons}]$

(b) $\begin{bmatrix} +\text{cons} \\ -\text{voc} \end{bmatrix} \rightarrow \emptyset \ / \ \underline{\quad} \ [\text{-seg}] \ [+\text{cons}]$

(8) (c) $\begin{bmatrix} +cons \\ -voc \end{bmatrix}$ → ∅ / ___ [-seg] %

(8c) is the rule for final consonant deletion (5). However, note that
(8b) can be readily combined notationally with (8c), rather than with
(8a), yielding (9a). (9b) is then equivalent to (8a).

(9) (a) $\begin{bmatrix} +cons \\ -voc \end{bmatrix}$ → ∅ / ___ [-seg] $\left\{ \begin{matrix} [+cons] \\ \% \end{matrix} \right\}$

(b) $\begin{bmatrix} -cons \\ +voc \end{bmatrix}$ → ∅ / ___ [-seg] [-cons]

I believe that the rules of (9) are the appropriate ones for characterizing elision and absence of liaison in French. The remainder of
this paper will provide evidence for why there is no truncation rule.

3.1 It is questionable whether vowels and true consonants (excluding liquids and glides) ever function as a natural class as claimed by
the truncation rule (4), so that this rule is dubious as evidence in
favor of a set of features. It may also be for this reason that Zwicky
was unable to find any example, other than the French truncation
rule, in support of his complement notation. On the other hand, there
are phonological rules where consonant and pause, as in (9a), function
as alternate environments--for example, vowel nasalization and l-
vocalization in French (Schane 1968:48, 80), r-deletion in certain r-
less dialects of English, and, perhaps, obstruent devoicing in German
and Russian.
3.2 Under the old framework consonants which are an exception
to the truncation rule almost without exception are also an exception
to the rule for final consonant deletion--e.g. sec, sens, sept, net.
Given the reformulation proposed in (9) such words would be an exception to rule (9a), rather than to two different rules, the truncation
rule (4) and final consonant deletion (5).
3.3 The consonants which regularly undergo deletion include most
of the obstruents and nasals. On the other hand, the only vowel which
is regularly deleted (other than the a of the feminine article and pronoun la) is schwa. Hence, rule (9b) could be rewritten in a less
general fashion to apply uniquely to schwa whereas it would not be
possible to restrict truncation rule (4) uniquely to schwa while at the
same time allowing it to delete all the consonants which must be deleted. [2]
It should also be noted that in order for a vowel to be deleted,
whether it be the deletion of schwa or exceptionally of a different
vowel, the vowel must be stressless. Consequently, truncation rule

(4) should contain the specification [-stress] in addition to [α consonantal, - α vocalic]. The added condition that a segment must be unstressed in order to undergo truncation would apply vacuously to consonants since consonants are inherently without stress. But one could seriously question whether this use of vacuous rule application is not an abuse since in French [stress] is not a feature available for marking consonants. If consonant deletion and vowel deletion are separate processes then this problem will not arise.

3.4 In French Phonology and Morphology I showed that in order to account for the intricacies of elision and liaison, the truncation rule has to be cyclic. It is for this reason that vowels are deleted before both vowels and glides. Now in underlying representations most initial glides are represented as vowels and I proposed a word-level rule which converts prevocalic high vowels to glides. For example, a form such as l'ouie [lwi] has as its underlying representation ((la#) (ui#)). At the word-level cycle the initial vowel of ui# is converted to the glide w. The next cycle applying to the phrase (la# wi#) truncates the vowel of la before the glide.

Milner has shown that gliding cannot be a word-level rule since it fails to take place whenever the preceding word ends in a consonant-liquid cluster--for example, une faible ouie [fɛbl ui]. Let us assume then that gliding is a postcyclic rule. What this means is that at the time the truncation rule applies between words, there are not yet any glides (these still being represented as vowels)--e.g. (la# ui#). As a consequence there is no longer any need for vowels to be deleted before glides and it is sufficient to state that vowels are deleted uniquely before vowels. Aside from arguments for vacuous rule application, the environment for consonant deletion and that for vowel deletion would no longer be strictly complementary.

3.5 If vowels need be deleted only before vowels (and never before glides), then 'h aspiré' words, such as la honte [la õt], can have h in the underlying representation. The h is subsequently deleted by an obligatory rule ordered after vowel deletion. In French Phonology and Morphology I was forced to set up an underlying obstruent, the velar spirant x, as the initial segment of 'h aspiré' words. I was unable to posit h due to vowel deletion before glides. Once we recognize that vowels are never deleted before glides we can set up underlying glides, y, w, and h, whose presence will explain the absence of elision for forms such as le yod, le watt, la honte, etc.

3.6 If there is no truncation rule then do we still need a cycle? First let us see why the truncation rule necessitates a cycle. There are instances of optional liaison--for example:

(10) des camarades anglais
    (a) de kamaradəz ãglɛ
    (b) de kamarad ãglɛ

It is the nonliaison form (10b) which is of interest because the inflectional S (the plural morpheme), phonetically [z] (see (10a)), has been deleted even though the following word begins with a vowel. As a consequence of this deletion the schwa of kamaradə finds itself in prevocalic position and is obligatorily deleted--in all styles of French there are no occurrences of prevocalic schwa with the exception of 'h aspiré' words. On the other hand, for the liaison form (10a), the schwa is retained as it is followed by a consonant. In northern French and colloquial styles this schwa would also be deleted, but would not necessarily be in certain southern dialects, some formal styles, poetry, and songs. Dell (1970) has shown that the rule for the deletion of schwa in (10a), depending on dialect or style, is one of many 'late' rules of schwa deletion. These rules constitute a separate phenomenon from the obligatory deletion of schwa whenever the next morpheme or word begins with a vowel.

In French Phonology and Morphology I proposed that the optional deletion of the plural S in (10b) be an extension of the final consonant deletion rule; hence the condition X in (5). (The exact constraints on X are not particularly relevant for the discussion here.) Making use of the concept of a cycle I showed how the nonliaison form (without schwa or S) of des camarad(e)(s) anglais is derived.

(11)

(1)	$((deS\#)_{Art}$	$(kamaradə+S\#)_N$	$(ãglɛz+S\#)_{Adj}\%)_{NP}$	underlying form
(2)	$((deS\#)_{Art}$	$(kamaradə+S\#)_N$	$(ãglɛ +S\#)_{Adj}\%)NP$	truncation (4)
(3)	$((deS\#)_{Art}$	$(kamaradə \ \#)_N$	$(ãglɛ +S\#)_{Adj}\%)_{NP}$	final consonant deletion (5)
(4)	$(deS\#$	$kamaradə \ \#$	$ãglɛ +S\# \% \ )_{NP}$	remove innermost parentheses
(5)	$(de \#$	$kamarad \ \#$	$ãglɛ +S\# \% \ )_{NP}$	truncation (4)
(6)	$(de \#$	$kamarad \ \#$	$ãglɛ \ \# \% \ )_{NP}$	final consonant deletion (5)
(7)	$de \#$	$kamarad \ \#$	$ãglɛ \ \# \%$	remove final parentheses

Line 1 shows the underlying representation of des camarades anglais with the appropriate syntactic bracketing and labeling. The rules are applied first to the innermost parenthesized constituents, i.e. to the individual words. The truncation rule (line 2) applies only to the stem final [z] of anglais since this is the only word which has a segment followed by a + juncture, which is in turn followed by a segment agreeing in consonantality. Final consonant deletion (line 3) deletes the final S of camarades. The rule may be applied to a plural noun; however, articles and adjectives are not affected by this rule. In line 4 the innermost, i.e. word level, parentheses and their labels have been removed and the set of rules will be reapplied to the whole noun phrase. The truncation rule (line 5) deletes the final S of des since this segment is followed by a word boundary, which is in turn followed by a consonantal segment. The same rule also deletes the final schwa of camarades as this vowel is followed by a word boundary and a vowel. Final consonant deletion (line 6) deletes the plural S of anglais; this segment is now in phrase final position, i.e. it is the final segment of a noun phrase. In line 7 the parentheses and labeling have been erased.

Note that what is critical here is that both the schwa and S of camarades must be deleted, the S because it is in final position and the schwa (subsequent to the deletion of the S) because it will precede the initial vowel of anglais. This means that final consonant deletion must precede schwa deletion, i.e. truncation. However, independently we know that the truncation rule (4) is ordered before final consonant deletion (5). Otherwise for a plural form in phrase final position the stem final consonant preceding the inflectional S would not be deleted--see (12b).

(12) (a) ãglɛz+S#%   underlying form
         ãglɛ +S#%   truncation (4)
         ãglɛ   #%   final consonant deletion (5)

     (b) ãglɛz+S#%   underlying form
        *ãglɛz #%   final consonant deletion (5)
        _____   truncation (4)

Because of the ordering required in (12), we see in (13) that the schwa would not be appropriately deleted if there were no cycle.

(13) deS#kamaradə+S#ãglɛz+S#%   underlying form
      de #kamaradə+S#ãglɛ +S#%   truncation (4)
     *de #kamaradə #ãglɛ   #%   final consonant deletion (5)

A cycle is therefore needed for phrases such as des camarades anglais if the truncation rule is to apply after final consonant deletion, which it must if the schwa of camarades is to be deleted (by the truncation rule) subsequent to the deletion of the final S. However, if we substitute the rules of (9), allowing them to apply in the order given there, and furthermore if we modify (9a) to accommodate the plural morpheme (i.e. incorporate into (9a) the condition X), then we can derive the form [de kamarad ãglɛ] without recourse to the cycle.

(14) deS#kamaradə+S#ãglɛz+S#%   underlying representation
      de #kamaradə   #ãglɛ   #%   consonant deletion (9a)
      de #kamarad   #ãglɛ   #%   vowel deletion (9b)

It remains to make explicit the conditions under which liaison takes place and to formalize more adequately the phonological rules in (9). Following suggestions by Milner and by Dell let us say that liaison is a consequence of the number of word boundaries. Normally each word is preceded and followed by a # boundary. There will then be two such boundaries between every pair of words--the boundary belonging to the end of the first word followed by the one denoting the beginning of the second word. There will also be an extra pair of # boundaries denoting the beginning and end of a phonological phrase. Liaison can then be defined as the phonological effects due to the removal of one of these word boundaries. That is, the syntactic component or perhaps the readjustment component would delete one of the # boundaries between words just in those cases where liaison is to take place. This approach would be in keeping with the traditional account of liaison, which maintains that words entering into liaison form a close-knit construct (i. e. behave as a phonological word). The underlying representation of <u>des camarades anglais</u> without liaison would then be that shown in (15a) whereas the form with liaison would be represented as in (15b).

(15) (a) ##deS#kamaradə+S##ãglɛz+S##
      (b) ##deS#kamaradə+S #ãglɛz+S##

We now allow consonant deletion to apply whenever the consonant is followed by a single boundary (either morpheme or word boundary) and a following consonant, or else whenever it is followed by a boundary and a word boundary (actually all the relevant examples will involve two word boundaries). The vowel deletion rule will apply between two vowels separated either by a single boundary or by double boundaries.

(16) (a) $\begin{bmatrix} +\text{cons} \\ -\text{voc} \end{bmatrix} \rightarrow \emptyset / \underline{\quad} [-\text{seg}] \begin{cases} C \\ \# \end{cases}$

      (b) $\begin{bmatrix} -\text{cons} \\ +\text{voc} \end{bmatrix} \rightarrow \emptyset / \underline{\quad} [-\text{seg}] \; (\#) \; V$

In (17a) we give the derivation for (13a) and in (17b) for (13b).

(17) (a)   ##deS#kamaradə+S##ãglɛz+S##   underlying form
           ##de #kamaradə   ##ãglɛ   ##   consonant deletion (16a)
           ##de #kamarad   ##ãglɛ   ##   vowel deletion (16b)

     (b)   ##deS#kamaradə+S# ãglɛz+S##   underlying form
           ##de #kamaradə+S# ãglɛ   ##   consonant deletion (16a)
                                              vowel deletion (16b)
           _____

It is important to note that a vowel is deleted only where the
boundaries are followed by another vowel, but not where the vowel is
simply followed by ## (for example, at the pause), as is the case for
consonants. Consequently, schwas are retained in final position
when not prevocalic and may subsequently be deleted by one of the
late schwa dropping rules. Finally, note that the upper environment
of rule (16a) and the environment of rule (16b) cannot be collapsed
notationally, for (16b) contains the parenthesized # lacking in (16a).
Here then is further evidence that it was wrong to combine consonant
deletion before consonant and vowel deletion before vowel as a single
process.

Note, incidentally, that the proposal to treat liaison as an adjust-
ment in the number of word boundaries allows us to eliminate entirely
the set of conditions X from rule (16), for, as we have noted, these
conditions, which are basically syntactic or stylistic, are to be
handled earlier in the grammar--either in the syntactic component
or by means of readjustment rules. Consequently, final consonant
deletion can be formulated uniquely in phonological terms. On the
other hand, with the cycle the conditions on X must appear in the
formulation of phonological rule (5). Furthermore it just so happens
that the surface form of a word when liaison fails to occur is always
identical to the surface form at the pause and it is for this reason
that I incorporated the conditions on X into rule (5). Yet the formulation of (5) provides no explanation for this surface identity. In
rule (5) the pause and the conditions on X are alternate environments
having no obvious relationship to each other. Now what is happening
in the case where a word fails to undergo liaison is that its surface
manifestation is the same as its 'citation' form and the citation form
of a French word is equivalent to a one-word phrase or to a word at
the pause. Under the new proposal where prepausal position is
represented as ___##, absence of liaison by ___##V, and liaison by
___#V, the environment for absence of liaison is automatically in-
cluded in that for prepausal deletion--that is, both deletions occur
precisely because the consonant is followed by ##. We therefore
have an explanation for the identity of surface forms where there is
absence of liaison and where they occur at the pause.

The most important point of this section is that the rules of (16) allow us to dispense entirely with the cycle. I believe it is evident that something as questionable as the cycle--particularly when it pertains to segmental phenomena--is slim justification for the truncation rule. [3]

4. I have provided several reasons which lead me to believe that the rules of (16) are the appropriate ones for French elision and liaison and are to be preferred to rules (4) and (5). Nonetheless, as with a discarded mistress, I retain a sentimental attachment to the 'French truncation rule'.

NOTES

[1]The left-hand side of both (6a) and (6b) should actually read: [α cons, - α syll, - α son], for the rules as given by Chomsky and Halle incorrectly delete liquids. However, the amended rule would not delete final nasals. Now it is true that most instances of nasal deletion can be attributed to vowel nasalization--e. g. bon # → [bõ], and the deletion of the nasal consonant could therefore be incorporated into the vowel nasalization rule. But a nasal consonant would still not be appropriately deleted in those cases where it is not preceded by a vowel--e. g. dorm+ons, dor(m)+s; journ+ée, jour(n). Consequently, both the truncation rule and the rule for final consonant deletion must apply to nasals as well as to obstruents. Using the features [consonantal], [syllabic], and [sonorant], I am unable to write a truncation rule which deletes obstruents, nasals, and vowels, but excludes liquids and glides. What conclusions should we draw then for this feature framework?

[2]I believe that the vowel deletion rule should really be general (i. e. in principle it should apply to all prevocalic unstressed vowels) and the conditions where it fails to apply should be separately stated in the readjustment component. See Schane (1973) for further discussion. However, if it turns out that the exceptional contexts should be built directly into the rule itself, then we would need to restrict the rule as suggested in the main body of the paper.

[3]Milner proposes to do away with the cycle. He retains the truncation rule and the rule for final consonant deletion but at the cost of adding a third rule, one which specifically deletes schwa in the context preceding ##, in order to account for its absence in the non-liaison form of des camarad(e)(s) anglais. He claims that this rule is independently needed for instances of schwa deletion at the pause. Such a rule, however, would be one of the late schwa deletion rules proposed by Dell. In the case of des camarad(e)(s) anglais we are dealing with the obligatory (!) deletion of a prevocalic schwa.

Milner's third rule then actually duplicates the vowel deletion part of his truncation rule. On the other hand, the rules of (16) do not lead to such duplication. Recall further that (16a) and (16b) are no more complex than (4) and (5). As we noted in (8) there are actually three cases--(i) vowel deletion before vowel, (ii) consonant deletion before consonant, (iii) consonant deletion before pause. Rule (4) notationally combines cases (i) and (ii), whereas rule (16a) notationally combines cases (ii) and (iii).

REFERENCES

Chomsky, Noam and Morris Halle. 1968. The sound pattern of English. New York, Harper Row.
Dell, François. 1970. Les règles phonologiques tardives et la morphologie derivationelle du français. Unpublished Ph. D. dissertation, Massachusetts Institute of Technology.
Milner, J.-C. 1967. French truncation rule. Quarterly Progress Report, No. 86. Cambridge, MIT Press. 273-83.
Schane, Sanford A. 1968. French phonology and morphology. Cambridge, MIT Press.
_____. 1973. The treatment of phonological exceptions: The evidence from French. In: Papers in linguistics in honor of Henry and Renée Kahane. Ed. by Kachru, Lees, Malkiel, and Saporta. Urbana, University of Illinois Press.
Zwicky, Arnold. 1970. Squib: Class complements in phonology. Linguistic Inquiry. 1.262-64.

'DIME CON QUIÉN ANDAS, DECIRTE HE QUIÉN ERES' OR THE ROLE OF LINGUISTS IN LANGUAGE DEPARTMENTS*

JEAN CASAGRANDE

University of Florida

Linguistic Symposia in Romance Languages I and II underscored a number of areas of linguistic studies which those attending these meetings have in common. In creating this workshop, the organizers of LSRL III have tried to capture another aspect of academic life shared by many attending. In what follows, I will outline and illustrate the role of linguists in language departments. I hope to show that this increasingly frequent situation is beneficial to both the departments and their linguists.

Although I have drawn from experiences of linguists in departments of Romance languages, what will be said here can be extended in scope to include other modern languages. I hope that this sketch of our situation will create enough interest to spark a lively discussion about the role of linguists in language departments and about areas of study which might prove valuable.

This paper has four parts. The first part briefly reviews a well-known pseudo-problem: the dichotomy between description and prescription. The second attempts to dispell a misconception about the nature and purpose of linguists, namely that they are, by nature of their training, capable of devising language teaching methods. The third part of this paper illustrates one type of contrastive research which can be carried out by linguists in language departments. In this part, I will take a problem of translation and solve it in terms of the structure of the languages involved. The fourth part shows the close relationship that exists between the teaching and research that linguists in language departments engage in.

Description and prescription: A happy couple. At the outset it will, I think, prove valuable to distinguish between the linguist in a linguistics department and the linguist in a language department. As all such distinctions, this one will have to be made on the basis of generalizations. In particular, I will assume a linguistics department where no language per se is taught in order to maintain a clear distinction between the two. As a rule, sharply divergent views are held about language in a linguistics department on the one hand and language in a language department on the other. The language department is interested in teaching students a standard language or languages and training them in the evaluation of the related literatures. The goal of the language teacher and student alike is to arrive at the closest possible approximation of a standard language in linguistic performance. In some cases, Latin American Spanish, for example, there are several possible standards. In such instances, the standard is only defined as a social dialect. In other cases, French, for example, the standard is the bourgeois speech of the 16th district in Paris. Here the goal is identified geographically and sociologically. The equivalent of this prescriptive tendency in one's native tongue is found in the early grades of school where efforts are made to 'correct' certain speech habits. This general effort toward conformity for the sake of clarity, social grace, acceptance in society, etc. falls under the heading of prescriptive grammar.

The attitude toward language within a linguistics department is quite different. There is a tradition of tolerance and diversity in linguistic scholarship. In the Western linguistic tradition this attitude is rather recent, stemming from the work of comparativists in the 19th century. In attempting to discover the relationship of languages, the comparativist used geographic and social dialects which the prescriptivist would have condemned as incorrect. So generally speaking, the attitude of the linguist towards language in all its forms is one of description while the attitude of the language teacher is one of prescription.

At first, it would appear that descriptive and prescriptive tendencies are incompatible and mutually exclusive. The purely descriptive approach to language acquisition would accept all language behavior regardless of the socio-economic or geographic background of a speaker, irrespective of his state of mental or physical health. It is clear that such an extreme has to be avoided if only because of the chaotic nature of the uncontrolled subject matter which would result from a strictly descriptive tendency. The purely prescriptive tendency is also inadequate but for different reasons. The prescriptive approach to language acquisition would exclude a great deal of normal, acceptable speech behavior on the grounds that this or that expression has not yet been accepted by the appropriate academy or blessed by the prose of a great author. Taken individually these two approaches are to be rejected because each fails to incorporate the good aspects of the other.

The role of the linguist, and of the language teacher, is to find the proper balance between these two tendencies. Structure courses that emphasize the standard language and language courses that allow flexibility on the descriptive-prescriptive axis avoid the pitfalls just outlined. In a lecture on the mid-vowel system of French, the linguist can describe both the highly systematic set of three mid-vowels south of the Loire River and the more irregular system of six mid-vowels north of the Loire, identifying the latter as the standard language.

Using the same reasoning in the case of language teaching, some linguists have even suggested teaching the more regular three vowel system before the more complex six vowel system of the standard language.[1] They argue that approximating the speech of native speakers of a nonstandard dialect is better than failing to approximate the more complex and nonsystematic standard dialect.

The interaction of description and prescription is highly desirable. I believe it constitutes a healthy balance between both extremes. It prevents the descriptivist from accepting everything as grammatical, especially errors of performance. It forces the prescriptivist to admit the existence of other acceptable, though not most socially desirable, modes of expression. What then might have appeared to be a frustrating situation for the linguist in a language department (and in fact for linguists everywhere since many languages are indeed taught in linguistics departments) turns out to be a felicitous one.

In the historical context it appears that we are returning to the more stable situation after a brief period of separation of prescription and description, as witnessed by the history of linguistics before the 19th century.

Linguist does not necessarily mean pedagogue. The goals and purposes of small groups, minority groups as it is fashionable to say these days, are often misunderstood. Linguists are no exception. Hence, the general public regards linguists as polyglots. People are unimpressed if you don't speak a couple more languages than the East-European immigrant who lives next door, speaks five languages, and sells shoes. This type of misunderstanding stems from polysemy. The term 'linguist' has at least two meanings. There is another misunderstanding--this one on the part of language teachers--regarding the purpose and goals of linguists. To many a language teacher, linguists are, or claim to be, authorities on language teaching. In other words, being a linguist unquestionably qualifies a person to supervise teachers, to write language manuals, and to pontificate about language teaching. This is, of course, absolutely false. This situation stems from the World War II era when the established foreign language departments were unable to respond to the sudden need for training military personnel in critical foreign languages. With their experience in the study of lesser-known languages, linguists were able to fill the gap and teach Burmese, Swahili, and other non-Indoeuropean languages. Applying in particular the idea of intensive contact, the so-called 'Army method' was quite successful for its purpose. This success led some to try to apply the same methods to the customarily taught languages and, before he knew it, the linguist was telling the language teacher how to conduct his class. Since they had no systematic linguistic training, many teachers welcomed the linguist's guidance. But many teachers soon grew weary of new methods that solved as few problems as the old methods. Many teachers to this day view the linguist as responsible for the 'linguistic method' and its failure.

So much for this past mistake. What do today's linguists think of their position regarding teaching? What do we assembled here think about our role with respect to language teaching? This question needs to be answered individually, according to one's training, one's interests, and one's aspirations. By and large, however, I think that even the specialists in language acquisition will agree that the role of linguists in language departments is to describe the language and contrast its structure with the language native to the students, not to establish methods for teaching. This is not to deny that there are many earnest and capable linguists working very diligently sharpening and modifying the works of Lado, Newmark, Di Pietro, and others.

Let us consider contrastive analysis not for the purpose of evaluating its theoretical claims (the large bibliography on the subject is sufficient indication that this evaluation is being carried out) but rather in an attempt to separate its steps. Then let us see to what extent a linguist who, for one reason or another, is not working on language teaching methods or on language acquisition can participate in the work of contrastive analysis.

It seems that contrastive analysis could be broken down into three steps. Given two chunks of linguistic structure, one from L_1 the other from L_2, step one consists in describing or analyzing these two chunks of structure. Step two consists in identifying the similarities and differences of these two chunks of structure and step three consists in predicting problems of interference as viewed by Lado (1957, 1961), degrees of 'nonknowing' as viewed by Newmark (1966) or errors in performance as viewed by Di Pietro (1970). This last step is the stumbling block, the step on which applied linguists cannot find agreement. It is the least empirically founded and the most difficult to state.

While controversy about the relative merits of the power of pre-
dictability of CA continues to rage, it is quite possible to do work on
the other two steps. This leads us into what I consider to be a major
activity of linguists in language departments: description and contrast.

Description and contrast. There is no need to acquaint the linguists assembled here with the activities they are constantly engaged
in themselves. However, there are scholars in this room and readers
of the proceedings of this symposium who might welcome the oppor-
tunity to get a taste of some work of descriptive and contrastive nature.
In order to keep both groups interested I will illustrate with a still unpublished analysis. [2] To add to the attraction, I will use this analysis
as an argument against one of the reviewers of Robert Di Pietro's
book Language Structures in Contrast.

In a hypothetical class on French stylistics and translation, a no
less hypothetical student, call him John Hughes for easy reference,
translated (1) by (2).

(1) La police était certaine d'appréhender le voleur.
(2) The police were certain to catch the thief.

John Hughes' instructor was quick to catch the mistake, correcting it
to (3) and indicating that (4) is also a paraphrase of (1).

(3) The police were certain of catching the thief.
(4) The police were certain that they would catch the thief.

John Hughes was puzzled and concluded that certain in French and
certain in English don't mean the same thing. Wrong conclusion. In
what follows, we will examine the structure of sentences of the type
of (1) and (2) and conclude that certain and sûr in French and certain
and sure in English have the same meaning but differ in terms of the
constraints which must be placed on the structures in which these adjectives may occur.

Let us first eliminate John Hughes' conclusion which was the
possibility of a lexical difference. In the following set of sentences,
a and b are equivalent, i. e. one translates the other.

(5a) Jules Verne was certain of it.
(5b) Jules Verne en était certain.

(6a) Paul is a sure friend.
(6b) Paul est un ami sûr.

(7a) This is certain.
(7b) Cela est certain.

(8a) It is certain that the sun will rise tomorrow.
(8b) Il est certain que le soleil se lèvera demain.

In (9a) and (9b), however, the meanings of the verbs are different.

(9a) Thieu will still demand weapons.
(9b) Thieu demandera encore des armes.

This semantic difference remains, no matter what structure <u>demand</u> and <u>demander</u> 'ask' are used in. [3]

(10a) Thieu's demands are to be reckoned with.
(10b) Les demandes de Thieu seront exhausées.

(11a) Demand equal time!
(11b) Il se demande pourquoi elle boude.

In other words, in (9-11), <u>demand</u> has the meaning of <u>exiger, re-vendiquer,</u> and <u>demander</u> the meaning 'ask', 'beg', 'request'. [4] On the other hand, even the second dictionary meaning of <u>certain</u> is the same for both languages as shown by the translation of Sagan's novel:

(12a) Un certain sourire.
(12b) A Certain Smile.

Furthermore in both sentences (1) and (2) the meaning of certainty is present, the difference residing in <u>WHO</u> is certain. In (1), <u>la police</u> is certain of something while in (2) the author of the sentence is certain of something--a very important distinction.

   Now that it is established that <u>sûr</u> and <u>sure, certain</u> (Fr.) and <u>certain</u> (Eng.) have the same lexical meaning, let us investigate the structure of the two sentences. In showing that the adjectives under scrutiny are lexically and semantically equivalent, we have identified a structural property of sentences (1) and (2). We found that the grammatical subject of the <u>est certaine</u> in (1) was also its semantic subject, [5] but that the semantic subject of <u>were certain</u> in (2) was the author of the sentence and not <u>la police</u>. Now let us find evidence in support of this assumption.

   If it is the case that the grammatical subject of <u>certain</u> in sentences of the same type as (1) is also its semantic subject, then it should also be the case that a statement which asserted that this subject is not certain of the same thing would prove to be contradictory. [6]

(13) *<u>Jean</u> est certain d'arriver à l'heure mais <u>il</u> n'en est pas certain.

(14) <u>Jean</u> est désireux d'arriver à l'heure mais <u>il</u> n'en est pas certain.

(15) Jean est certain d'arriver à l'heure mais je n'en suis pas certain.

Our prediction was correct: (13) is ungrammatical while (14) and (15) are grammatical.

Following the same line of reasoning, we would expect that a sentence of the same type as (2) followed by a statement of uncertainty on the part of its author should yield a contradiction. It does:

(16) ⌐*John is certain to arrive on time

but ⎰ I doubt it.
⎱ I am not certain about it.
⎳ I tend to think he won't.

But there is no contradiction in (17),

(17) John is certain to succeed but he is not sure of it.

a fact which is predicted by our assumption. It is possible for the author of sentence (17) to express his certainty about an event while acknowledging someone else's doubt about it.[7]

In short, we have formulated a hypothesis (that the relation of the adjectives in question with their respective subjects is not the same for (1) and (2) and we have tested the validity of this hypothesis with the contradiction test. What this test has shown is that, somehow, the structural relation of the elements of (1) is different from that of (2).

Another test of our hypothesis has to do with nominalized forms of the adjectives in question. Here we hope that the nominalized forms will not have the same distribution. If they do not, then we will have shown yet another way that (1) and (2) differ. The derived nominals <u>certitude</u> and <u>certainty</u> correspond to <u>certain</u> (Fr.) and <u>certain</u> (Eng.) respectively. Sentence (19) is a translation of (18).

(18) Sa certitude lui vaut bien des succés.

(19) His certainty is bringing him much success.

Similarly (21) translates (20).

(20) Sa certitude d'arriver à l'heure me surprend.

(21) His certainty of arriving on time surprises me.

(in (18-21) it is the person who the author of these sentences is speaking of who is certain, not the author himself. Suppose we combine the nominals of sentences (20) and (21) with (22) and (23).

(22) Jean est certain d'arriver à l'heure.

(23) John is certain to arrive on time.

Our assumption about the structure of these sentences would predict that the French sentence would be grammatical since its nominal would reflect the structural relation of all other French sentences considered here, namely that the grammatical subject refers to the person who is certain of something. (24) is indeed grammatical.

(24) Jean est certain d'arriver à l'heure mais sa certitude me surprend.

Our assumption about the structure of these sentences does not predict that the English sentence formed by conjoining (23) and (21) is grammatical. In fact, it is incongruous.

(25) John is certain to arrive on time but his certainty surprises me.

Let us compare (24) and (25). On the one hand, sentence (25) is incongruous because John's certainty is unexpected. On the other hand, John's certainty is a natural consequence in (24). In other words, certainty in (25) is not a nominalization of the string John is certain in (25), but rather the result of independent knowledge on the part of the author of (25) that John is certain of arriving on time, a thought not expressed in (23). (24), however, is not incongruous because certitude is a nominal which corresponds in meaning to the string Jean est certain in (22). The difference between (24) and (25) can be accounted for if there is a structural difference between (22) and (23). That is precisely what is claimed in our assumption. We conclude that our assumption that there is a structural difference in the relation of certain (Eng.) and certain (Fr.) with their respective subjects provides us with one simple explanation for two different phenomena: the cases of contradiction and the cases of incongruity.
    As a further test of our assumption about the structural relationship of certain (Eng.) and certain (Fr.) with their semantic subjects

let us consider what other grammatical subjects can be found before
these adjectives. There is no question that verbs like be sure, be
certain and their French equivalents require thinking semantic subjects. There are no sentences such as

(26) *My old shoes are certain of their fate.

(27) *Our conviction was sure of the outcome.

(28) *Ces allumettes en sont certaines.

(29) *Vos efforts sont sûrs du succès qui les attend.

It would be absurd to imagine a human language in which shoes and
matches are capable of thought. Hence the semantic subject of certain must be capable of thought. No such restriction, however, need
be placed on strictly grammatical subjects. Combining these restrictions with our assumption about the structural relationship of certain
(Eng.) and certain (Fr.) with their subjects, we can predict that given
constructions of the type illustrated by (1) and (2), we can replace the
subject of (1) by nouns characterized as 'thinking' while any noun form
will do for (2).

(30) ?Le grizzly était sûr de reconnaître l'odeur de l'homme.

(31) The grizzly was sure to recognize man's odor.

(32) *L'étui à cigarettes du professeur est certain de disparaître.

(33) The professor's cigarette case is certain to disappear.

(31) and (33) are grammatical because the semantic subjects of sure
and certain, i.e. the authors of these sentences, are, of course,
human. (32) is not grammatical because the semantic subject of certain is an inanimate object. (30) is possible if and only if the subject
of sûr is personified. On the basis of the sentences examined hereto-
fore, the predictions made by our assumption are correct: in English
the grammatical subjects of sure and certain may or may not be
human, while their French equivalents must be human. But there
are, in French, sentences which the second part of this assumption
fails to predict.

Let us digress a moment to examine these sentences. Consider
(34) and (35).

(34) Il est certain que Jean arrivera à l'heure.

(35) C'est sûr!

These sentences have nonhuman grammatical subjects. We need to weaken our assumption to allow (34) and (35) while excluding sentences like (27), (29), and (32). Let us, therefore, specify the type of nonhuman grammatical subject which French certain and sûr may have. They may have sentential noun phrases as their subjects as (36-38) illustrate.

(36) Cela est certain.

(37) Son arrivée est certaine.

(38) Qu'il arrivera à l'heure, c'est certain.

The same is true of English.

(39) This is certain.

(40) His arrival is certain.

(41) That he will arrive on time is certain.

English and French have grammatical correspondences which relate sentences like (34) and (42) on the one hand to sentences like (38) and (41) on the other. In classical transformational grammar the derivation of (42) from (41) is called SENTENCE EXTRAPOSITION.

(42) It is certain that he will arrive on time.

This brief digression shows that there are cases in French where the grammatical subject of certain is not also its semantic subject. But since EXTRAPOSITION applies to both languages our assumption about the relation of certain (Fr.) and certain (Eng.) to their respective subjects can still be restricted to sentences like (1) and (2). In other words, we will disregard cases of EXTRAPOSITION, and keep in mind that in both languages the adjectives in question can have sentential noun-phrases as grammatical subjects.

We will now attempt to show how sentences (1) and (2) are structurally different. We will start by demonstrating that (1) and (43) share a grammatical correspondence.

In (1) and (43), the semantic subject of the verb in the main clause is the same as the grammatical subject of the verb in the main clause.

(1) La police est certaine d'appréhender le voleur.

(43) The police are certain of catching the thief.

If we can show that the understood subjects of appréhender and catching in (1) and (43) respectively are the same as the subjects in their respective main clauses, we will identify a structural relation at work in these sentences as the result of a known type of ellipsis referred to in transformational grammar as EQUI NOUN PHRASE DELETION.

To show that (1) and (43) are indeed cases of EQUI NOUN PHRASE DELETION we will make use of other processes of French and English. In the case of English, we will use stressed forms of the pronoun to show that at some stage in the derivation of the sentence in question, a pronoun of a certain type was a part of the lower clause. We will base our argument on the fact that there are no sequences like She, himself; He, themselves, etc., because a stressed form must agree with the unstressed form. We will use the same principle in the case of French sentences, but the argument will hinge on agreement of tout.

Let us take up the English case first. In sentence (44), the stressed form himself must have been derived from another third person pronoun, as is the case in (45).

(44) Mannix was certain of catching the bandits himself.

(45) Mannix was certain that he himself would catch the bandits.

The stressed pronoun cannot refer to bandits. If it did, it would be themselves as in (46).

(46) Mannix was certain that he would catch the bandits themselves.

Finally, himself must be derived from another third person pronoun. It cannot stand alone.

(47) *Himself is going to catch you.

Given that there was a third person pronoun in (44) at some stage, it follows that EQUI NP DELETION must have deleted it.

We now turn to the argument for French.

In (48), toute agrees with la police in gender and number.

(48) La police est certaine d'appréhender les voleurs toute seule. Elle ne demandera pas à l'agent 007 de l'aider.

As (49) and (50) show, toute refers to la police.

(49) La police est certaine que, toute seule, elle viendra à bout des voleurs.

(50) La police est certaine d'appréhender les voleurs tous seuls.

Examples (51) and (52) show that toute seule, which gets its morphology via agreement, requires the existence of a feminine subject for appréhender.

(51) *La police est certaine d'appréhender tout seul les voleurs.

(52) La police est certaine d'appréhender toute seule les voleurs.

For EMPHATIC PRONOUN FORMATION and AGREEMENT to apply, an antecedent subject of the subordinate verb is needed. We have seen that this understood subject is not randomly chosen, as (51) illustrates, but that the inflections on himself and toute seule are the same as featured in the understood pronoun. We conclude that (1) and (43) are cases of EQUI-NP-DELETION.

We have seen that French and English are structured similarly with respect to the application of EXTRAPOSITION and EQUI-NP-DELETION to sentences with certain (Fr.) and certain (Eng.) in the main clause. We are now left with the cases where French and English differ, as illustrated in examples (30–33).

(30) ?Le grizzly était sûr de reconnaître l'odeur de l'homme.

(31) The grizzly was sure to recognize man's odor.

(32) *L'étui à cigarettes du professeur est certain de disparaître.

(33) The professor's cigarette case was certain to disappear.

We have seen that (30) is odd and (32) ungrammatical because both involve a violation, the same violation, in fact, which can be found in their English equivalents.

(51) ?The grizzly was sure of recognizing man's odor.

(52) *The professor's cigarette case was certain of disappearing.

When EQUI-NP-DELETION applies to sentences with the adjectives
in question in the main clause, the subordinate clause takes the form
'of VERB-ing' in English and 'de VERB-INF' in French. This tells
us that (1) and (41) are cases of EQUI-NP-DELETION, but not (2). It
implies that (2) and all other sentences of English with <u>sure</u> or <u>certain</u>
in their main clause and an infinitive in the subordinate clause are of
an altogether different type. Furthermore, the fact that we know that
<u>the police</u> in (2) is not the semantic subject of <u>certain</u> suggests that
it could have been placed as grammatical subject of <u>certain</u> by some
operation. Let us assume a grammatical correspondence between
(2) and a sentence which is its semantic equivalent, namely (53).

(53) It was certain that the police would catch the thief.

The rule which places <u>the police</u> as subject of <u>certain</u> has a name: it
is SUBJECT RAISING. To test whether it is indeed SUBJECT RAIS-
ING which relates these sentences we need only consider a case of a
pseudo-noun-phrase to which we can attach no semantic or syntactic
property relating to <u>sure</u> and <u>certain,</u> and see if the grammatical
correspondence still obtains.

(54) It was certain that there would be a mob at Dub's.

(55) There was certain to be a mob at Dub's.

(56) It was sure that all hell would break loose.

(57) All hell was sure to break loose.

It does obtain. Pseudo-nouns like <u>there</u> can be raised to become the
subject (grammatical) of <u>certain</u>. The noun-like portion of the idiom
<u>All hell broke loose</u> in (56) can also be raised to the position of sub-
ject of <u>sure,</u> in (57). We conclude that SUBJECT RAISING applies to
<u>sure</u> and <u>certain</u>. This correspondence also accounts for the gram-
maticality of (31) and (33). In other words, (31) and (33) are also
cases of SUBJECT RAISING.

Now let us see whether SUBJECT RAISING applies to <u>sûr</u> and <u>cer-</u>
<u>tain</u> (Fr.). First, (1) and (58) are not synonyms.

(1) La police est certaine d'appréhender le voleur.

(58) Il est certain que la police appréhendera le voleur.

Second, although (59) is grammatical, (32) is not.

(59) Il est certain que l'étui à cigarettes du professeur diaparaîtra.

(32) *L'étui à cigarettes du professeur est certain de disparaître.

Third, pseudo-noun-phrases like <u>sa bourse</u> in the idiom <u>sa bourse</u> <u>est ouverte à</u> cannot be raised as subjects of <u>certain</u>.

(60) Il est certain que sa bourse est ouverte à ses amis.

(61) *Sa bourse est certaine d'être ouverte à ses amis.

Fourth, pseudo-noun-phrases like <u>sa bourse</u> in the same idiom <u>sa</u> <u>bourse est ouverte à</u> can be raised as subjects of predicates other than <u>certain,</u> like <u>sembler</u>.

(62) Il semble que sa bourse est ouverte à qui que ce soit.

(63) Sa bourse semble ouverte à qui que ce soit.

Of the four brief arguments above, the first three show that SUBJECT RAISING does not apply to <u>certain</u> (Fr.) and the fourth shows that SUBJECT RAISING is a rule of French.

We are now in a position to return to John Hughes and his translation problem. John, you will recall, had translated (1) by (2). His instructor had explained that (2) is not a translation of (1) but that either (3) or (4) would have been appropriate translations of (1). John had incorrectly concluded that the meanings of <u>certain</u> (Eng.) and that of <u>certain</u> (Fr.) were different, at least in part. We have just seen that there is no semantic difference between <u>certain</u> (Eng.) and <u>certain</u> (Fr.), but rather that the interplay between the rules of grammar on the one hand and the lexical items under consideration on the other is the real cause of this difference. In English and in French, there are lexical items which carry the same meaning in both languages and there are rules which move constituents in the same way. English <u>sure</u> and <u>certain</u> behave like <u>seem</u> and can trigger the rule of SUBJECT RAISING. French <u>sûr</u> and <u>certain</u> do not trigger the rule of SUBJECT RAISING. Unless used in the impersonal construction <u>il est sûr/certain que . . .,</u> <u>sûr</u> and <u>certain</u> (Fr.) often trigger EQUI-NP-DELETION, yielding an infinitive in the subordinate clause. The English sentence, (example 2) is derived by means of SUBJECT RAISING while the French sentence (example 1) is

114 / JEAN CASAGRANDE

derived by means of EQUI-NP-DELETION. John Hughes didn't know
that. Nor did his instructor. In fact, they didn't need to know it to
translate properly, as witness the instructor's remarks. However,
better than knowing the proper translation is the explanation of the
phenomena involved in this difficulté de traduction. The table below
was conceived with other John Hughes' in mind.

TABLE 1.

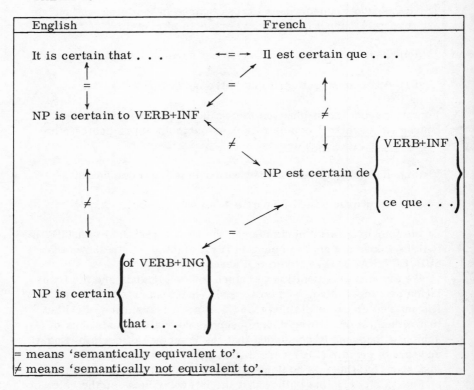

= means 'semantically equivalent to'.
≠ means 'semantically not equivalent to'.

Now a few words about what strikes me as an unfair criticism of
the more recent form of contrastive analysis, as exemplified by
Di Pietro's Language Structures in Contrast. In his recent review of
this book in Language Learning, R. Wardhaugh stated that:

. . . the difficulty with accepting transformational grammar
is that too much is to be taken on trust. For example, the concept of competence and performance and the recognition of
deep-surface distinctions must somehow be related to any contrastive statements that are made. Competence and performance
are useful concepts within linguistic theory, but they turn out to

be slippery to handle in practice, particularly in work in contrastive linguistics. Much the same observation can be made about deep structure and surface structure: a statement that all languages have the same deep structure really tells us nothing . . .

I cannot disagree with Wardhaugh's belief that a competence oriented theory is likely to prove insufficient when predicting the performance of students. Furthermore, I don't want to argue about the relative merits of the predictive power of any form of contrastive analysis. I would like, however, to take up Wardhaugh's claim that a language theory which incorporates two or more levels of structure is 'too slippery to handle'. What the descriptive portion of this paper proves is precisely the opposite. Though no mention by name was made of deep and surface structure and though no effort was made to identify a specific structure as 'the deepest', it should be very clear that were there not at least two levels of structure in the theory we adopted, it would be impossible to speak of EQUI-NP-DELETION and SUBJECT RAISING. Since the explanation just given depends crucially on the existence of these or similar or equivalent rules, and since these rules allow us to EXPLAIN a structural difference between two languages, it follows that a theory like that of classical transformational grammar is justified even in contrastive linguistics.

Not only do the findings given in this analysis justify a linguistic theory of the type of TG, but they also point to any linguistic theory which does not have at least two levels of structure equivalent in some way to deep and surface structure as inappropriate to describe this aspect of language.

As another aside on the topic of this description, it is most interesting to note that the distinction between certain (Fr.) and certain (Eng.) is very similar to Chomsky's celebrated examples with easy and eager.

(64) John is easy to please.

(65) John is eager to please.

In 'Current Issues in Linguistic Theory' Chomsky showed how the structures of (64) and (65) are necessarily different because a number of variations of these sentences yield asymmetry. Hence, (64) is related to (66) and (67) in some way but (65) does not have the equivalent, as shown by (68) and (69).

(66) To please John is easy.

(67) It is easy to please John.

(68) *To please John is eager.

(69) *It is eager to please John. (It = impersonal)

Similarly, (65) is related to (70) and (71) in some way but (64) does
not have the equivalent, as shown in (72) and (73).

(70) John's eagerness to please . . .

(71) John is eager to please Mary.

(72) *John's easiness to please . . .

(73) *John is easy to please Mary.

At the time he wrote this article Chomsky didn't know about EQUI-
NP-DELETION, SUBJECT RAISING, EXTRAPOSITION, etc. Subsequent work by him and others was to yield these rules. His point,
however, was that linguistic theory must account for the distribution
found in (64-72). We have just seen that the same type of condition
needs to be placed, not just on the theory we adopt but also on contrastive analysis. Presumably, anyone wanting to do a contrastive
analysis of the data given here would have to make use of the concepts outlined above. Indeed, theory, description, and application
are but interrelated parts of a whole.
     I have illustrated one of several possible types of research activi-
ties that linguists in language departments engage in. A glance at the
contents and bibliographical materials of Generative Studies in
Romance Languages and Diachronic Studies in Romance Languages
will show that other areas of more historical, theoretical, applied,
and descriptive nature are also carried out by this very group. I have
limited my presentation to a fairly detailed analysis because I wanted
to make my point in depth instead of breadth. Hopefully, the discussion which will follow the fourth and last part of this paper will
draw upon some of the areas of research which I didn't develop here.

     Courses. Before concluding I wish to discuss the teaching aspect
of the role of linguists in language departments. I will not single out
courses in dialectology, lexicology, history of specific languages,
etc., although they deserve careful consideration. My remarks in
this section will bear on structure courses, that is, courses which
describe the structure, be it phonological, syntactic, or semantic,
of one or more languages.

As I view it, the content of courses taught by linguists in language departments is closely connected with the content of their research. Their purpose is to make available to students generally not trained in linguistics those insights about the nature of language gained by practicing linguists. The body of research from which materials for these courses is drawn is often written in a technical way: what may be a simple argumentative development to a linguist may require many steps and much effort for a neophyte. Terminology and methodology, in short, can create a barrier to understanding. So, the job of the linguist teaching nonlinguists is to translate the cryptic statements of the specialist into statements that will be clear and simple to the neophyte. This activity of translation is equally as difficult a task as that of making original contributions. A good balance of both activities can contribute to the general well being. Linguists in language departments are called upon to engage in both activities.

Before enumerating the advantages which can be gotten by taking structure courses, I want to emphasize that structure courses do not replace the very hard work needed in nonnative language acquisition. Nor do structure courses replace language practice courses, including the exercise of translation which I don't mean to malign here. But structure courses can supplement all these courses. What is more, a language course can be intellectually stimulating, a welcome change from the necessary but nevertheless unintellectual drudgery of second language memorization.

Rather than preaching about the usefulness of structure courses, I will quote from comments written by students who have taken structure courses given by linguists in language departments.

A graduate student who held a teaching assistantship in French reported the following:

A student in my beginning French class asked me why 'y' was placed before the verb in French while 'here' comes generally after. I told him that French, like other Romance languages, has clitic pronouns while English does not. I explained that clitics are much like endings on words, that they are sort of part of the verb, and that, depending on the syntactic construction, they could be before (vous les y trouverez), after (Trouvez-les-y), or on both sides of the verb (Les-y trouverez-vous ?)

Another teaching assistant in a language structure course wrote that she had

. . . noticed that my students were confusing the uses of stressed and unstressed pronouns. For example, I often

found sentences like *Il et sa femme sont venus directement
des Etats Unis. From our discussion on clitics I knew why
this was ungrammatical. I was able to explain that unstressed
pronouns are cliticized and cannot be conjoined but that the
stressed ones can be . . .

The instructors of the structure courses which these teaching assistants had taken drew some of their lectures from work on clitics by
Perlmutter (1969, 1971), by Kayne (1969, 1972), by Dinnsen (1972),
and others, which they summarized and otherwise translated to make
it available to nonlinguists.

Teaching assistants are more readily convinced of the importance
of structure courses then their nonteaching peers, because they can
and do put to test the explanations acquired in structure courses. A
case in point is the author of the following.

This course has helped me to better teach my students Spanish
pronunciation. I have tried some exercises that I have made
up myself using what I learned in this course and . . . IT
WORKED!

Another student writes:

Besides having a greater interest in students learning to look
at language analytically, I feel that I am better prepared (in a
small way) to guide them along these lines.

In a particular structure course, the instructor's first lecture
illustrated the generality of rules. He identified three types of rules:
a widely distributed rule, a rule limited to a language family, and a
language specific rule. The students were told that these are arbitrary points on a wide scale but, nevertheless, they should compare
all new rules to these three types. Here is a student's reaction to
this approach.

Keeping in mind the three types of rules has helped me acquire
a perspective on language in general. Previously, when faced
with a linguistic problem I tended to accept it as such, without
investigating it any further. I now find that it helps to classify
it, if possible, as one of the three types of rules. Labeling the
thing, knowing if it is really different from English, or just
looks like it on the surface, and knowing finally, when there is
a difference between English and the foreign language, which
is more the exception to language in general.

Drawing from work by Robin Lakoff (1968), María-Luisa Rivero (1970, 1972) and many others, the instructor of the course referred to in the following quote outlined a number of principles of abstract grammar: higher predicates, the predicate hierarchy, the imperative and subjunctive as subordinate moods, negation as a predicate, si as a world-creating verb, etc. This approach prompted one student to make the following remark.

> Then there is abstract grammar. What I like about it is its universality. I find it reassuring to have something big like this to lean on. I know that whatever other language I may study will have this or a similar underlying pattern. I am not at all sure that abstract grammar has a direct application in language teaching but it seems to me that if we know many more such 'reasons behind language' it will inevitably make them easier to learn or to teach. For my mind, it is a palliative for alien forms, since I know that underneath all languages are the same in this way.

This next quote has to do with rule ordering and constraints on rule application.

> What turns me on in this type of course is that instead of identifying a sequence as ungrammatical, as I did before, with no general explanation of its ungrammaticality, I can state (or try to state) the more general reason for why that sequence is starred. So, instead of saying that *María se cree ser hermosa or *Marie se trouve être jolie are not acceptable and nothing more, one can say that BE INSERTION is blocked in sentences with a class of verbs including creer, encontrar in Spanish, and croire, trouver in French, when OBJECT RAISING has applied.

Implied in this remark is the realization that the explanation will also account for the ungrammatical status of (73) and (74), while the identification of a sequence as ungrammatical will not make predictions about similar cases.

(73) *Paul trouve la sauce être succulente.

(74) *Tous nos amis la trouve être succulente.

Both (73) and (74) have a slightly different structure than (75).

(75) *Marie se trouve être jolie.

This is so because (73-75) violate the explanation in the quote above, to the effect that the verb être may not be inserted under certain conditions. Exclude some of those conditions and you get grammatical sequences.

(76) Marie s'imagine être jolie.

(77) Paul trouve que la sauce est succulente.

The verb imaginer is not a member of the verb class which, together with ETRE INSERTION yields ungrammatical sequences, so (76) is grammatical. In (77), OBJECT RAISING, a rule which takes the subject of a subordinate clause and makes it the object of the next higher clause, did not apply.

This last quote and subsequent comment on it constitute just another example of the generalizations which practicing linguists make about languages and which students in linguistically oriented courses can make theirs. One can easily imagine how in a literary stylistic analysis one might be able to go beyond the 'linguistically superficial' remarks which apply to specific sentences. Think how much more general, and perhaps informative, a stylistic analysis might be which referred to syntactic rules and constraints in a piece of literature than one which is bound to data available superficially only.

More yet can be gained from structure courses than I have shown here. In the words of yet another student,

... the most significant learning takes place not in the facts and formulae learned, but in the apprehension of the questioning process necessary to obtain these facts. It is the comprehension of this process which is really involved in the understanding of any discipline or system. Thus, the most important concepts of a course must be those which guide that process of questioning and make it possible. In your course there seem to be three such basic guides ...

Once a scholar understands the questioning process, that is, the methodology, of a discipline he can make intelligent use of that discipline in his own field, and have intelligent exchanges with specialists in his newly acquired field of knowledge.

In his research and in his teaching the linguist is in the unusually advantageous position of creating a bridge between the sciences and the humanities. I can imagine no thinker who would not admit that translating the jargon of his profession into everyday language does not constitute a good exercise. The reactions of students and colleagues not trained in linguistics, frustrating though they may be, can be of value to linguists in language departments. These reactions may appear naive or old-fashioned, and perhaps they are, but they stand a good chance of being novel enough to deserve a serious look. The position of linguists, straddling the fence between the two cultures can be frustrating but, in the long run, it is beneficial.

A word about the title. This well-known proverb was uttered by Sancho Panza in one of his famous lucid moments. I don't wish for this proverb to be interpreted in the context of Sancho's thoughts, something like 'I must be crazy to be doing this.' Instead, I propose that we take this proverb out of its Quixotic context and apply it literally to linguists in language departments. 'Tell me your company and I'll tell you who you are.' That's just what I have tried to do.

NOTES

*I am pleased to acknowledge support from the National Endowment for the Humanities and from the Department of Romance Languages, as well as from the Center for Neuro-behavioral Linguistic Research, University of Florida. I am indebted also to the several colleagues and students whose ideas have contributed to this paper.

[1]See A Drillbook of French Pronunciation by Valdman et al.

[2]Some of the examples and arguments presented here are extracted from an unpublished paper entitled 'Sûr et certain en français et en anglais'.

[3]Demander also has a meaning equivalent to demand, require. Le Petit Robert gives it as the seventh sense of the word, and it is restricted to inanimate subjects.

(a) Votre proposition demande reflexion.

(b) Ce voyage demande trois heures.

[4]In connection with (11b), note that demand cannot be made reflexive, while ask, the equivalent of demander, can be made reflexive:

(a) *He demanded himself why she was pouting.

(b) He asked himself why she was pouting.

(c) Il se demandait pourquoi elle boudait.

[5]Throughout this paper I will use the term 'semantic subject' loosely to cover two different concepts. Semantic subject will mean what is generally understood in classical generative grammar as deep structure subject. It will also refer to the author of an assertion of the type It is sure that . . . There is, of course, no syntactic evidence that a semantic subject in this second sense of our term is also a syntactic subject at any time in a derivation. This second meaning of semantic subject is dependent on an integrity condition. When you say that you are sure of something you either believe it or you are

lying. Here we are assuming that speakers are honest about their statements. The term semantic subject is used here in this unorthodox manner in order to present a complex and little understood relation in as simple a way as possible.

[6]We are following the convention that calls for underscoring pronouns and their co-referential antecedents.

[7]There seem to be dialect differences with respect to judgments about (17). But this does not change the fact that (17) is not strictly contradictory. It appears to be at first. More work is needed on this topic.

REFERENCES

Casagrande, Jean. 1972. Sûr et certain en français et en anglais. Unpublished paper.

Casagrande, Jean and Bohdan Saciuk. 1972. Generative studies in Romance languages. Rowley, Mass., The Newbury House.

Chomsky, Noam. 1964. Current issues in linguistic theory. In: Fodor and Katz 1964.

Dinnsen, Daniel A. 1972. Additional constrains on clitic order in Spanish. In: Casagrande and Saciuk 1972.

Di Pietro, Robert. 1970. Language structures in contrast. Rowley, Mass., The Newbury House.

Fodor, Jerry A. and Jerrold J. Katz. 1964. The structure of language. Englewood Cliffs, N. J., Prentice-Hall.

Kayne, Richard S. 1969. The transformational cycle in French syntax. Unpublished Ph. D. dissertation, Massachusetts Institute of Technology.

_____. 1972. Subject inversion in French interrogatives. In: Casagrande and Saciuk 1972.

Lado, Robert. 1957. Linguistics across cultures. Ann Arbor, Mich., University of Michigan Press.

_____. 1961. Language testing. New York, McGraw-Hill.

Lakoff, Robin T. 1968. Abstract syntax and Latin complemention. Cambridge, Mass., MIT Press.

Najam, Edward. 1966. Language learning: The individual and the process. Bloomington, Ind., Indiana University Press.

Newmark, Leonard. 1966. How not to interfere with language learning. In: Najam 1966.

Perlmutter, David. 1969. Les pronoms objets en Espagnol. Langages. 14. 81-133.

_____. 1971. Deep and surface structure constraints in syntax. New York, Holt, Rinehart, and Winston.

Rivero, María-Luisa. 1970. La concepcion de los modos en la
gramática de Andres Bello y los verbos abstractos en la gramática
generativa. Mimeographed.
_____. 1972. On conditionals in Spanish. In: Casagrande and
Saciuk 1972.
Valdman, Albert et al. 1971. A drillbook of French pronunciation.
2nd ed. New York, Harper and Row.
Wardhaugh, Ronald. 1971. Review of Di Pietro (1970). Language
Learning. 21.247-48.

CONSTRAINTS ON CLITIC INSERTION IN SPANISH*

MERCEDES ROLDÁN

The Balch Institute, Philadelphia

The statement about clitic attachment that appears in the traditional Spanish grammars is succinct: (1) A clitic must follow the verb (enclitic) if the latter is an infinitive, an affirmative imperative, or a gerund.
Examples:

(1.1) Despedir<u>se</u> no es ir<u>se</u>.
'Saying good-bye is not (the same as) leaving.'

(1.2) Al ir<u>se</u> Juan Pedro quedó solo.
'When John left Peter was left alone.' (The subject of the infinitive S is obligatorily extraposed into the predicate.)

(1.3) Te vi hacer<u>lo</u>.
'I saw you do it.'

(1.4) Descríbame<u>lo</u>!
'Describe it to me!' (2nd polite)

(1.5) Imitémos<u>lo</u>!
'Let's imitate him!'

(1.6) No conociéndo<u>lo</u> nos va a ser difícil dar con Pedro.
'Not knowing him, it will be hard for us to find Peter.'

(1.7) Si hay que hacer<u>lo</u>, hay que hacer<u>lo</u>.
'If it's got to be done, it's got to be done.'

124

(2) It must precede the verb (proclitic) otherwise, i. e. if it is indicative, subjunctive, or a negated imperative:

(2.1) Lo veo y no lo creo.
       'I see it and I don't believe it. '

(2.2) Aunque lo viera no lo creería.
       'Even if I saw it I wouldn't believe it. '

(2.3) No me lo describa!
       'Don't describe it to me!'

(2.4) Que me lo describa!
       'Have him describe it to me!'
       (3rd sing., compare with 1.4)

(2.5) Digo que te calles!
       'I insist that you shut up!'

(2.6) No lo imitemos.
       'Let's not imitate him. '

Exception. (3) A clitic can neither immediately precede nor follow a past participle; it must be raised to a verb phrase above it:

(3.1) Sin haberlo visto.
       'Without having seen it. '

(3.2) Habiabiéndolo visto.
       'Having seen it. '

(3.3) Lo hemos visto.
       'We have seen it. '

(*vístolo and *lo (clitic) visto)

This exceptional case will be accounted for by ordering clitic climbing before clitic attachment and making the former obligatory for the past participle.

The generalization has been proposed that a clitic must follow the verb if the latter is the first word of the sentence but it is 'attracted' to pre-verb position by any lexical material preceding the verb. Example (2.1) will not constitute a counter-example to this observation because clitic attachment must be ordered before the rule that optionally deletes the pronominal subjects of finite verbs; this is a very late rule of the grammar. Nevertheless, the generalization is wrong: it fails to account for the non-finite verbs when they are preceded by a complementizer, an article or sentence negation, as in examples (1.2), (1.6), and (1.7). In these cases the clitics are not 'attracted' as the rule would predict.

I want to propose that the correct generalization that will account for all the cases of clitic attachment is the following: a clitic must be attached to the right of the verb if the subject has been removed prior to the application of clitic attachment, and it is attached to the left of the verb if the sentence has a subject before the verb. Some rules that delete the subject and must precede clitic attachment are illustrated in the examples of set (1): (1.1) deletion of a generic indefinite subject, (1.2) extraposition of the subject into the predicate, (1.3) subject raising, (1.6) and (1.7) equi NP deletion.

The validity of the rule I am proposing is challenged by the behavior of the imperatives. Compare (1.4) and (1.5) with (2.3) and (2.6). If we order imperative subject deletion before clitic attachment, we can account for the affirmative forms but not for the negative forms. If we reverse the order, the affirmative forms are left unaccounted for. The only way out of this dilemma is to have two partially different derivations for the affirmative and the negative imperatives. The imperative transformation, which is preceded by negative lowering, applies only to non-negated sentences. This transformation erases the subject of an imperative sentence after the clitics have been generated but before their attachment. All other semantically imperative sentences are eligible for subjunctive reduction, a transformation that also deletes the subject but is ordered after clitic attachment. I wish to argue that this solution is not ad hoc, and that it reflects, in fact, the native speakers' intuitions about the imperatives. The traditional Spanish grammars list only an affirmative form for the imperative, and they say that the negative forms are 'borrowed' from the subjunctive. This intuition is based on the fact that the second person imperatives have a contrasting form that occurs only in the affirmative, in the negative they have the subjunctive form. The behavior of the clitics lends additional force to this interpretation.

Apparent counterexamples to the rule I am proposing are the following:

(4.1)ʲ Tú cállate la boca . . . (ahora me toca hablar a mí).
   'You shut your mouth . . . (now it's my turn to speak).'

(4.2) Así vivimos yo y mis gatos, yo ordenando la casa y
ellos desordenándo<u>la</u>.
'This is the way I and my cats live, I tidying up the house
and they messing it up.'

In example 4.1 the subject is contrastive. Compare with:

(4.3) Cállate la boca (que quiero dormir).
'Shut up (I want to sleep).'

Observe that a subject is not permissible in the non-contrastive
situation of (4.3):

(4.4) *Tú cállate la boca (que quiero dormir).

The traditional Spanish grammars claim that the subject of the
imperative form is not deleted but rather extraposed into the predicate, and then, optionally deleted. The paradigm that appears in the
Academy grammar is as follows:

(4.5) Ven tú. etc.

If this is the correct rule, then the need to introduce a contrastive
subject in (4.1) after the imperative transformation is obviated. The
imperative subject is first extraposed into the predicate. Clitic
attachment applies then. Later the subject can be moved back to
initial position for emphasis.[1]
As for example (4.2), the two parallel sentences <u>yo . . . y ellos</u>
<u>. . .</u> have a verb <u>vivir</u> gapped.

(4.2') Yo vivo ordenando la casa y ellos viven desordenándo<u>la</u>.

The pronouns are subjects of <u>vivir</u>, the subjects of the gerunds have
been erased by equi NP deletion prior to the deletion of <u>vivir</u>.

Clitic formation. All clitics are transformationally derived and,
obviously, clitic attachment must be preceded by the various rules
that generate the clitics. Clitic attachment is a postcyclical rule: it
must follow object topicalization, which is a postcyclical rule.
Clitic formation, as we shall see, is a cyclical rule. Cliticization
must follow passive in order to prevent the generation of such non-
sentences as (5.1), which would be the outcome of applying passive
to (5.2):

(5.1) *Ella la fue vista, pero al marido no.
'She her was seen, but to her husband wasn't.'

(5.2) La vieron a ella pero al marido no.
'They saw her but not her husband.'

Passive is a cyclical rule. It must precede several rules that delete the subject. Otherwise it would not be possible to account for the clitics in the following examples:

(5.3) Conócete a tí mismo!
'Know yourself!'

(5.4) Luis dijo que se fueran.
'Louis said for them to leave (reflexive).'

(5.5) Los chicos no quieren lavarse las manos.
'The children don't want to wash their hands.'

(5.6) El espejo$_i$ lo$_i$ vi romperse$_i$ en mil pedazos.
'The mirror, I saw it break in one thousand pieces.'

The subject of (5.3) has been deleted by the imperative transformation (a cyclical rule). The underlying structure of (5.4) is:

(5.7) Luis dijo que ellos fueran (inchoative).

The clitic se is derived by the inchoative reflexive transformation (see Roldán 1971). Its source is the subject ellos which is extraposed to the predicate. Inchoative reflexive must, therefore, precede subject deletion. The antecedent of the clitic se in (5.5) is the subject of lavar which has been deleted by equi NP deletion. Therefore, clitic formation must precede equi. The antecedent of se in (5.6) is the pronoun lo which has been raised to the higher sentence but only after cliticization has applied.
Compare (5.6) with (5.8):

(5.8) El espejo$_i$ lo$_j$ vi romperlo$_j$ en mil pedazos.
'The mirror, I saw him break it in one thousand pieces.'

The first lo of sentence (5.8) is the raised subject of the complement which is obligatorily cliticized, in the second cycle, because it is a pronoun. The second lo is a redundant repetition of the object of the lower sentence el espejo. The formation of this redundant clitic, which is cyclical, triggers object topicalization, a postcyclical rule.

Now consider examples (6.1) and (6.2). Their respective underlying structures are (6.3) and (6.4):

(6.1) Luis se dejó dar gato por liebre (por alguien).
'Louis allowed himself to be shortchanged.'
('Louis allowed himself to be served cat instead of hare.')

(6.2) Al enfermo háganlo revisar por un buen especialista.
'The sick person, have him examined by a good doctor.'

(6.3) Luis dejó [$_S$ alguien dio a Luis gato por liebre].

(6.4) Hagan [$_S$ un buen especialista revise al enfermo].

Although the antecedents of the clitics of these two sentences are in the lower predicate, they must be attached to the higher verb. Sentences (6.5) and (6.6) are ungrammatical:

(6.5) *Luis$_i$ dejó $\left\{ \begin{array}{l} \text{darle}_i \\ \text{darse}_i \end{array} \right\}$ gato por liebre.

(6.6) *Al enfermo hagan revisarlo por un buen especialista.

Subject raising could account, clumsily, for (6.2), but it can not account for (6.1). It could be possible to apply the following transformations to the underlying structure (6.4): in the lower cycle passive, subject raising--the loss of the subject causes the deletion of the passive auxiliary as well as the infinitivization of the verb.

We generate the intermediate structure (6.7):

(6.7) Hagan al enfermo [$_S$ revisar por un buen especiali~'

Optional cliticization of the raised object ge~ in the correct predicate.

A serious flaw of this derivatio~ be generated in the intermediate leaving no traces. But, more dan derivation will not account for exan cliticized in this case in the indirect is not eligible for the passive transfo.

Both examples will be accounted fo. Chomsky's proposal, we separate pass. object movement.[2] In this way, we can

inflection of the embedded verb, and its change into an infinitive, by the fact that subject extraposition is a very early cyclical rule: it is the first rule of passivization. Therefore, it must also precede cliticization. But observe that cliticization may not apply in these examples until the cycle of the higher verb: (6.5) and (6.6) are ungrammatical. This indicates that cliticization has to be constrained to apply only to finite sentences.

Cliticization. The following rule, with the introduction of variables between the verb that controls cliticization and the NP's that are to be cliticized, will generate the clitics of (6.1) and (6.2) in the cycle of dejar and hacer respectively, if tree-pruning is applied to the lower sentence when it loses its inflection:

$$\text{S. D.: } [_S \text{ NP - V - X - NP - (NP) - Y]} \Rightarrow$$
$$\phantom{\text{S. D.: } [_S }1 \quad \ 2 \ \ \ 3 \ \ \ 4 \quad \ \ 5 \quad \ 6$$

$$\text{S. C.: } 1, 2, 3, \quad 4 \qquad + 4, 5 \qquad + 5, 6$$
$$\phantom{\text{S. C.: } 1, 2, 3, \quad 4 \ \ }[\text{Clitic}] \qquad [\text{Clitic}]$$

Object raising. The clitics se and lo respectively of sentences (6.3) and (6.4) are, therefore, triggered by the higher verbs dejó and haga, but generated in the predicate of the lower infinitives dar and revisar. If they are allowed to remain in that position, clitic attachment will attach them to the wrong verb, generating the undesirable sentences (6.5) and (6.6). To prevent this, the clitic and redundant NP must be raised to the higher sentence by the following rule of object raising.

Object raising

$$\text{S. D.: } [_S \text{ NP - V - Vinf. - Clit , (NP) - Y]} \Rightarrow$$
$$\phantom{\text{S. D.: } [_S }1 \quad \ 2 \ \ \ \ 3 \qquad \ \ 4 \qquad \ 5$$

$$\text{S. C.: } \quad 1 \quad \ \ 2 \ \ 4 \ 3 \qquad \ \ \ 0 \qquad \ \ \ 5$$

Minor Rule, applying to dejar, hacer, verbs of the senses (oir, ver) and possibly to a few others.

se familiar with 'subject raising' will notice that this rule is identical to subject raising, and that it applies in those cone subject raising cannot apply, i. e. to the complements of gering verbs which have no subject. Thus then, 'object subject raising' must be accounted for by one and the Roldan 1972).

Clitic climbing. When there is a series of verbs with clitics in a complex VP the clitics can sometimes be transported to progressively higher sentences and all the way to the top. For example:

(8.1) Quisiera poder estar haciéndomelo ahora.

(8.2) Quisiera poder estármelo haciendo ahora.

(8.3) Quisiera podérmelo estar haciendo ahora.

(8.4) Me lo quisiera poder estar haciendo ahora.
['I wish I could be making it for myself right now.']

Which contrasts with:

(9.1) Espero poder estar haciéndomelo muy pronto.

(9.2) *Me lo espero poder estar haciendo muy pronto.
['I expect to be able to be making it for myself very soon.']

Clitic climbing must precede clitic attachment. It must, of course, follow cliticization, which is a cyclical rule.

The fact that a clitic cannot cross the verb esperar, but does cross querer is only one of the many puzzles connected with this rule. Clitic climbing is restricted by many constraints. Some have to do with tree structure, or with whether the higher verb has clitics of its own. But there are cases in which one would expect clitic climbing to apply, yet it blocks. A few of these cases which I cannot explain will be discussed below.

Rivero (1970) has observed that clitic promotion is blocked by the presence of an S node in the path of the clitic. For example:

(10.1) Quiero que sigas haciéndomelos.

(10.2) Quiero que me los sigas haciendo.

(10.3) *Me los quiero que sigas h
['I want you to go on m

Compare with:

(10.4) Me los quieres seguir haci
'Do you want to go on makin

Clitics can be transported across the complementizer <u>que</u> and the preposition <u>a</u>, <u>por</u>, and <u>de</u>. But not all the time:

(11.1)   Tenemos que hacer<u>lo</u>.

(11.2)   <u>Lo</u> tenemos que hacer.
        ['We've got to do it.']

But:

(11.3)   Hay que hacer<u>lo</u>.

(11.4)   *<u>Lo</u> hay que hacer.
        ['It's got to be done.']

(11.5)   Vine a saludar<u>los</u>.

(11.6)   <u>Los</u> vine a saludar.
        ['I came to greet them.']

But:

(11.7)   Renuncio a saludar<u>los</u>.

(11.8)   *<u>Los</u> renuncio a saludar.
        ['I give up (trying to) greet them.']

(11.9)   Están por entregár<u>mela</u>.

(11.10)   <u>Me</u> <u>la</u> están por entregar.
        ['They are about to give it to me.']

But:

(11.11)   Muero por conocer<u>la</u>.

(11.12)   *<u>La</u> muero por conocer.
        ['I am dying to meet her.']

(11.13)   Acabamos de ofrecér<u>selos</u>.

        <u>Se</u> <u>los</u> acabamos de ofrecer.
        ['We've just offered them to him.']

But:

(11.15) Venimos de entregár<u>selos</u>.

(11.16) *<u>Se</u> <u>los</u> venimos de entregar.
['We are back from delivering them to him. ']

Clitic climbing is blocked by the presence of any other constituents in the path of the clitic, including the other prepositions.

(12.1) Quisiera no volver a ver<u>te</u>.

(12.2) *<u>Te</u> quisiera no volver a ver.
['I wish I would not see you again. ']

Compare with:

(12.3) No <u>te</u> quisiera volver a ver.

(12.4) Convinieron en encontrar<u>se</u>.

(12.5) *<u>Se</u> convinieron en encontrar.
['They agreed to get together. ']

(12.6) Deseamos mucho ver<u>te</u>.

(12.7) *<u>Te</u> deseamos mucho ver.
['We very much wish to see you. ']

Compare with:

(12.8) Mucho <u>te</u> deseamos ver.

(12.9) Los vi a ellos matar<u>la</u>.
['I saw them kill her. ']

(12.10) *Se <u>la</u> vi a ellos matar.

Compare with:

(12.11) <u>La</u> vi matar.
['I saw her (get) killed. ']

Clitics always climb in a block. It is not possible to promote only one of a series of clitics and leave the other(s) behind. Compare examples (13.1)-(13.3) with (13.4)-(13.6):

(13.1) Tengo que ir a pedírselo.

(13.2) Tengo que írselo a pedir.

(13.3) Se lo tengo que ir a pedir.

(13.4) *Tengo que irle a pedirlo.

(13.5) *Le tengo que ir a pedirlo.

(13.6) *Lo tengo que irle a pedir.
['I have to go ask him for it. ']

Similarly, if a clitic is promoted to the side of another, the two become fused, so to speak, and from here on they have to move together:

(14.1) Tienes que verlo hacerlo.

(14.2) Tienes que vérselo hacer.

(14.3) Se lo tienes que ver hacer.
['You have to see him make it. ']

Observe that (14.4) is also grammatical:

(14.4) Lo tienes que ver hacerlo.

Here the higher clitic has been moved; the lower clitic has not been promoted up to it and, consequently, there is no violation. Compare with:

(14.5) *Lo tienes que verlo hacer.

After the higher clitic has been removed, the lower clitic can not climb. This suggests that clitic climbing must be a cyclical rule.

In general, a clitic cannot be promoted up to a verb phrase that already has clitics of its own. For example:

(15.1) <u>Me</u> voy a buscar<u>los</u>.

(15.2) *<u>Me</u> <u>los</u> voy a buscar.
['I am leaving to look for them.' (inchoative)]

Sentence (15.2) is grammatical with the reading: 'I am leaving in
order to look for them for me', where both clitics come from the
lower VP. Compare (15.1) and (15.2) with (15.3) and (15.4):

(15.3) Voy a buscar<u>los</u>.

(15.4) <u>Los</u> voy a buscar.
['I am going to look for them.']

An exception to the above generalization are the constructions of
the type <u>hacer hacer,</u> in which the higher verb can be <u>hacer,</u> 'make',
<u>dejar,</u> 'let', a verb of the senses such as <u>ver,</u> 'see', <u>mirar,</u> 'look',
and a few others. These constructions do allow climbing up to an-
other clitic. The higher clitic is the subject of the complement which
has been promoted by raising. Examples are sentences (14.1)-(14.3)
and also:

(16.1) <u>Le</u> hice leer<u>lo</u>.

(16.2) <u>Se</u> <u>lo</u> hice leer.
['I made him read it.']

But these constructions have the peculiar restriction that only non-
reflexive third person clitics that are not coreferential with the higher
subject or clitic can climb:

(17.1) <u>Lo</u> hice suicidar<u>se</u>.

(17.2) *<u>Se</u> <u>lo</u> hice suicidar.
['I made him kill himself.']

(17.3) Luisa$_i$ lo oyó maldecirla$_j$.

(17.4) *Luisa se la oyó maldecir.[3]
['Louise heard him curse her.']

Compare with:

(17.5) Luisa$_i$ lo oyó maldecirla$_j$.

(17.6) Luisa se la oyó maldecir.

(17.7) La oyeron nombrar<u>me</u>.

(17.8) *<u>Me la</u> oyeron nombrar.
['They heard her mention my name.']

Compare with:

(17.9) Me oyeron nombrar<u>la</u>.

(17.10) <u>Me la</u> oyeron nombrar.
['They heard me mention her name.']

And, again, compare the above with 17.11 and 17.12:

(17.11) Me oyeron llamar<u>la</u>.

(17.12) *<u>Me la</u> oyeron llamar.
['They heard me call her.']

Not surprisingly, there is wide discrepancy among native speakers about the grammaticality of some of the examples that I have discussed above.

Clitic climbing is a colloquialism. In all the pairs of examples that I have presented above, the member of the pair that has undergone climbing is more colloquial than the one that has not. The rule is very frequent in spoken Spanish. It applies to all the so-called auxiliaries and quasi-auxiliaries: <u>haber</u>, <u>estar</u>, <u>tener</u>, <u>poder</u>, <u>deber</u>, and to most of the verbs of high frequency. However, it fails to apply to some very frequent verbs such as <u>morir</u> 'die' and <u>esperar</u> 'hope'. This appears to be a new rule of Spanish, the application of which has not yet been extended to all the verbs of the language and probably never will be. Thus, although clitic climbing is an easy rule to state, it is one of those rules that only native or nearly native speakers use correctly.

Conclusion. In his Ph. D. dissertation, 'Root and Structure Preserving Transformations', (1970) Joseph Emonds claims that he can account for the Spanish clitics by means of the following rules:

(1) VP $\longrightarrow$ (Cl) V

(2) Cl $\longrightarrow$ (Ref) (II) (I) (III)

The clitic nodes would be empty in deep structure and filled in during the cycle. He then proposes a post-cyclical transformation that exchanges the position of the verb and the clitics for the infinitive verbs. This paper shows that this account is both observationally and explanatorily inadequate.

It is observationally inadequate because it would generate the wrong verb-clitic order in imperative sentences, which are finite but the clitic follows the verb, and in sentences having a past participle, which is non-finite, yet it can be neither preceded nor followed by clitics.

It is explanatorily inadequate because it would not be able to account in a non-ad hoc way for examples (6.1) and (6.2) discussed in this paper, where the clitic must be attached to the higher verb although it is an object of the lower verb. In Emonds' grammar, clitic climbing would have to be stated as a lowering rule, in direct contradiction with its semantics, and the rule would have to be enormously complicated. Other rules that would be complicated are: passive, object topicalization, the double object constructions, and, finally, the observation that, in non-contrastive sentences, clitics are in complementary distribution with non-pronominal direct and indirect objects.

NOTES

*I am indebted to Fred W. Householder and David Perlmutter for comments on an earlier version of this paper. Their observations led me to expand my analysis considerably. But they are not responsible for the conclusions nor for the claims I have made here.

[1]Observe that the imperative sentences have no person ending, which indicates that the subject of these sentences is deleted before subject-verb agreement, which is a late rule, applies:

(a) ¡Cómelo! (familiar form)
'Eat it!'
(b) ¡Cómalo! (polite form) (a is the subjunctive morpheme)
'Eat it!'

The substandard first plural imperative

(c) ¡Lo hagamos!
'Let's do it!'

has a person ending--i.e. it has gone through subject-verb agreement, but the proclitic shows that this is not a 'real' imperative

but a 'borrowed' one. The standard first and second plural imperatives,

(d) ¡Hagámoslo!
     'Let's do it!'
(e) ¡Háganlo!
     'Do it!'

which have undergone subject-verb agreement and take enclitics, are
exceptions to the generalization.

[2]This does not mean that I accept Chomsky's formulation of the
passive transformation. But I do agree with him that agent raising
and object movement are two (or more) rules.

[3]The reason for this restriction is, of course, that in (17.2), raising causes a reflexive clitic to occur in surface structure in a simplex
sentence whose subject is not coreferential with the clitic; while in
(17.4) the nonreflexive clitic occurs in the same simplex sentence as
its coreferential antecedent. The two forms are in violation of the
rules for Spanish reflexivization.

REFERENCES

Emonds, Joseph. 1970. Root and structure preserving transfor-
    mations. Unpublished Ph. D. dissertation, Massachusetts Institute
    of Technology.
Real Academia Española. 1931. Gramática de la lengua española.
    Madrid, Espasa-Calpe.
Rivero, María Luisa. 1970. A surface structure constraint on
    negation in Spanish. Language. 46.640-66.
Roldán, Mercedes. 1972. In defense of raising. Paper read at the
    LSA Meetings, December 1972.
_____. 1971. Spanish constructions with 'se'. Language Sciences.
    18.15-29.
Ross, John R. 1969. A proposed rule of tree-pruning. In: Modern
    studies in English. Ed. by David Reibel and S. Schane. Englewood
    Cliffs, N.J., Prentice-Hall.

DEEP AND SURFACE ORDER
OF THE SPANISH CLITICS

ROBERT K. SZABO

University of Texas, Austin

1. Introduction. Perlmutter has shown that a surface structure
constraint is necessary to handle the ordering by person of the Spanish
clitic pronouns. Dinnsen has shown the need for a constraint on the
order of cases of the clitics. I will present evidence from Spanish and
French to show that stating clitic case order in terms of surface structure involves an inherent loss in generality. Thus, in order to explain one presumably unified phenomenon, clitic ordering, two distinct mechanisms are required if one is to avoid loss of generality:
Perlmutter's surface structure constraint (SSC) to explain ordering
in terms of person, transformation(s) to account for ordering in terms
of case.

In addition, I will examine the behavior of reflexive clitics in two
dialects, and show that the facts for one dialect are best handled transformationally, whereas those for the other dialect are best done in
terms of surface structure. In accounting for the facts in each of the
two dialects without loss of generality, one is forced to the conclusion
that these two dialects (which differ on the surface only in that one
allows a small group of clitic sequences disallowed in the other) differ
not in the details of their rules and ordering, but in the very types of
mechanisms they use.

2. Clitic case order. Clitics take any one of three cases: Benefactive, Dative, Accusative. In addition, they are either plus or
minus Reflexive. As Dinnsen has shown, Benefactive clitics must
precede Datives, and Datives must precede Accusatives, in a transitive, irreflexive, and antisymmetric relationship. (They must, of

course, also conform to Perlmutter's SSC, which constrains the order of persons.) This ordering could be expressed by the SSC (100) below, CASORDER.

CASORDER (100) BENEFACTIVE DATIVE ACCUSATIVE

CASORDER alone, however, is insufficient to account for the data, since there exists a class of exceptions to it. In these exceptions, the clitic not conforming to CASORDER is a Reflexive clitic in left-most position. (There are no examples where more than one clitic fails to conform to CASORDER.) Reflexive clitics, in fact, appear on the surface only in leftmost position. [1]

(95) Te me le echaste encima. [2]
      'You threw yourself on him (on me).'

(1) No te me indisciplines.
     'Don't become undisciplined on me.'

In (95) the order of cases is Accusative, Benefactive, Dative; in (1) Dative, Benefactive. In both, the leftmost clitic is reflexive. Sentences with a non-leftmost Reflexive are ungrammatical, as in (2) and (3) below. In these examples, as in all the examples I quote, the full form of the sentence (without the clitics and with the NP's they came from) is grammatical--the ungrammaticality is due to the clitics.

(2) *Te me maté.
     'I killed myself for you.'

(3) *Te me lavé las manos.
     'I washed my hands for you.'

Sentences (2) and (3) conform both to CASORDER and to Perlmutter's SSC: an additional constraint is needed. We can account for this ungrammaticality by positing a separate SSC like (101) below.

(101) +Reflexive   -Reflexive

Unfortunately, allowing (101) and Casorder to operate simultaneously would rule out the grammatical sentence (95).

The alternative is to combine (101) and CASORDER. This move, however, requires us to use feature notation, since clitics must be described in terms both of reflexivity and case.

(OOB) [+REFLEXIVE] $\begin{bmatrix} \text{BENEFACTIVE} \\ \text{-REFLEXIVE} \end{bmatrix} \begin{bmatrix} \text{DATIVE} \\ \text{-REFLEXIVE} \end{bmatrix} \begin{bmatrix} \text{ACCUSATIVE} \\ \text{-REFLEXIVE} \end{bmatrix}$

Neither of these alternatives seems desirable, as they involve mechanisms additional to those proposed by Perlmutter. But I see no other alternatives in terms of SSC's.

As I show later, however, reflexivity and case ordering of the clitics are easily handled transformationally, with a generality that is necessarily absent from any surface structure explanation.

3. Mirror image. The Royal Academy grammar notes that complements to the Spanish verb normally occur in the order Accusative, Dative, Benefactive. Deviations from this order are, in general, due to topicalization--moving the complement to the head of the sentence. In (4) below, the complements are as follows: la carta 'the letter' is Accusative, a mí 'to me' is Dative, and para ti 'for you' is Benefactive.

(4) Escribió la carta a mí para ti.
'He wrote the letter to me for you.'

The normal order of the clitics, on the other hand, is Benefactive, Dative, Accusative, precisely the mirror image of the order of the complements to which they correspond. Any surface structure solution to case order must of necessity claim that this mirror-image relationship (MIR) is accidental; transformationally the relationship is quite straightforward (see Section 4).

Of course, one could always claim that this mirror-image relationship (MIR) is an accidental fact about Spanish. If this were so, we would not expect to find the same or a similar relationship in French.

In terms of case, French has the same order (as Spanish) of the postverbal nominal complements (Accusative, Dative, Benefactive) as illustrated in (5) below. We would therefore expect the case order of the clitics to be Benefactive, Dative, Accusative, as in Spanish. (I am ignoring the clitics y and en, which do not seem to bear on the point in question, i. e. the order of the personal clitics.) The predicted order can be observed in (103) and (117) below, and in (149).

(5) J'ai donné le livre à Jean pour toi.
'I gave the book to Jean for you.'

(103) Roger te l'avait recommandé.
'Roger had recommended it to you.'

(149) Tu vas me lui obéir!
'You will obey him (for me)!'

In (103) we note the clitic order Dative, Accusative, in (149) the order Benefactive, Dative.

The constraints on the order of the French clitics are usually stated in chart form, as in Perlmutter's SSC (121) below.

(121) Surface structure constraint on clitics:

Nom	ne	me	III	III	y	en
		te	ACC	DAT		
		nous				
		vous				
		se				

As the presence of $\mathrm{III}_{Acc}\ \mathrm{III}_{Dat}$ in the chart shows, the situation in French regarding MIR is the same as Spanish in that there are exceptions. The resemblance is complete, in that the exceptions form a small, well-defined group which is easy to explain transformationally.

All the exceptions to MIR are due to the fact that III_{Dat} must follow III_{Acc}, contrary to what MIR would lead us to expect. This can easily be accounted for by positing a transformation taking $\mathrm{III}_{Dat}\ \mathrm{III}_{Acc}$ to $\mathrm{III}_{Acc}\ \mathrm{III}_{Dat}$. (I will refer to this transformation as LLF, or lui/le Flip.)

An analysis with MIR and LLF predicts that there will be sentences conforming to (121) whose ungrammaticality will be due solely to violations of MIR. This turns out to be the case. Perlmutter notes that while the sequence me lui is grammatical in some constructions (as predicted by (121)), it is not grammatical in others.

(149) Tu vas me lui obéir!
       'You will obey him (for me)!'

(145) *Ton cousin me lui a recommandé.
       'Your cousin recommended me to him.'

In (149) the order of cases is Benefactive Dative (predicted by MIR), in (145) it is Accusative Dative (violates MIR). As the only difference between the me lui in (149) and the one in (145) is the order of cases, the ungrammaticality of (145) must be due to a violation of MIR.

Therefore, since French displays the same MIR as Spanish, the claim that the MIR of Spanish is accidental cannot be true. As MIR cannot be expressed solely in terms of surface structure, any surface structure constraint solution to the problem of case ordering must necessarily miss the generalization involved.

4. Transformations. The general form of a transformation that takes items from the right-hand side of a verb, and places them in a

mirror-image order on the left side, is presented in T1 below.

T1	S. D.	Verb	Item 1	(Item 2	(Item 3))
Obligatory	1	2	3	4	
	S. C. 4+3+2+1	$\emptyset$	$\emptyset$	$\emptyset$	

The details of this transformation are not at all crucial. None of the following, for example, is crucial: (1) Whether or not cliticization takes place in the base, before T1 applies, as a part of the operation of T1, or even after T1 has applied (although this last possibility looks quite inelegant). (2) Whether the clitics are placed by the verb one at a time, or all at once. (3) What the bracketing of the string 4+3+2+1 really looks like: one could have it all sister nodes, all Chomsky-adjoined, or have a separate clitic node for just the clitics, sister to the Verb node.

Consider possibility (2): suppose we want to place the clitics by the verb one at a time. To do this we need a left-to-right iterative transformation that must be able to apply to its own output. The validity of such transformations is highly dubious, of course, but it is not clear that they definitely do not exist. Thus if it should turn out that for some reason clitics must be moved one at a time, this will only count against my proposal insofar as left-to-right iterative transformations (applying to their own output) are shown to be invalid. At that, I rather doubt that there are any good reasons to move clitics one at a time.

Whatever T1 really looks like, it must place the clitics to the left of the verb in an order which is the mirror image of the order of their corresponding constituents at the time of application of T1. Then, after T1 has applied, a reflexive-clitic-moving transformation can apply (this only for those dialects that move them, of course). Such a transformation might look like T2 below.

T2	S. D.	(Clitic)	(Clitic)	Clitic +Reflexive	(Clitic)
Obligatory		1	2	3	4
	S. C.	3 1	2	$\emptyset$	4

If we assume that at this level of derivation only the complement clitics are under the verb node (besides the verb), then we can re-write T2 as the more elegant-looking T2A.

T2A	S. D.	$[_\text{V} X \left[\begin{array}{c} \text{Clitic} \\ \text{+Reflexive} \end{array} \right]$	$Y]_\text{V}$
Obligatory		1 2	3
	S. C.	2 1	3

144/ ROBERT K. SZABO

Again, the details are unimportant.

5. Dialects. In looking at the treatment of reflexive clitics, one can observe two dialects. [3] In one dialect, all clitic sequences where MIR would predict a non-leftmost reflexive clitic, are disallowed. There is no support for a reflexive clitic movement transformation like T2. In this dialect there are no surface violations of MIR.

In the other dialect, the reflexive clitic always occurs in leftmost position (among the clitics), even when this produces surface violations of MIR. [4] The facts of this dialect can be accounted for by positing a reflexive movement transformation T2, which acts after MIR is imposed by the clitic placement transformation T1. Reflexive movers find both (95) and (96) below grammatical; Reflexive non-movers find only (96) to be grammatical.

(95) (*) Te me le echaste encima.
(Yourself (on me) on you threw).
'You threw yourself on him (on me).'

(96) Te le comiste el pan a Miguel, pero a mí no te me lo comas.
'You ate up Miguel's bread (on him), but don't you eat up
mine (on me).'

To account for the Reflexive non-moving dialects I see no alternative to an SSC disallowing non-leftmost reflexives (i.e. (101)). In this dialect, perfectly good deep structures, such as that of (95), can become acceptable surface structures only if the appropriate deletions happen to take place.

The Reflexive-moving dialect, on the other hand, not only does not require a SSC, but in fact cannot have one: to account for the facts in the most general way possible, we are forced to posit T1 (and thus MIR) and T2. Not only does a SSC solution lose the generalization of MIR, but it requires additional mechanisms--either feature notation or ordered SSC's.

6. Conclusions. In examining clitic ordering, Perlmutter has found that a SSC is necessary to handle clitic ordering by person. As clitic ordering is presumably a unified phenomenon, we would like to be able to make the general statement that clitic ordering is handled by SSC's. Perlmutter, for example, predicts from the universality of SSC's (to handle clitic ordering) that 'the order of clitics in surface structure will be determined solely by a surface structure constraint . . . the only properties of clitic pronouns that can be relevant to this order are properties that are present in surface structure.' [5] We have seen that this cannot be the case. Two distinct

mechanisms are required if one is to avoid loss of generality: Perl-mutter's SSC to explain ordering in terms of person, transformation(s) to explain ordering in terms of case.

Similarly, we would expect to find that dialects differing very little on the surface would differ little in their systems of rules. But in examining two dialects that both disallow non-leftmost reflexives, we were forced to the conclusion that one dialect does this by a SSC, the other by a transformation. The dialects are highly similar, but we are forced to posit two distinct mechanisms to account for their differences in the most general way possible.

Is it plausible that what we would like to describe as a trivial dia-lect difference should require mechanisms so different? Is it plausible that a single phenomenon such as clitic ordering should require two completely different mechanisms?

NOTES

[1] Perlmutter's (189), (190), and (191) look like counter-examples. But in the dialects I am investigating, they are not all grammatical: (189a), (190a), and (191) (second reading) are not grammatical. In an expanded version of this paper (forthcoming), I explain the dialects where (189a) and (190a) are grammatical. I don't as yet know what to do about the second reading of (191), if it is indeed grammatical for any group of Spanish speakers.

[2] This example is from Perlmutter, p. 219. Examples (1)-(5) are mine; (100), (101), and (00B) are adapted from Dinnsen; and all the rest are from Perlmutter.

[3] Actually, I have observed four (and there are probably five or maybe even more) dialects with respect to moving/not moving spurious se and reflexives. I discuss these in an expanded version, forthcoming.

[4] I am assuming here that I'm dealing with speakers who accept three-clitic sequences. The arguments hold for two-clitic speakers, but need to be presented in pairs.

[5] Perlmutter, p. 218.

REFERENCES

Dinnsen, Daniel. 1972. Additional constraints on clitic order in Spanish. In: Generative studies in Romance languages. Ed. by J. Casagrande and B. Saciuk. Rowley, Mass., Newbury House.
Perlmutter, David. 1970. Surface structure constraints in syntax. Linguistic Inquiry. 1(2).187-257.
Royal Academy Grammar (Real Academia Espanola. 1931. Gramática de la lengua espanola. Madrid, Espasa-Calpe.

WHERE DOES IMPERSONAL <u>SE</u> COME FROM ?*

MARGARITA SUÑER

Cornell University

Sentences with impersonal <u>se</u> present a problem because syntactically they are subjectless sentences but semantically one understands them to have an unspecified, impersonal, human Agent or Experiencer:

(1) Se comfa tortillas.
'One ate tortillas.'

(2) Se vive bien aquf.
'One lives well here.'

The question is whether this [-def, +human] Agent is just part of the meaning, and therefore properly belongs to the semantic component of the grammar or whether this Agent is also part of the syntactic component and should hence appear in the deep structure as a dummy symbol which never gets filled lexically. The choice is then between two possible DS's for (1):

(3)

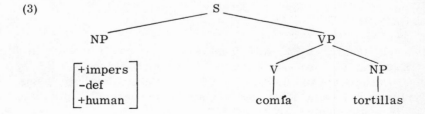

and

(4)

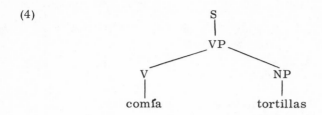

A principled choice must be made in order to determine which one of these two possible solutions is more valid than the other. Our first consideration should be the examination of the use of the dummy symbol or empty node in the first tree. Chomsky (1965:129) uses a dummy symbol to derive an agentless passive (The man was fired). Chomsky's motivation for the use of this dummy symbol seemed to be semantic, i. e. when one sees a sentence like The man was fired, one understands that there is somebody or a circumstance that caused the firing. The problem is that, should we motivate the use of empty nodes through semantic reasons, then in a sentence like:

(5) Edgardo compró un libro para Juan.
     'Edgard bought a book for John.'

we would be justified in using an empty node for the argument that is missing (i. e. from where or from whom Edgard bought the book). The verb comprar 'to buy' is a four-argument verb (at least): the entity who does the buying or Agent; the thing bought or Theme; the receiver of the thing bought or Goal; and the Source or place or person from which the object was bought. Consequently, at any time an argument for any verb is not stated, a dummy symbol could be used to indicate this.

This stand could be extended ad absurdum when we picture trees with two or three empty nodes to show that an equal number of arguments of the verb are missing. For example:

(6) Juan comió ayer.
     'John ate yesterday.'

could be said to have the DS:

(7)

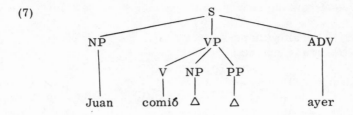

as opposed to (8) which has all of its arguments realized:

(8) Juan comió tortillas con las manos ayer.
     'John ate tortillas with his hands yesterday.'

It is said that deep structure grammatical relations are the ones that determine the meaning of a sentence (Chomsky 1965:162), but Shopen (1972) has shown quite convincingly that 'No syntactically motivated deep structure could provide unique grammatical relations for each semantic function' (210) and that presuppositions are a property of the verbs themselves and therefore, cannot be a property of empty nodes.

In the Spanish sentence <u>Se comía tortillas</u>, we understand an unspecified human Agent but this is a semantic interpretation based on the lexical meaning of the impersonal SE plus the verb, and as such it should be confined to the realm of the semantic component which will provide a semantic interpretation for the sentence.

The only valid justification for permitting the use of empty nodes in the deep structure would be syntactic. [1] For example, if it would be possible to capture a generalization by saying that every sentence in Spanish has a syntactically motivated deep structure subject, the use of empty nodes could be justified. [2] But we cannot find a principled way to maintain such an assertion when there are Spanish sentences like:

(9) Llovió a cántaros anoche.
     'It poured last night.'

(10) Hacía frío la semana pasada.
     'It was cold last week.'

(11) Había muchas flores en el jardín.
     'There were many flowers in the garden.'

In conclusion, we must reject the use of empty nodes for semantic reasons and consequently we feel justified in choosing the second deep structure tree (4) and the concomitant arguments for Se comía tortillas.

Moreover, if we allow impersonal SE to be inserted transformationally, this transformation would read something like:

(12) Impersonal SE Insertion T. (oversimplified)

SD: # X Y [+V] Z
     1 2 3   4   5

Cond. : 2 ≠ [NP, S]
         3 can only be a clitic

SC: 1 2 SE 3 4 5

((3) might not be necessary if transformations are assumed to be strictly ordered and if the Impersonal SE Ins. T. is ordered before any other T that moves clitics up to the verb).

Impersonal SE is one of the Spanish clitics. If we accept that it is introduced transformationally, we also need to accept all the implications that this approach entails.

Perlmutter (1970) in exploring the implications of the fact that object pronouns (i. e. clitics) in Spanish are strictly ordered finds that transformational rules cannot block certain ungrammatical sentences; hence, he concludes:

It is necessary to strengthen grammatical theory by the addition of surface structure constraints or output conditions which the output of the transformational component must satisfy . . . This constraint is to be interpreted as a template or filter . . . (1970:188)

that is, it will discard sentences generated by the transformational component which do not agree with the constraint. The final shape of his SSC is:

(13) SE II I III (1970:213)

This is a positive output constraint because it states the grammatical sequences of clitics. By being positive it correctly predicts the impossibility of having two or more consecutive clitics from the same 'slot' (i. e. it rules out not only *le le but also *le les). It also predicts that SE must be the first clitic in the series.

At this point it is pertinent to ask about the explanatory power of a device such as a SSC. It has none. A SSC does not explain anything.

It is merely an expression of despair, like throwing one's arms up in the air and confessing that in spite of all the powerful machinery we have at our disposal, we are not able to filter out ill-formed sentences so we give up and add an extra piece of machinery at the end of the production line in order to discard the 'bad sentences'.

Chomsky (1970:4-5) writes:

> The gravest defect of the theory of transformational grammar
> is its enormous latitude and descriptive power . . . Therefore
> a critical problem in making transformational grammar a
> substantive theory with explanatory force is to restrict the
> category of admissible phrase markers, admissible transfor-
> mations, and admissible derivations, . . . If descriptive power
> is enormous, the theory is rather uninteresting . . . permit-
> ting a broader class of 'derivational constraints' within particular
> grammars is a step towards a worse theory; . . .

Therefore, the goal of linguists should be to constrain the limitless power of transformational grammar because only a small part of what transformations could do seems necessary for characterizing natural languages. SSC's or output filters instead of constraining the gram- mar have the opposite effect. They open a new realm of possibilities where everything is permitted.

Linguists should then try to find other workable alternatives and leave the overtly powerful SSC's or filters aside until all other re- sources have been exhaustively explored and discarded. This is what we will do by examining the interpretive approach (cf. Jackendoff, 1968).

Suppose that pronouns and clitics are introduced at the base by the PS rules. Then, since there are several kinds of se's in Spanish (impersonal, reflexive, reciprocal, etc.), we have to decide how many se's are listed in the lexicon. The simplest solution is to assume that there is only one se in the lexicon whose meaning is highly indeterminate, something like third person singular or plural and that it takes the rest of its meaning from the context it is used in by means of semantic interpretation rules.

Assuming for the moment that the semantic values of se can be determined by semantic interpretation rules, if we are to weaken the power of the grammar by discarding SSC's in general, we must be able to show that the surface form of the clitic sets can be accounted for by PS rules. Perlmutter thinks that trying (13) as a PS rule 'would immediately encounter insuperable difficulty. Only two of them will be pointed out here' (243).

His first insuperable difficulty is that clitics may occur in SS with a verb other than the one with which they have been generated.

This is because clitics can move up to higher verbs. Examples:

    (14a) Quería mostrár<u>melo</u>.
    (14b) <u>Me lo</u> quería mostrar.
            'He wanted to show it to me.'

This is not such an insuperable difficulty. Perhaps with the exception of impersonal <u>se</u>, all other clitics belong with the lower verb in the verb phrase, provided the verbs have the same subject; so that they could be generated in DS with the lower V and they could be moved up to the higher V by a movement T although they would be interpreted in SS as going together with the lower V. The fact that they belong with the lower V in the VP is true regardless of the number of verbs within the same VP.

    (15a) Debía haber podido ayudar<u>lo</u>.

    (15b) Debía haber<u>lo</u> podido ayudar.

    (15c) <u>Lo</u> debía haber podido ayudar.
            'I should have been able to help him.'

In (15) there are four verbs, nevertheless the clitic <u>lo</u> should be generated with <u>ayudar</u> 'to help' and interpreted by means of a semantic interpretive rule as belonging with <u>ayudar</u>, which is the lowest V of the VP, regardless of the surface position of the clitic.
    Why is it necessary to state 'perhaps with the exception of impersonal <u>se</u>'? Because suppose we have sentences like:

    (16a) <u>Se</u> debe regar<u>las</u> todos los días.

    (16b) <u>Se las</u> debe regar todos los días.

    (16c) Debe regár<u>selas</u> todos los días. [3]
            'One must water them (fem) every day.'
            It is necessary to water them (fem) every day.'

In (16) it is easy to see that <u>las</u> belongs with the lower V <u>regar</u> 'to water' but it is not so easy to determine whether impersonal <u>se</u> was generated with <u>deber</u> 'must' or <u>regar</u>. Both verbs are syntactically subjectless although semantically it is understood that a [-def, +hum] Agent is performing the actions. But since both verbs have the same subject, or rather lack of it, it is immaterial to determine with which V impersonal <u>se</u> is generated. We could allow clitics to be generated freely with each verb by a PS rule and have a semantic interpretation

rule which requires that if more than one se is generated in a sentence
they need to be [-coreferential]. If they are not, the S is discarded
as ungrammatical. This is the reason for the ungrammaticality of
sentences like (17) and (18) (cf. Contreras and Rojas 1972):

(17) *Se puede arrepentirse.
'One may repent onself.'

(18) *Se quiere arrepentirse.
'One wants to repent oneself.'

Compare (17) and (18) with (19) and (20):

(19) Se prohibe bañarse.
'Bathing is prohibited.'
'One prohibits bathing.'

(20) Se mandó detenerse al sol. (Ramsey 1956:19.35)
'The sun was ordered to stand still.'
'One ordered the sun to stand still.'

In (19) and (20) the consecutive verbs have different syntactic subjects
or different semantic referents, i.e. in (19) somebody does the pro-
hibiting while somebody else does the bathing, and in (20), one did
the ordering but the sun is the one supposed to stand still. Consequently, the two se's in each S are [-coreferential] and the sentences
are grammatical.

Moreover, sentences (17) and (18) show Perlmutter's SSC to be inadequate. His SSC rules out as ungrammatical only sequences of
consecutive clitics from the same slot and therefore does not filter
out sentences like (17) and (18).[4] On the other hand, the interpretive
approach handles the facts adequately just by making use of the notion
of coreferentiality.

Perlmutter's second objection to having the constraint stated as a
PS rule is that he believes that 'this stratagem would still require
the spurious se rule' (244). I do not see how this is necessarily true.
If all pronouns and clitics are introduced by PS rules, there would be
no pronouns or clitics introduced by transformations, hence the
spurious se rule, which is a T, will not be necessary.

Another inadequacy of Perlmutter's analysis is that his SSC was
motivated by sequences of two clitics, but it also predicts that sequences of more than two clitics are grammatical; he shows that this
is so for three consecutive clitics although he gives no examples having four clitics in succession. The constraint, as stated, says that
each slot may optionally be filled but it also claims that when fully

specified all four may be filled. He discussed this for French and explains the ungrammaticality of the sentence:

(133) *Je ne se les leur y en pense (229)

by saying that 'there is no underlying structure which the transformational component would convert into (*133)'. Nevertheless, for Spanish there are some sentences that, though not very common, are grammatical:

(21) Se te mandó flores para mí.
'Somebody sent you flowers for me.'

(22) Se te escribió una carta para nosotros.
'Somebody wrote a letter for us on your behalf.'

(23) Se me dio un libro para ti.
'Somebody gave me a book for you.'

The constraint predicts that when the complements are pronominalized the outcomes would be grammatical sentences, but the facts disprove such a prediction:

(21b) *Se te me las mandó.

(22b) *Se te nos la escribió.

(23b) *Se te me lo dió.

Although the clitics are in the order required by the output constraint the sentences are ungrammatical. From these three examples it seems impossible to have all four clitics in the same sentence. Even though the constraint, in accordance with the lexicalist hypothesis, would be a PS rule, the same problem would present itself; there is no way to prevent the generation of sentences like (21b), (22b), and (23b), consequently it is necessary to modify our PS rule so that it reads 'three clitics is the upper limit tolerated by the language'. The revised rule reads:

(24) Clitic $\longrightarrow$ (SE II I III)$_1^3$

to be interpreted as: the Clitic node is optional but if it is chosen one must select at least one clitic though no more than three. [5]

Finally, it seems pertinent to justify the postulation of the node clitic. Perlmutter believes that 'there is no possible motivation for

the node 'Clitic' in underlying structure' (246) but this belief stems
from the hypothesis that clitic pronouns in Spanish are underlying
NP's. Although later he admits:

> Clitic movement transformations, however, move only
> clitics; other NP's are unaffected by these rules. Further-
> more, it is just an accident of Spanish that all the clitics happen
> to be NP's. In the South Slavic languages, for example, the so-
> called 'auxiliary verbs' are clitics as well, and undergo clitic
> movement transformations. It is therefore necessary for lin-
> guistic theory to provide the grammars of particular languages
> with a means of identifying certain lexical items as clitics and
> referring to them in rules (246-47).

The interpretive hypothesis generates clitics directly, therefore
the problem of changing a node label from NP to Clitic or creating
one in the course of a derivation does not exist.

One may ask why it is necessary to have a node Clitic dominating
the entire clitic group. The answer is simple: because the entire
clitic group behaves as a unit with respect to movement transformations. It must be remembered that Spanish clitics come before a
finite verb but after an infinitive, gerund, or affirmative imperative
verb form, and moreover, clitics may move up to the verb of the
higher sentence. Hence, since it seems impossible to generate them
in all of their surface positions, movement transformations are
needed. When discussing movement transformations and the node
Clitic, Perlmutter writes:

> . . . it would be difficult, if not impossible, to show that a
> node over the entire clitic group is needed to achieve this re-
> sult. The rule in question may simply refer to clitics, which
> would all undergo it individually simply because they are all
> clitics (248).

Assume that the fact the rule 'may simply refer to clitics' will posit
no problems in spite of there not being a clitic node. But suppose we
have a S like:

(25) Quería comérselo.
    'He wanted to eat it up.'

where the infinitive has two clitics (se and lo) attached to it. These
clitics may move up to the higher verb (i. e. up to quería). The
movement transformation that does this has to be optional since the
clitics may also stay with the infinitive. Now, if we follow

Perlmutter's reasoning that the node Clitic cannot be motivated since clitics may all undergo a movement rule individually we may end up with ungrammatical sentences such as:

(26a) *Se quería comerlo.

(26b) *Lo quería comerse.

because the movement transformation needs to be optional and it might just move one of the clitics and not the entire group. Therefore, we need a node Clitic to make sure that when the optional movement transformation applies it moves the whole clitic group to obtain the grammatical:

(27) Se lo quería comer.
      'He wanted to eat it up.'

To sum up, it has been shown in this paper that if the standard transformational theory approach is chosen and impersonal se is inserted by means of a transformation, one implication will be the acceptance of an extremely powerful device, namely, SSC's or output filters.

Perlmutter's SSC for Spanish clitics was shown to be inadequate in more than one way. First, it is able to discard as ungrammatical only sequences of consecutive clitics from the same slot. Second, his SSC, as stated, claims that optionally all four clitic slots may be filled. This fact is disproved by observing what actually happens in the language. It was postulated that the filter needs to be restated as (SE II I III)$_1^3$.

The interpretive theory which introduces pronouns and clitics at the base was presented as a viable alternative; the semantic values of pronouns and clitics would be given by semantic interpretation rules. Perlmutter's objections to introducing (SE II I III) as a PS rule were contested and found to be unwarranted. The interpretive approach was found adequate for handling Perlmutter's objections and moreover, it can handle non-consecutive sequences of se by referring to the feature [±coreferential].

Finally, the node clitic was justified provided there is a transformation which moves clitics around.

This paper, merely a first step in the investigation of Spanish clitics, moves towards what I consider the right direction: towards constraining the power of the grammar. Interpretive theory seems to provide an adequate model for providing these constraints.

NOTES

*I would like to thank Mark Goldin and Charles Bird for their comments and suggestions.

[1]Emonds (1970) makes a principled syntactic use of empty nodes. Empty nodes are generated by the PS rules for a purpose. They are generated to receive those constituents which are shifted around through the application of movement transformations. That is to say, phrase nodes cannot be moved unless there is an empty duplicate node to receive it. The only exception to this condition is root transformations (a transformation which applies only to main sentences and direct quotes). Empty nodes must be non-empty at some stage of the derivation of a sentence. Empty nodes play no part in semantic interpretation; their motivation is purely syntactic. By using empty nodes for his structure preserving hypothesis, Emonds is able to constrain the power of transformations.

[2]I am grateful to Tim Shopen for pointing this out to me.

[3]Non-Argentinian native speakers find (16c) odd. If se were generate with deber, this example implies that the clitic has moved down, i. e. a T would be moving the clitic from a higher S into a lower one, a fact which is rather suspect. On the other hand, if we allow se to be generated freely with any verb, it could have been generated with regar. The ungrammatical:

*Se debe regárselas todos los días.

will be discarded by the constraint which requires that se's be [-coreferential].

[4]Perlmutter might have thought of another way of blocking these sentences; but if so, he does not mention it in his article.

[5]I am perfectly aware that for a PS rule (24) looks strange. I have never seen a syntactic rule which requires the specification of a lower and an upper limit. I am conscious that I am proposing a rather powerful abbreviatory device; my justification for it is that rule (24) really captures the facts of the language, namely, that any combination of two or three Spanish clitics is grammatical if kept in the order of (24), but sequences of four clitics are not allowed.

The node Clitic would be introduced in the expansion of VP:

VP—→ . . . (Clitic) V . . .

REFERENCES

Chomsky, Noam. 1970. Some empirical issues in the theory of transformational grammar. Indiana University Linguistics Club.

Chomsky, Noam. 1965. Aspects of the theory of syntax. Cambridge, MIT Press.
Contreras, H. and J. N. Rojas. 1972. Some remarks on Spanish clitics. Linguistic Inquiry. 3.385-92.
Gruber, Jeffrey. 1970. Studies in lexical relations. Indiana University Linguistics Club.
Jackendoff, R. 1968. An interpretive theory of pronouns and reflexives. Indiana University Linguistics Club.
Perlmutter, David M. 1970. Deep and surface structure constraints in syntax. Linguistic Inquiry. 1.187-256.
Ramsey, Marathon M. 1956. A textbook of modern Spanish. Revised by R. K. Spaulding. New York, Holt, Rinehart and Winston.
Shopen, Tim. 1972. A generative theory of ellipsis: A consideration of the linguistic use of silence. Indiana University Linguistics Club.

THE EVOLUTION OF ROMANCE CLITIC ORDER

DIETER WANNER

University of Illinois

1.1 Perlmutter has called attention to the problem of clitic order
by presenting a solution which he proposed as a candidate for universal
status (cf. Perlmutter 1968, 1970).[1] The supporting data were drawn
mainly from Spanish and French, thus making this proposal highly at-
tractive for some further testing on Romance languages. The following points may serve as a summary of Perlmutter's conclusions:

(1a) In languages where clitics obey a special ordering constraint, the resulting order is due to a surface structure
constraint (SSC) (Perlmutter 1970:217).

(1b) Such a constraint is to be stated positively rather than
negatively by means of a chart notation such that each slot
in the chart is defined in its relative order with respect
to the other slots by transitive, antisymmetric, irreflexive
precedence relations (215).

1.2 I tried to show in an earlier paper (Wanner 1972) that Perlmutter's conclusions cannot be fully supported when the data base is
extended to include languages other than Spanish and French: Modern
Italian offers a situation which transcends with its specific complexity
the SSC approach as originally presented. The following modifications
are necessary:

(2a) In addition to the positively stated main SSC a supplemen-
tary negative constraint may be required. This amounts
to a partial falsification of the claim of transitivity (cf.
(1b)).

(2b) Clitic order can be the result of a reordering process
applying to the output of the SSC, a denial of the un-
qualified validity of the antisymmetry requirement.

(2c) Also due to a post-constraint rule (morpho-phonological
alteration of a clitic) the irreflexivity requirement may be
violated.

I concluded that study by pointing out that what is vitiated by the facts
of Italian (in my interpretation) is not the notion of the SSC itself,
but only its global domain: Instead of holding true for any stage of
derivation after it is met, it may be the case, as it is for Italian,
that the SSC has only a local extension (i. e. at its level of application,
but not beyond) such that eventual later rules can contradict it.

1. 3 In this paper I propose to consider the implications which
Perlmutter's SSC approach to clitic order has for the historical
evolution of the Romance languages. Among the statements which can
be derived from Perlmutter (1970), the following are relevant here:

(3a) Since an SSC is not connected to any part of the grammar
of a specific language it has an arbitrary nature; given this
basic arbitrariness it is to be expected that there are rather
extensive fluctuations from one stage of a language to another.

(3b) The universality of the SSC ordering of clitics (for those
languages which do have a specified clitic order) and the
rigidity of the ordering relations predict that no language
should be found in a transition stage where for a given
clitic combination one and the same speaker may produce
or accept two conflicting orders.

(3c) The arbitrariness of the order within the clitic SSC denies
the possible existence of a drift involving clitic order in
any given language (and much less in a language family)
which could not be explained in terms of purely clitic-
internal categories.

I will show here that all of these phenomena which are ruled out
a priori by the SSC approach do exist and that therefore Perlmutter's
proposal must be modified again such that the data can be described
and explained. It will become clear that the cumulative effect of the
required revisions demands the formulation of an entirely new clitic
account.

2. In the tradition of Romance linguistics the clitic ordering problem has received considerable attention. The data for most of the Romance languages and dialects in their various stages of evolution are very well researched. This makes it possible to attempt a reinterpretation of the whole problem taking advantage of the efforts of a great number of Romance scholars. As a result, this paper will not contain any new data which would not have been accessible before in published form.

With respect to the original condition of (basically) free word order in Latin, two ordering types are found in Romance; they are generally referred to as illum mihi and mihi illum. illum mihi stands for the ordering principles 'third person clitics precede second and first person clitics'; and 'accusative precedes dative'. Schematically, languages with the type illum mihi therefore have the skeletal clitic order shown in (4):

(4) illum mihi: [III, acc] – [III, dat] – II, I

For the type mihi illum the ordering is exactly the mirror image of (4):

(5) mihi illum: II, I – [III, dat] – [III, acc]

All modern Romance languages and dialects (with a very small number of exceptions)[2] belong to type (5). Thus Modern Portuguese, Spanish, and Catalan exhibit the following SSC's for clitics (cf. (6), (7), and (8), respectively):

(6) Portuguese (cf. Vázquez Cuesta 1961:335-39)
    se – II – I – [III, dat] – [III, acc]

(7) Spanish (cf. Perlmutter 1970:213)
    se – II – I – III

(8) Catalan (cf. Badía Margarit 1962(I): 192-210)
    se – II – I – [III, dat] – [III, acc] – en – hi

(French, Provençal, Italian, and Rumanian present the same structure which, however, is complicated by some special deviation in each case.) This unified picture contrasts sharply with the situation in the thirteenth century. Whereas Portuguese, Spanish, most Northern and all Southern Italian dialects already conform to the order type (5), the other languages and dialects, Catalan, Provençal, French, some Northern and most Central Italian dialects, showed orderings of type (4). Consequently all of these went through an order change sometime after the thirteenth century.

The important aspects of this evolution are (a) the unidirection-
ality of the clitic order changes; no language changed in historical
times from type (5) to (4), but many exchanged (4) for the newer (5);
and (b) the fact that the same changes took such a long time and apparently occurred independently. It will be interesting to have a
closer look at some of the languages which changed their clitic order.

3.1 The full SSC for Modern Italian contains eight slots (for a detailed discussion, cf. Wanner 1972):

(9) Surface structure constraint for Modern Italian[3]

mi	vi	ti	ci	$\begin{Bmatrix}\text{gli}\\\text{le}\end{Bmatrix}$	si	ne	$\begin{Bmatrix}\text{lo}\\\text{la}\\\text{li}\\\text{le}\end{Bmatrix}$
1	2	3	4	5	6	7	8
[1 sg]	[2 pl] [loc]	[2 sg]	[1 pl]	$\begin{bmatrix}\text{3 sg}\\\text{dative}\\\text{-refl}\end{bmatrix}$	$\begin{bmatrix}\text{3 refl}\\\text{unspeci-}\\\text{fied sub-}\\\text{ject}\end{bmatrix}$	[gen]	$\begin{bmatrix}\text{3 acc}\\\text{-refl}\end{bmatrix}$

All combinations of two or more pronouns are acceptable in principle; the only combinations which may not occur are those made up of
clitics from slots 1, 2, 3, 4 with 5 (i.e. *1 > 5, *2 > 5, *3 > 5,
*4 > 5). Their non-occurrence is the reason for the postulation of a
negative constraint supplementing the main SSC (9) (cf. (2a) above).
    Compare now (9) with the SSC expressing the state of affairs in
Old Florentine (cf. Castellani 1952(I):79-105; Lombard 1934:73):

(10) Surface structure constraint for Old Florentine (up to end
      of the thirteenth century)

$\begin{Bmatrix}\text{lo}\\\text{la}\\\text{li}\\\text{le}\end{Bmatrix}$	$\begin{Bmatrix}\text{(l)i}\\\text{le}\end{Bmatrix}$	mi	vi	ti	ci	si	ne
8	5	1	2	3	4	6	7

The slots in (10) have been identified in accordance with the Modern
Italian SSC (9) for easier reference. The functions indicated there
remain constant.[4] The significant change, then, is the order

assigned to slots 8 and 5 which occupy the first two positions in Old Italian in reverse order with respect to (9).

The combination of [III, acc] with [III, dat] has special morphological manifestations in Old Italian as _lili_ for a masculine dative, and as _lele_ for a feminine dative; in both cases the first syllable of the combination may represent either number and gender of the non-reflexive accusative. Starting from this situation at the beginning of the thirteenth century, we can distinguish a series of small changes leading to the overall change in type.

Consider first the evolution of the combination of 8 with 5. The following steps can be distinguished:

(11a) _lili_ > _lile_; _lele_ unchanged; ca. 1250.[5]
(11b) _lile_, _lele_ > _(g)liele_ invariable; ca. 1300.
(11c) invariable _gliele_ dies out; ca. 1520.
(11d) occasionally in the 15th century the invariable _gliele_
        (= [III, acc] - [III, dat]) is replaced by variable forms
        glielo, _gliela_, _glieli_, _gliele_ (= [III, dat] - [III, acc]).
        This order is normal from about 1500 on.

This chain of changes represents therefore a partial change of type (from (4) to (5)) mediated through a series of independent phonological alterations. Next consider the combinations consisting of clitics from slots 8 and 1, 2, 3, 4, 6, 7 where 8 originally preceded:

(12a) _lo mi_ is the only order found up to the end of the 13th
        century.
(12b) sporadically at end of the 13th century, rarely in the
        first half, and increasingly in the second half of the
        14th century _mi lo_ or _me lo_ is found.
(12c) the change is completed in the first decades of the
        15th century.

The evolution of the combinations 5 and 6 (cf. (13)), and 5 and 1, 2, 3, 4 is slightly different (cf. (14)).

(13a) _gli si_ is normal up to the end of the 14th century.
(13b) from then on up to the 19th century _si gli_, _se gli_ are
        used; in the 17th, 18th, and 19th centuries _gli si_ appears
        occasionally.
(13c) in the 19th century the combination finally reverts back to
        gli si.

(14a) _gli mi_ is stable up to about 1400.

(14b) from 1400 on <u>mi gli</u> is stable throughout the 15th and 16th
centuries, but alternating with <u>gli mi</u> in the 17th, 18th, and
19th centuries.

(14c) in the 20th century this grouping became altogether inad-
missible (cf. under (9)).

All of these changes affect the order of clitic elements directly.
A number of other changes took place approximately during the same
period; specifically those clitics with a final vowel <u>i</u> (and which do not
have this vowel as a gender/number marking) lower it to <u>e</u> when they
stand in combination with a clitic from slots 7 or 8 (<u>ne</u>; <u>lo</u>, <u>la</u>, <u>li</u>, <u>le</u>):

(15a) <u>mi ne</u> > <u>me ne</u>; ca. 1250.

(15b) <u>(g)li ne</u> > <u>gliene</u>; beginning ca. 1300, completed by 1400
and stable thereafter.

(15c) <u>mi lo</u> > <u>me lo</u>; beginning at end of the 13th century (obviously somewhat later than the prerequisite order rever-
sal (12b)); completed ca. 1450.

The chart (16) summarizes the sequence of the various changes leading to the Modern Italian condition as expressed in (9) (the numbers
and letters referring to the stages identified in the text above):

(16) Time chart for changes in Italian clitic order

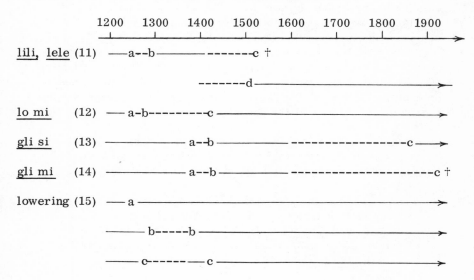

To sum up: the salient features of the discussed Italian changes
are the postposing of the [III, acc,-refl] clitics from first to last position, and the somewhat less drastic shift of [III, dat, -refl] from second
to fifth position. Together these two changes result in a typological
change from (4) to (5). The changes took place between the end of the
thirteenth and the beginning of the sixteenth centuries. These centuries are generally characterized by the rather rapid changes which
occurred in the language as opposed to the apparently stable periods
before and after.

What are the reasons behind these changes? Most of them allow
no more than a straightforward acknowledgment of the fact that an
order reversal has taken place, but they do not offer any clue as to
what the conditioning factors were. Thus, due to the claimed autonomy
of clitic ordering within the grammar, the data do not contain anything
beyond factual information. Only the combinations [III, acc] - [III, dat],
i. e. lili and lele, are structured differently; their surface forms contain a certain degree of ambiguity for their analysis. If it could be
shown that these modifications were reinterpreted early as containing
not the actual 'accusative-dative' sequence, but on the other hand
'dative-accusative', then it would be possible to explain the change
from e. g. lo mi to me lo as a motivated analogy on the basis of the
reinterpretation of lili, lele. However, the appeal of such a solution
vanishes quickly when we look at the sequence of events: lo mi starts
showing inverted forms mi lo as early as the last years of the thirteenth century whereas gliele (i. e. the form developed from lili,
lele) shows its first traces of reinterpretation only in the fifteenth
century. In other words, the change from invariable gliele ('acc'. >
'dat'.) to variable glielo etc. ('dat'. > 'acc'.) is clearly a consequence of a previously completed order reversal from 'accusative' >
'dative' to 'dative' > 'accusative' as evidenced by me lo. Thus again,
no explanation is contained in the data itself, and consequently one
important implication of the SSC approach is not supported by the
facts.

A further serious problem consists in the rather well-documented
existence of idiolect internal variation with respect to clitic order.
Consider these cases pointed out by Castellani (1952. I):

(17) lo ci and ci lo at the end of the 13th century (in the
      idiolect of the writer of f. 1280-98:56.6 and 56.4)
      ne gli and glie ne; ne le and le ne in Boccaccio's
      Decameron (cf. Castellani 1952. I:87) lo mi and me lo
      in the Decameron (92)

Since all the texts considered are autographs they reflect the language
of their authors as accurately as possible for historical periods;

especially authoritative is the Decameron due to the care which went into its final version.

It will not do to dismiss these 'transitional' stages as non-representative on the grounds that they show the opposite, namely that the idiolect under discussion has no SSC on clitics; in other respects the orderings are very firm. Nor would it be very convincing to argue that the variable clitic order might have been exploited for stylistic purposes. Given that the clitic elements constitute a rather unexpressive area of syntax to carry stylistic information in their mutual order, the consideration leads to an impasse. It appears then that the only conceivable explanation of this situation lies in the acceptance of the fact that, contrary to the claim made by the SSC approach, variable ordering can be a property of an individual's grammar in specific instances even though otherwise the clitics obey rigid surface ordering.

Finally, the evolution of Italian clitics yields one other interesting observation: Modern Italian has contradictory order in the combination of slots 6 and 8 (si and lo, la, li, le), since both se lo (as predicted by the SSC (9)) and lo si (not contained in (9)) are acceptable. However, they have different functions: se lo represents a combination of a [III, refl] pronoun with a non-reflexive accusative of the third person; lo si on the other hand consists of the [III, acc, -refl] clitic with the unspecified subject morpheme si. In Old Italian the two expressions were identical in the form of lo si. I have shown (Wanner 1972) that the Modern Italian conditions require a considerable modification of the SSC approach (cf. (2b)): contrary to its implications, the remote origin of the constituents represented by clitic elements may have a bearing on their relative order in a given clitic sequence even though this different origin is not manifested phonologically on the surface. This is the case with lo si vs. se lo. If the Modern Italian situation is surprising, it is even more surprising to find that it originated from a situation where this functional difference, based on global information, did not exist.

In short, the historical evolution of the Italian clitics is puzzling, and it contradicts the SSC approach in three important points.

3.2 Let me turn now to the other languages which underwent the same typological change. For Old Provençal the following constraint must have been operative (cf. Elsner 1886; Brusewitz 1905; Brunel 1926:xxix-xxxi):

(18) [III, acc] - [III, dat] - II, I, se - o - en - i[6]

Modern Provençal has a SSC very much like the ones quoted above for Portuguese, Spanish, and Catalan:

(19) se - II - I - [III, dat] - [III, acc] - ié - en - o

It will be useful to establish the temporal sequence of the various
events. The first major change to occur was, as in Italian, the order
reversal of lo me to me lou which started sporadically in the fifteenth
century and was completed in the eighteenth century. The two non-
reflexive third person pronouns exchanged positions between the beginning of the seventeenth and the middle of the eighteenth century.
The change from III - II, I to II, I - III took place during the seventeenth century. Finally, the two clitics with locative and genitive
reference (i/ié and en) switched order in the nineteenth century from
en - i to ié - en (actually n'i'en). Consider the corresponding time
chart (20):

(20) Time chart for changes in Provençal clitic order

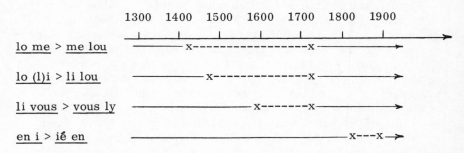

Again, as in the Italian case, the same two basic difficulties with
the SSC approach arise: contradictory orders of the same clitic
group are found within the speech of one author (cf. especially
Brusewitz 1905:27-32) and the same directionality of the change can
be observed. There is no clue from within the clitic system as to
what had happened exactly or for what reason it had happened. In the
case of Provençal the possibility of an explanation in terms of an
analogical reanalysis of a superficially ambiguous clitic group does
not exist: the combination [III, acc] - [III, dat] has clear forms directly corresponding to the pronouns in isolation: lo(u), la, les for
the accusative, (l)i (or various other spellings such as l'y, ly, l'i)
for the dative, thus yielding la li, lai, or li la, etc. Significantly
this combination follows the lo me group in carrying out the order
reversal. [7]

3.4 Catalan offers the same picture as Provençal. The modern
order is given in (8), repeated here for convenience:

(8) se - II - I - [III, dat] - [III, acc] - en - hi

Compare it to the old arrangement (cf. Par 1923:511-13; 1928:60-61):

(21) [III, acc] - [III, dat] - II, I, se - ho - hi - en

Unfortunately, there is no study available which would trace the evolution through the documents up to the modern period; therefore I cannot give a more detailed account of the temporal sequence of events. The similarity of the starting point and of the result with the Provençal formulae suggests, however, a close resemblance also for what concerns the evolution.

3.5 French offers difficulties similar in complexity to those found in Italian. Its clitic system changed from order type (4) to (5). In addition, in its modern stage it still has clear vestiges of the old clitic ordering, since the positive imperative, characterized by the fact that the clitics follow the verb, shows most combinations in the reverse order of that found with clitic combinations preceding the verb: tu me le donnes contrasts with Standard donne-le-moi! The question of the French clitic order and especially clitic placement (the question of enclisis vs. proclisis)[8] has been debated extensively, revealing a number of interesting facts which tie in with the problem concerning us here.

Old French had the following clitic ordering constraint (valid for the twelfth century; cf. Meyer-Lübke 1899:800-02):

(22) [III, acc] - [III, dat] - II, I, se - en - y

This order is heavily changed in Modern French:

(23) (subject - ne -) II, I, se - [III, acc] - [III, dat] - y - en[9]

In enclitic position (in the case of the affirmative imperative) the old order is basically preserved:

(24) [III, acc] - [III, dat] - II, I - y - en[10]

However, in popular speech, this variant constraint (24) is not regularly in effect and (23) takes over in both cases thus reducing French to the size of the other Romance languages in this respect: donne-me-le!, donne-nous-le! may be found with no difference in clitic order with respect to the statement or question order (est-ce que) tu me le donnes(?), (est-ce que) tu nous le donnes(?). The one big difference between French and the other Romance languages lies in the fact that the order reversal left intact the 'accusative-dative' order of the two non-reflexive third person pronouns (cf. le lui, le leur, etc.).

Thus the only major change (disregarding the case of en - y becoming y - en) is the order reversal le me to me le etc. Its first instances occur in manuscripts of the middle of the thirteenth century; it lingers on to pick up momentum only in the sixteenth century; the change is finally completed in the first decades of the seventeenth century. Although it thus lasts somewhat longer than the Italian change, it falls nevertheless together with the other Romance order switches illum mihi > mihi illum which all took place between the thirteenth and the seventeenth century.

The classical explanation for this change is outlined in Meyer-Lübke (1899:800-02). He assumes the operation of two principles to determine clitic order. The first one is of rhythmical nature requiring the phonologically 'heavy' clitics (les, lui, leur, nous, vous, moi, toi) to be placed in second position within any clitic combination. The 'lighter' clitics (me, te, se, le, la) precede the heavy elements. This principle accounts very well for the Old French situation, and also for the particular clitic order found with the affirmative imperative in Modern Standard French. The second principle is of 'grammatical' nature requiring that the dative be placed before the accusative. This later principle is responsible for the order switch of le me to me le, a case where the rhythmical principle is not applicable because both clitics have the same degree of 'heaviness'. The actual uniformity of the order 'dative-accusative' was achieved through analogical extensions replacing the rhythmical principle gradually with the grammatical one (le nous should not have changed according to the first principle; when it finally followed suit--this happened considerably later than the reordering of le me to me le--it was attracted by the other constructions of the type 'dative-accusative').

This explanation did not go unchallenged. Of the alternative accounts the one presented by Brusewitz (1905:32-36) is the most interesting for present purposes. He also accepts the first rhythmical principle. However, he proposes instead to abandon the second grammatical principle since it is burdened with problems. His explanation is that the considerable number of pronominal verbs (reflexiva tantum) in French resulted in the development of a special relation between the clitic subject pronoun and the reflexive pronoun which was then perceived as a unit; thus, je-me lave, tu-te laves, nous-nous lavons, etc. As a result, the semantically much more loosely connected third person accusative clitics (le, la, les) appearing with such a reflexive construction were not able to break up the special nexus between the subject and reflexive clitics such that they were placed after this combination; from (je) le me suis dit one reaches through the intermediary of je-me suis lavé the new order je-me le suis dit. Brusewitz's evidence is the fact that the order reversal of le me to me le coincides in time with the gradual increase in use of the subject clitics, so that the greater frequency of the subject-reflexive nexus demanded more and more the postposing of the loosely connected non-reflexive clitic.

It is not my intention to assess the relative merits of each theory; rather I would like to show how the implications made by the SSC approach to clitic ordering impose an a priori choice on the two accounts presented here for French. We are forced to favor Brusewitz over Meyer-Lübke on the basis of the fact that Brusewitz's theory makes crucial reference to conditions and categories which are directly represented in clitics in their surface shape. Both the rhythmical principle (common to Meyer-Lübke and Brusewitz) and the special-nexus solution (Brusewitz) are defined in terms of clitics or can be defined as such; the distinguishing properties responsible for the clitic order show up directly on the surface. On the other hand, the grammatical principle of an order shift imposed by the category of case goes beyond the clitic domain. In the clitics of the first and second person, which prompted the introduction of the grammatical principle, there is no surface distinction between accusative and dative. In the one instance where the two cases are superficially marked on clitics, in the non-reflexive third person pronouns, the principle does not apply since le lui, le leur etc. remain unchanged throughout the evolution of French.

Both of the accounts presented here can only be regarded as interesting speculations since they are not sufficiently supported by proper evidence. So far, thus, all cases of the typological clitic order change in Romance, in Italian, Provençal, Catalan, and French, remain unaccounted for.

4.1 The picture which emerges from the study of the evolution of Romance clitic order does not yield too much encouragement for upholding the SSC approach to clitic order. I have discussed evidence showing (a) that transitional stages do exist; (b) that the syntactic source of the clitic elements may be relevant to their order on the surface; (c) that there are practically no arbitrary fluctuations in surface clitic order; and (d) that a drift evolution within the family of Romance languages does exist (cf. points (3a-c) above).

The similar changes in the various languages did not occur at exactly the same time. Not exactly the same changes occurred in all languages which did undergo changes. Only French offers sufficient evidence to enable one to attempt an explanation in terms of clitics; in the other languages studied there is not even a hint of what may be at the root of the evolution. Yet the picture as a whole does not make the impression of an unorganic accumulation of accidents. The initially discussed typological change appears to be a reality, otherwise it would be quite incomprehensible why it is not just one combination which changes its order ('accusative-dative' to 'dative-accusative') but also a second one, III - II, I to II, I - III. In addition the languages which do not undergo any change also conform to the general pattern.

Any account of these phenomena which attempts to approach a level of meaningfulness must provide for a considerable degree of factual complexity. It must provide a means of expressing surface regulation of clitic order. The most likely candidate for a true surface constraint is the subpart of the Italian SSC (9) placing slots 1 - 2 - 3 - 4 - 5 - 6; this order does not follow from anything else, placing apart the singular and plural clitics of the first and second person. The solution must also be prepared to offer an explanation for the globally conditioned split in Modern Italian and for the clearly syntax-related difference between the two clitic orders in Modern French. It will also have to include possible information on phonological peculiarities: the rhythmical principle for French does make sense to a certain degree; all the phonological mergers of clitics in special combinations are to be accommodated. Finally a connection must exist between clitic order and morphological markings: the inability of Italian gli/le to occur together with mi, vi, ti, ci belongs to this category. In other words, contrary to what the assumptions of the SSC approach are, the relative order of clitics in combination may be interestingly connected with other aspects of the grammar.

4.2 I will now present a framework which will take all such considerations into account; it does not constitute a motivated theory, but only a speculative delimitation of any forthcoming acceptable solution for these problems.

The requirements for a successful account of the occurring clitic phenomena listed so far could be met by the following system shown in (25).

The solution must contain:

(25a) a basic ordering principle for clitics which is ultimately related to the major constituent order, i.e. which assures a connection to syntax;

(25b) a principle allowing the ordering stipulation (a) to be interpreted in two directions, i.e. which allows left-to-right and right-to-left application reflecting the two possible linear arrangements;

(25c) idiosyncratic principles which are related to phonology and morphology taking care of language specific complications.

The basic ordering principle (25a) can be envisaged as a transformational process of clitic placement (a copying transformation reproducing a [NP, +PRO] constituent in proclitic position before the verb). By operating on one NP at a time, scanning through the NP's dependent on the verb, first the surface direct object immediately to the right of the verb would be copied to the position immediately to the left of the verb; the indirect object NP would be copied subsequently ending up in a position to the left of the 'direct object clitic-verb' nexus. [11] In this way the ordering principle would be the mirror image representation of the normal constituent structure determining the order 'dative-accusative' for third person non-reflexive clitics. As it has been shown, the order 'dative-accusative' implies empirically also the order 'non-third person--third person'. That a grammatical principle to this effect does not lack motivation entirely can be seen from the fact that at least in Romance languages another area of syntax, namely subject-verb agreement, is sensitive to a similar hierarchy among grammatical persons: if the subject contains a first person, the verb will show a first person form; if it contains no first but a second person, the verb agrees with the second person; only in those cases where the subject is exclusively third person does the verb take on the corresponding third person endings. The two principles together define a linear clitic order of the type <u>mihi illum</u> (cf. (5)):

(26) I, II > [III, dat] > [III, acc]

Any other constituent to be expressed by a clitic element will have to conform to this basic ordering principle by not breaking it up. Typically we observe that the third person reflexive pronoun <u>se</u> is closely associated with I and II; and the locative and genitive clitics usually do not disrupt this basic sequence either; they are placed after (i. e. to the right of) the non-reflexive third person clitics. The syntactic connection motivating these specific placements remains, however, to be identified. [12]

The second requirement is the double interpretation principle (25b). It is necessary because in looking at the medieval stage of Romance we actually find two implementations of the basic principles, namely (4) and (5). The two orders result from the left-to-right reading in the case of (5), and from the mirror image right-to-left reading in the case of (4). This double directionality can be incorporated into the grammar in a meaningful way. Clitic elements in the Romance languages depend on the verb. It seems natural to express this verb dependency in the basic ordering principle such that the verb is the axis around which the clitics are copied:

(27a) Proclisis: I, II - [III, dat] - [III, acc] - Verb
       (corresponds to type mihi illum = (5))

(27b) Enclisis: Verb - [III, acc] - [III, dat] - I, II
       (corresponds to type illum mihi = (4))

All medieval Romance languages knew both proclisis and enclisis.
In Old French the difference was very strictly observed, whereas
Provençal, for example, handled it in its historical phase rather
loosely. Increasingly after the thirteenth century the proclisis vs.
enclisis principle was lost, all Romance languages now exhibiting
basically proclisis. This suggests that all Romance languages might
have known a preliterary phase where the proclisis vs. enclisis
principle was operative and where the enclitic order was exactly the
reverse of the proclitic arrangement. However, it appears that such
a situation is not stable since all of the Romance languages must have
given up a strict interpretation of this double principle of clitic order
very early, before the thirteenth century, concentrating on one order
for both proclisis and enclisis. But the choice between the two possible directions for interpreting the basic ordering principle appears
to be free: Catalan, Provençal, French, and Italian chose enclisis
while the others chose proclisis. The final dismantling of the proclitic vs. enclitic placement of clitics falls roughly in the period between 1300 and 1600, in the same period, thus, which also saw the
reshuffling of the clitic ordering. Since the new clitic placement was
mainly proclitic it is not surprising that the various languages with
enclitic order switched to proclitic order.
     A few examples will illustrate the scope of stipulation (25c) allow-
ing for the statement of idiosyncratic properties of clitic ordering.
This category provides the explanation for the merger of the Old
Spanish ge in the [III, dat] - [III, acc] combinations ge lo etc. with the
reflexive pronoun se, a phonetic evolution which eludes the regular
change [ž] > [š] > [x]. The phonetic similarity between reflexive [şe]
and non-reflexive [še] (after devoicing) together with the singular
status of ge in the clitic system led the two elements to merge.
     The phonetic influence can also be observed in the case of French:
there must be a rhythmical principle at play with respect to the preservation of le lui, le leur against all expectations. It will derive most
probably from the oxytone intonation characteristic of French phonetics which requires a 'heavy' element to be placed last in a linear
arrangement as long as no other stronger principles postulate a
different order. In this way it is assured that the 'heavy' and not
the 'light' element bears the greater stress.
     I have already mentioned the connection of clitic order with mor-
phology in the discussion of the behavior of Italian gli/le. If these

clitics would bear a lexical exception feature to the effect that they
may not be preceded by any other clitic, the resulting picture would
be satisfactory: these elements would be exceptional in the same way
that some morphemes are exceptional in inflection. Their exception-
ality is not very strongly motivated since judgments by speakers on
sentences containing clitic combinations with gli/le are typically less
clear. Thus the peculiarity could disappear at any time, in the same
way that it entered the language of the nineteenth century.

    The overall mode of operation of such a system determining clitic
order would fluctuate between two poles: on the one hand, clitic
order could be the exclusive result of transformational processes,
directly reflecting the syntax and the grammar of the language in
general. On the other hand, clitic order could be stated by a superficially arbitrary constraint as in the SSC approach. But any such
arbitrary constraint would be the degenerate result of transformational
processes such that it is not surprising to find that even in the most
complicated surface regulated situation there may be features which
can only be described in the light of the transformational origin of the
constraint. In the same way that the basically transformational order
can be superseded by a constraint growing out of it, this constraint
can at any time be revoked returning clitic order to a more 'natural'
state. Thus clitic order can be seen as the expected result of otherwise operative grammatical principles. The ossification of a complex
situation into a constraint then would not be significantly different
from the collapse of the derivational account of inflectional forms
changing to a partially arbitrary surface patterning (paradigmatic
condition) which, however, still reflects the earlier derivational
motivation of the forms to a certain degree. Clitic elements therefore, behave as other morphemes do; thus they are part of language
in a very natural sense.

    4.3 I would like to conclude my considerations with a critical
rejection of the account for clitic ordering just described. Each one
of the assumptions and stipulations made above may be justified. In
their totality, however, they fail. The system is far too rich. I
did not spell out how one could actually account for a given clitic
system (or better, how the speaker accounts for it). The problem is
that the proposed categories transcend the domain of empirically
falsifiable phenomena or categories. There are two catch-all
assumptions: first, the situation of the Romance languages does not
provide direct evidence for the double directionality principle (25b).
Notice that it was necessary to push back its full applicability to the
preliterary period. It can only be saved through strong arguments
establishing it not necessarily as a phylogenetic, but as an ontogenetic
principle. [13] Second, the real problem is the stipulation (25c)

providing room for unrestricted idiosyncrasies. But to account
fully for the clitic system of any of the Romance languages requires
a heavy dosage of corrective assumptions to eliminate the harm done
by the more plausible, but over-generalized principles (25a) and
(25b).

If a clitic account is to make sense in terms of language and the
particular language under investigation it must be very powerful because the relevant data cannot be subsumed under one easy heading.
The price for the versatility of the theoretical apparatus is the dilu-
tion of its meaning as a psychologically valid and scientifically sound
model. I suggest here in lieu of a positive conclusion that clitic order
as such is not a suitable topic since clitics are not autonomous in the
grammar. They are embedded in the grammar and they are actively
part of it; thus they must be accounted for in terms of the grammar as
a whole.

NOTES

[1]For present purposes Perlmutter (1970) will be considered exclusively. There has been considerable discussion of this aspect of
grammar, especially for Spanish; cf. Suñer (1973); Contreras and
Rojas (1972); Dinnsen (1972); Otero (1972); Roldán (1971); Roldán
(1973); Szabo (1973). The arguments presented here do not relate
directly to the problems discussed in these studies which are mainly
concerned with the adequacy of the clitic account for Spanish. This
paper will rather establish the insufficiency of the SSC approach in
general, based on arguments offered by the historical evolution.

[2]Cf. Menéndez Pidal (1950:343); Par (1928:61); Brusewitz (1905:
26); Lombard (1934:37). These studies point out the exceptional dialects of Hecho (Aragón); Mallorca; some Provençal cases; some
Northern Italian cases, respectively.

[3]loc means locative, i.e. a pronoun representing a structure
a/in + NP; ci and vi can be used interchangeably in this function.
gen stands for genitive, a clitic element representing the strings
di/da + NP.

[4]The order mi – vi – ti – ci is not necessarily acceptable to all
speakers, neither in Old nor in Modern Italian; but if these clitics
occur in combination, then it is always in the order given and in no
other.

[5]The data come from the meticulous works by Melander (1929),
Lombard (1934), Castellani (1952). The temporal arrangement is a
condensation of Castellani's description (1952.I:79-105).

[6]ho in Catalan and o in Provençal are sentential pronouns with
characteristics different from the regular [III, acc, -refl]. en is the
form for the genitive; i, ié for the locative clitic.

[7]Some dialects of Provençal have preserved the old order type (Brusewitz 1905:26).

[8]Foulet (1965), Wagner-Pinchon (1962), Lerch (1934, 1940), Melander (1935/36), Meyer-Lübke (1897), Gamillscheg (1957).

[9]en = genitive; y = locative; subject has to be specified since je, tu, il, etc. are clitics in Modern French; ne = negative preverbal particle. One general problem with (23) is that it must allow the clitic subject to follow the verb in questions (cf. (iii) vs. (iv)) even though the other clitics precede the verb:

(i)   il m'en a parlé
(ii) est-ce qu'il m'en a parlé?
(iii) m'en a-t-il parlé?
(iv) *a-t-il m'en parlé?

This situation also points to the existence of rules affecting clitic placement which operate on the output of the SSC; or else, the SSC (23) must be supplemented with conditions allowing this type of construction (cf. point (2b) above).

[10]Notice that in (24) 'subject' is not to be mentioned due to the fact that the imperative lacks a surface subject. ne cannot interfere since (24) holds only for affirmative second person imperatives.

[11]It should be pointed out that neither the assumption of an iterative rule of this type nor that of a remote constituent order 'V - direct object - indirect object - X' can be made safely. (I owe this observation to Richard Kayne.) For the sake of the argument I will disregard these difficulties for the moment. Since the whole approach outlined here will be rejected in the last section (cf. 4.3) this complication does not affect my position.

[12]Note that there might be some significance to the presence of the locative and genitive clitics since all the languages which have them belonged in their medieval stage to type (4), all the ones which lack them, at least now, belong to type (5). This opposes Portuguese and Spanish to Catalan, Provençal, French, and Italian.

[13]Cf. Szabo's (1973) contribution in this volume. He arrives at a similar conclusion on the basis of different arguments. But his attempt is not fully justified either so it cannot provide the necessary independent justification for my proposal.

REFERENCES

Badía, Margarit A. 1962. Gramática catalana. Vol. I. Madrid: Gredos (BRH Manuales 10).
Brunel, Clovis. 1926. Les plus anciennes chartes en langue provençale. Paris, Picard.

Brusewitz, Victor. 1905. Etude historique sur la syntaxe des pronoms personnels dans la langue des Félibres. Stockholm, Isaac
Marcus.

Castellani, Arrigo. 1952. Nuovi testi fiorentini del Dugento. 2 vol.
Florence, Sansoni.

Contreras, Heles and Jorge Nelson Rojas. 1972. Some remarks on
Spanish clitics. Linguistic Inquiry. 3(3).385-92.

Dinnsen, Daniel A. 1972. Additional constraints on clitic order in
Spanish. In: Generative studies in Romance languages. Ed. by
B. Saciuk and J. Casagrande. Rowley, Mass., Newbury House.
175-83.

Elsner, Alfred. 1886. Über Form and Verwendung des Perso-
nalpronomens im Altprovenzalischen. Kiel, Fiencke.

Foulet, Lucien. 1965. Petite syntaxe de l'ancien français. Paris,
Champion (3rd edition).

Gamillscheg, Ernst. 1957. Historische französische Syntax.
Tübingen, Niemeyer.

Lerch, Eugen. 1934. Historische französische Syntax. III:
Modalität. Leipzig, Reisland.

_____. 1940. Proklise oder Enklise der altfranzösischen Objekts-
pronomina? Zeitschrift für romanische Philologie. 60.417-50.

Lombard, Alf. 1934. Le groupement des pronoms personnels régimes
atones en italien. Studier i modern språkvetenskap. 12.19-76.

Melander, J. 1929. L'origine de l'italien me ne, me lo, te la, etc.
Studia neophilologica. 2.169-203.

_____. 1935/36. Enklise oder Proklise der tonlosen Objektspronomen
im Altfranzösischen. Studia neophilologica. 8.45-60.

Menéndez Pidal, Ramón. 1950. Orígenes del español. Madrid,
Espasa-Calpe (3rd edition).

Meyer-Lübke, Wilhelm. 1897. Zur Stellung der tonlosen Objekts-
pronomina. Zeitschrift für romanische Philologie. 21.313-34.

_____. 1899. Grammatik der romanischen Sprachen. III: Romanische
Syntax. Leipzig, Reisland.

Otero, Carlos. 1972. Acceptable ungrammatical sentences in Spanish. Linguistic Inquiry. 3(2).233-42.

Par, Anfós. 1923. Sintaxi catalana. Beihefte zur Zeitschrift für
romanische Philologie 66. Halle (Saale), Niemeyer.

_____. 1928. Curial e güelfa; notes lingüístiques y d'estil. Barce-
lona: Biblioteca Balmes.

Perlmutter, David. 1968. Deep and surface structure constraints
in syntax. Unpublished Ph.D. dissertation, Massachusetts Institute of Technology.

_____. 1970. Surface structure constraints in syntax. Linguistic
Inquiry. 1.187-255.

Roldán, Mercedes. 1971. Spanish constructions with se. Language Sciences. 18.15-29.

_____. 1973. Constraints on clitic insertion in Spanish. Appearing in this volume.

Suñer, Margarita. 1973. Where does impersonal se come from? Appearing in this volume.

Szabo, Robert K. 1973. Deep and surface order in Spanish clitics. Appearing in this volume.

Vázquez Cuesta, Pilar and María Albertina Mendes da Luz. 1961. Gramática portuguesa. (2nd edition). Madrid, Gredos.

Wagner, R. L. and J. Pinchon. 1962. Grammaire du français classique et moderne. (2nd edition). Paris, Hachette.

Wanner, Dieter. 1972. The misplaced clitics of Italian. Urbana, Linguistics Library, University of Illinois. Mimeographed.

PRENOMINAL ADJECTIVES
IN SPANISH PREDICATES

MARTA LUJÁN

University of Texas, Austin

Attributive adjectives in Spanish can precede or follow the noun they modify. It has been argued that adjectives in this function are transforms of relative clauses (Cressey 1966; Luján-Gough 1971, 1972). In particular, the prenominal adjective, when it does not carry the main stress of the phrase, is derived from an appositive clause. Since predicate nominals do not take appositive clauses,

    (1) *Es estudiante, que es estupendo.
        'He is a student, who is stupendous.'

it follows that prenominal adjectives should also be ungrammatical before predicate nominals. But they are not:

    (2) Es un estupendo estudiante.[1]
        'He is a stupendous student.'

Hence, if the hypothesis that attributive adjectives are transforms of relative clauses is to be maintained this adjective must come from another source.

The thesis of this paper is that the prenominal adjective of (2) is not an attributive adjective. Rather, it is the head of the phrase, and what looks like a predicate nominal on the surface is instead an adjectival phrase in underlying structure. The head of this phrase, the adjective, is in construction with an ndo-VP complement (ing-VP). The underlying string in (3) is mapped onto (2) by a transformation that deletes <u>siendo</u> in the complement and a rule that inserts the determiner <u>un-</u> before an Adj+NP substring:

(3) *Es estupendo siendo estudiante.
     'He is stupendous being a student. '

Accordingly, (2) is quite different in underlying structure from (4), where the predicate is nominal and the adjective is attributive, a transform of a restrictive clause:

(4) Es un estudiante estupendo.
     'He is a stupendous student. '

(5) Es un estudiante que es estupendo.

Instead, (2) is closer in basic structure to (6), where a predicate adjective, head of the predicate, is in construction with a manner adverbial:

(6) Es estupendo como estudiante.
     'He is stupendous as a student. '

There are several striking differences between the predicates of (2) and (4) which lend support to the hypothesis that these predicates are unrelated and, in fact, structurally distinct.

First, postnominal adjectives modify nouns in any structure. Thus, for any subject or object noun phrase like:

(7) el estudiante estupendo

there is a predicate nominal like:

(8) Es un estudiante estupendo.

But this implication does not hold for prenominal adjectives. A number of adjectives which can be prenominal in subject or object noun phrases are barred before nouns in predicates.

(9) el $\begin{Bmatrix} \text{obeso} \\ \text{alto} \\ \text{rubio} \end{Bmatrix}$ estudiante

(10) *Es un $\begin{Bmatrix} \text{obeso} \\ \text{alto} \\ \text{rubio} \end{Bmatrix}$ estudiante.

It is interesting to note that exactly the same adjectives cannot be followed by a manner adverbial.

(11) *Es $\begin{Bmatrix} \text{obeso} \\ \text{alto} \\ \text{rubio} \end{Bmatrix}$ como estudiante.

Second, there are restrictions on the kinds of adverbs that can appear before these prenominal adjectives. Adverbs like frecuentemente, constantemente, continuamente, etc. are ungrammatical here just as they are before adjectival phrases with manner adverbials:

(12) Es una tediosa tarea.
   'It is a tedious job. '

(13) *Es una frecuentemente tediosa tarea.
   'It is a frequently tedious job. '

(14) *Es frecuentemente tediosa como tarea.
   'It is frequently tedious as a job. '

But no restrictions hold for either the postnominal adjective in a predicate or the ordinary prenominal attributive adjective:

(15) Es una tarea frecuentemente tediosa.
   'It is a frequently tedious job. '

(16) la frecuentemente tediosa tarea
   'the frequently tedious job'

Third, the predicates where the adjective precedes the noun can appear in the progressive aspect; again, this is correlated with the grammaticality of the progressive in similar adjectival phrases.

(17) Está siendo un estupendo estudiante.

(18) Está siendo estupendo como estudiante.

But it is not possible to use a predicate noun phrase, with or without postnominal modifier, in the progressive aspect:

(19) *Está siendo estudiante.

(20) *Está siendo un estudiante estupendo.

(21) *Está siendo un estudiante que es estupendo.

Fourth, while the predicate nominal with a postnominal adjective allows an appositive clause headed by quien (who) or que (that), the predicate with the prenominal adjective cannot be followed by this kind of appositive clause; once again, the same is true of the adjectival phrase:

(22) Es un estudiante estupendo, $\begin{Bmatrix} \text{quien} \\ \text{que} \end{Bmatrix}$ merece todo mi respeto.
'He is a stupendous student, who deserves all my respect.'

(23) *Es un estupendo estudiante, $\begin{Bmatrix} \text{quien} \\ \text{que} \end{Bmatrix}$ merece todo mi respeto.

(24) *Es estupendo como estudiante, $\begin{Bmatrix} \text{quien} \\ \text{que} \end{Bmatrix}$ merece todo mi respeto.
'He is stupendous as a student, who deserves all my respect.'

Thus we see that predicates with prenominal adjectives differ from predicate nominals in four significant ways: many adjectives are excluded from these predicates, there are restrictions on the kinds of adverbs these adjectives can take, they allow the progressive aspect, and they cannot be followed by an appositive clause headed by quien or que. These differences suffice to establish that predicates with prenominal and postnominal adjectives are structurally distinct. Moreover, in each of these differences, the prenominal adjective behaves exactly like the adjective phrase. If we assume that the prenominal predicate adjective is really an adjectival phrase in underlying structure, then all of the differences noted will be a consequence of its basic structure. Thus, I will assume that the underlying structure of sentences like (2) is:

(25)

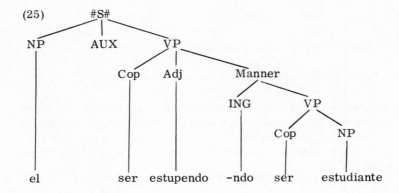

It follows from this deep structure that it is not possible to append an appositive clause introduced by quien or que to predicates with prenominal adjectives. Such clauses need an antecedent which is referential. Since both the noun and the head adjective in (25) are non-referential, neither could serve as antecedent. But just as a predicate adjective phrase can only stand as antecedent to a clause introduced by lo que and lo cual (which),

(26) Este estudiante es estupendo, lo que tu nunca serás.
'This student is stupendous, which you will never be.'

(27) Esta tarea es tediosa, lo cual me desespera.
'This job is tedious, which drives me crazy.'

the predicate with a prenominal adjective, unlike the predicate nominal with postnominal modifiers, allows only these relative pronouns in an appositive of which it is the antecedent. This fact follows from assuming an underlying structure like (25) for predicates of this kind:

(28) Es un estupendo estudiante, lo que tu nunca serás.

(29) Es una tediosa tarea, lo cual me desespera.

Adjectives which refer to a state or condition are constructed with the copula estar (cf. Luján-Gough 1972). Most adjectives may refer to a state or to a property and this semantic difference is overtly marked by the use of different copulas.

(30) Mi hermano está feliz. (state, condition)

(31) Mi hermano es feliz.

But the head adjective in (25) is clearly not a 'stative' adjective. Notice that inherently stative adjectives (i. e. those that refer only to states) are ungrammatical in parallel adjectival phrases:

(32) *Está asombrado como marido.
'He is astonished as a husband.'

(33) *Está asustada como niña.
'She is frightened as a girl.'

(34) *Está angustiada como mujer.
'She is anguished as a woman.'

And although these adjectives can be prenominal modifiers,

(35) El asombrado marido la miraba boquiabierto.
'The astonished husband was looking at her open-mouthed.'

(36) La asustada niña salió disparando.
'The frightened girl ran away.'

(37) La angustiada mujer lloraba desconsoladamente.
'The anguished woman cried unconsolably.'

they should be ungrammatical in predicates that derive from underlying structures like (25), and they are:[2]

(38) *Juan es un asombrado marido.

(39) *Ana es una asustada niña.

(40) *Mi hermana es una angustiada mujer.

By contrast, these adjectives can be postnominal modifiers of a predicate noun, since no restriction is placed on the predicate adjective of the embedded sentences from which these attributive adjectives derive:

(41) Es un marido asombrado.

(42) Es una niña asustada.

(43) Es una mujer angustiada.

A crucial point in this hypothesis is then that the head adjective in the underlying structure of predicates as shown in (25) must be non-stative. Thus, I am assuming that this semantic feature, which may be labeled 'STATE', plays a role in the subcategorization of adjectives. Accordingly, only adjectives negatively specified for this feature may be constructed with adverbials of the form 'como NP' (where NP is a property noun phrase; e.g. como hombre, como professor, como tarea, etc.) and 'ING-VP' (e.g. siendo hombre, estando enojado, escribiendo cartas, etc.). But adjectives positively specified for the feature [STATE] cannot be constructed with these adverbial phrases because 'como NP' and 'ING-VP' are instances of Manner Adverbial and stative adjectives are incompatible with this type of adverbial:

(44) *Está $\begin{bmatrix} \text{cortésmente} \\ \text{deliberadamente} \\ \text{inteligentemente} \end{bmatrix}$ enojado.

     'He is $\begin{bmatrix} \text{politely} \\ \text{deliberately} \\ \text{intelligently} \end{bmatrix}$ annoyed.'

(45) *Está $\begin{bmatrix} \text{cortésmente} \\ \text{deliberadamente} \\ \text{inteligentemente} \end{bmatrix}$ angustiado.

     'He is $\begin{bmatrix} \text{politely} \\ \text{deliberately} \\ \text{intelligently} \end{bmatrix}$ anguished.'

The non-occurrence of adverbs like frecuentemente, constante-mente, continuamente, etc. follows precisely from the specification [-STATE] in the head adjective in an underlying structure like (25). These adverbs are incompatible with adjectives which are not stative:

(46) Mi hermano está constantemente feliz.
     'My brother is constantly happy.'

(47) *Mi hermano es constantemente feliz.

Consequently, while the prenominal adjective in a predicate may be preceded by an adverb, this cannot be a frequency adverb:

(48) Es una extremadamente tediosa tarea.

(49) *Es una frecuentemente tediosa tarea.

(50) Es un muy estupendo estudiante.

(51) *Es un constantemente estupendo estudiante.

The specification [-STATE] in the head adjective in (25) is well motivated on independent grounds. It accounts for the occurrence of progressive aspect in predicates with prenominal adjectives:

(52) Está siendo un estupendo estudiante.

Stative adjectives are ungrammatical with the progressive aspect, but non-stative adjectives are not:

(53) Está siendo { paciente / prudente / justo } .

    'He is being { patient / prudent / just } .

(54) *Está { estando / siendo } { enojado / angustiado / contento } .

    'He is being { annoyed / anguished / happy } .

There are some adjectives, such as <u>aburrido</u>, which are ambiguous and have two widely different interpretations corresponding to the stative/non-stative distinction.

(55) Tenía un acompañante aburrido.
    'She had a bored/boring escort. '

(56) El aburrido accompañante permanecía callado.
    'The bored/boring escort remained silent. '

The specification [-STATE] in the head adjective of predicates like (25) allows us to derive another prediction concerning the interpretation of such adjectives. If an adjective like <u>aburrido</u> precedes a noun in a predicate, it should be unambiguous, and the meaning should correspond to its non-stative interpretation. This is indeed the case:

(57) Es un aburrido acompañante.
    'He is a boring escort. ' (but not: 'He is a bored escort. ')

Except for the fact that the VP in the Manner Adverbial in (25) cannot have a [-STATE] head adjective, no restrictions are placed on the form of these gerundive phrases. Thus, we should have a varied range of them, and we do:

(58) Es estupendo bailando.
     'He is stupendous dancing.'

(59) Es estupendo dirigiendo la orquesta.
     'He is stupendous conducting the orchestra.'

(60) Es estupendo manejando el autobús a la escuela.
     'He is stupendous driving the bus to school.'

Moreover, it must be also possible to have gerundive phrases which are of the form Cop+Adj, where the head adjective is stative, but where the copula estando has been deleted. Such sentences are in the language:

(61) Este hombre es inaguantable enojado.
     'This man is unbearable (when) annoyed.'

(62) *Este hombre es inaguantable estando enojado.

The transformations that map a structure like (25) onto what looks like a predicate nominal in (2) are the following:

(63) $\text{X} - \text{Cop+ING} - \begin{Bmatrix} \text{NP} \\ \text{Adj} \end{Bmatrix} - \text{Y} \Longrightarrow 1 - \emptyset - 3 - 4$

    where 2-3 is Manner

(64) $\text{X} - \text{Cop} - \text{Adj} - \text{NP} - \text{Y} \Longrightarrow 1 - 2 - \underline{un} + 3 - 4 - 5$

The first transformation deletes copulas siendo and estando before a noun phrase or an adjective which is part of a Manner Adverbial. The second inserts the determiner un- before a substring Adj+NP. The transformation that deletes the gerundive copulas has independent motivation. There is convincing evidence that the so-called 'adverbial' adjectives, constructed with verbs or verb phrases, derive from gerundive phrases by deletion of the copulas that introduce them. Thus, parallel to gerundive adverbials in (65)-(67) we have (68)-(70), which correspond to underlying strings (71)-(73).

(65) Llegó corriendo.
     'She arrived running.'

(66) Llegó trayendo regalos.
'She arrived bringing presents. '

(67) Tomaba la sopa haciendo mucho ruido.
'He ate the soup making a lot of noise. '

(68) Llegó cansada.
'She arrived tired. '

(69) Viven contentos.
'They live happily. '

(70) Lo esperaba muy ansiosa.
'She expected it very anxiously. '

(71) *Llegó estando cansada.

(72) *Viven estando contentos.

(73) *Los esperaba estando muy ansiosa.

It was noted initially that many adjectives which may function attributely in prenominal position are barred from the predicates whose syntactic properties we undertook to study:

(10) *Es un $\left\{ \begin{array}{l} \text{obeso} \\ \text{alto} \\ \text{rubio} \end{array} \right\}$ estudiante.

These adjectives, though non-stative, cannot be constructed with manner adverbials.

(11) *Es $\left\{ \begin{array}{l} \text{obeso} \\ \text{alto} \\ \text{rubio} \end{array} \right\}$ como estudiante.

(74) *Es $\left\{ \begin{array}{l} \text{obeso} \\ \text{alto} \\ \text{rubio} \end{array} \right\}$ deliberadamente.

This problem is left unsolved here, for it is beyond the scope of this paper to determine what semantic properties of a non-stative adjective define its compatibility with a manner adverbial. But it is investigation of this aspect which is likely to throw further light on the structure of the predicate with prenominal modifiers.

Conclusions. It was argued that predicates with prenominal adjectives are not predicate nominals in underlying structure, and that they are structurally distinct from predicate nominals with postnominal adjectives. Facts were presented which support the hypothesis that predicates with prenominal adjectives are instead adjectival phrases composed of a non-stative adjective and a gerundive Manner Adverbial. This hypothesis together with the assumption of the existence of two transformational rules, one of them independently motivated, predicts all of the facts and structural differences noted initially. Furthermore, they have allowed the derivation of new predictions, and these were borne out by the data.

NOTES

[1]This sentence is presented by Bolinger (1972) to illustrate the 'preposing of differentiating adjectives'.

[2]The fact that stative adjectives do not occur prenominally in predicates is of course evidence that this function is not equivalent to the attributive (pre- or postnominal) function. For adjectives in this function are transforms of relative clauses and are usually ambiguous between a stative and a non-stative interpretation (cf. Luján Gough, 1972).

REFERENCES

Bolinger, D. 1972. Adjective position again. Hispania. 55(1). 91–94.
Cressey, W. W. 1966. A transformational analysis of the relative clause in urban Mexican Spanish. Unpublished doctoral dissertation, University of Illinois.
Kuno, S. 1970. Some properties of non-referential noun phrases. In: Studies in general and Oriental linguistics. Ed. by Roman Jakobson and Shigeo Kawamoto. Tokyo, TEC.
Luján-Gough, M. 1971. Pre- and postnominal adjectives in Spanish. Presented at the summer meeting of the Linguistic Society of America at Buffalo, New York.
_____. 1972. Adjectives in Spanish. Unpublished doctoral dissertation, University of Texas.

(

DEFINITE AND INDEFINITE NP'S IN SPANISH

MARÍA-LUISA RIVERO

University of Ottawa

This study compares definite and indefinite NPs in Spanish and their modification by restrictive relative clauses in the subjunctive and in the indicative moods, as in the following paradigm:

(1a) Me interesa el LIBRO que tiene fotos. (Ind.)
      'I am interested in the BOOK which has pictures.'[1]

(1b) Me interesa el LIBRO que tenga fotos. (Ind.)
      'I am interested in that BOOK which might turn out to
      have pictures.'[2]

(1c) Me interesa un LIBRO que tiene fotos. (Ind.)
      'I am interested in a BOOK which has pictures.'

(1d) Me interesa un LIBRO que tenga fotos. (Subj.)
      'I am interested in a BOOK which might turn out to have
      pictures.'

In relatively recent work, philosophers (see, for example, Donnellan 1966 and Stalnaker 1972) have classified definite descriptions (1a)-(1b) as either referential or attributive. An example of a referential NP in Spanish appears in (1a). The NP in (1b) is an attributive definite description.

To clarify this distinction I will briefly discuss Donnellan's example Smith's murderer is insane and some of its Spanish equivalents. The definite description in the above example has two possible functions. It can be used in connection with a specific individual we have in mind, the 'referential' sense, or it can be used to state something about whoever murdered Smith, the 'attributive' sense. Spanish formally marks this distinction in its use of mood in the relative clause. If an example of type (2a) offers the same ambiguity as its English counterpart, (2b) can only be interpreted referentially, while (2c) is attributive.

(2a) EL ASESINO de Smith está loco.
      'Smith's MURDERER is insane.'

(2b) El que asesinó a Smith está loco. (Ind.)
      'The ONE who murdered Smith is insane.'

(2c) El que asesinara a Smith está loco. (Subj.)
      'The ONE who might have murdered Smith is insane.'

Philosophers have claimed that from a logical point of view, the distinction between referential and attributive definite NPs belongs to pragmatics (the study of linguistic acts and the contexts in which they are performed, the study of language in relation to its users). That is to say, that it has no semantic or syntactic consequences. This contention has not been discussed in a specific way by linguists. For example, McCawley (1970) has formalized the difference as if it were syntactico-semantic, ignoring Donnellan's claim, and Barbara H. Partee (1972) is not sure of the level to which the referential and the attributive belong.

Linguists have classified indefinite NPs (1c)-(1d) as specific or non-specific. (1c) contains a specific indefinite NP, while a non-specific NP appears in (1d). Specificity or the lack of it has been formalized as a syntactic-semantic aspect of indefinite NPs by a number of linguists (Baker 1966, Karttunen 1969, McCawley 1970). Some linguists think that the distinction is merely implied or presupposed (Dean 1968),[3] and others have doubts about its nature (pragmatic, semantic, syntactic) because of its parallelism with the distinction referential/ attributive found in definite descriptions (Partee 1972).

Modern philosophers, on the other hand, have in general assumed that the way definite and indefinite phrases refer is not comparable. I will show that linguistically speaking this is not true, and that definite and indefinite NPs refer, as far as certain natural languages are concerned, in a comparable (but not identical) manner.

This paper studies definite and indefinite NPs in Spanish in relation to their respective referentiality or specificity and concludes that referentiality in definite NPs and specificity in indefinite NPs is linguistically speaking, one unique phenomenon. The conclusion applies to opaque and transparent contexts in the same way. This possibility has been proposed by a number of linguists as I have already pointed out (see, for instance Partee 1972), but investigations of the issue have been neither detailed nor motivated.

A second conclusion is that the manifestation of referentiality-specificity in Spanish is both semantic and syntactic in nature; this means that there is at least one natural language in which the logical distinction between the referential and the attributive is not pragmatic, but belongs to the realm of grammar. Since referentiality and specificity are one and the same aspect of NPs, specificity too belongs to semantics and syntax and not to pragmatics. For the sake of the clarity of the exposition I will keep the terms 'referential'/'attributive' for definite NPs, and 'specific'/'non-specific' for indefinite NPs in my discussion.

The observation that Spanish marks many of its NPs as referential or specific and as attributive or non-specific at the level of surface structure is a clear demonstration that this distinction cannot be pragmatic. The following example is ambiguous in Spanish, but we are not dealing here with pragmatic ambiguity:

(3) La MUCHACHA rubia es francesa.
     'The blond GIRL is French.'

The ambiguity of (3) is syntactic and arises through the application of Relative Clause Reduction, a well-known transformation. In other words, the reduction of relative clauses in Spanish renders a definite NP ambiguous between a referential interpretation and an attributive one. Full relative clauses are not ambiguous in this way:

(4a) La MUCHACHA que es rubia es francesa. (Ind.)
      'The GIRL who is blond is French.' REFERENTIAL

(4b) La MUCHACHA que sea rubia es francesa. (Subj.)
      'The GIRL who might turn out to be blond, that one is French.' ATTRIBUTIVE

The same type of argument can be developed for indefinite specific and non-specific NPs. However, this discussion indicates that referentiality and specificity must be considered as a semantic-syntactic phenomenon in Spanish but it does not imply that we are dealing with one unique aspect of Spanish NPs. The rest of this paper will provide arguments which motivate my two hypotheses at the same time: (a) specificity and referentiality are the same aspect of NPs, and (b) this feature of NPs belongs to the realm of grammar.

Notice first that considering specificity and referentiality as one unique aspect of NPs has the advantage of providing an explanation for the fact that both specific indefinite NPs and referential definite NPs are modified by restrictive relative clauses in the indicative while their attributive and non-specific counterparts are modified by clauses in the subjunctive. Syntactic consequences of referentiality and specificity in Spanish which point out the parallelism of the two notions are not hard to find.

The conjoining of relative clauses in the indicative and in the subjunctive produces an ungrammatical (and not merely infelicitous) result, both for definite and indefinite NPs:

(5a) *Una CASA que sea espaciosa (Subj.) y que tiene jardín (Ind.) es nuestro ideal.
'*A HOUSE which is spacious (NON-SPECIFIC) and which has a garden (SPECIFIC) is our ideal.'

(5b) *La CASA que sea espaciosa (Subj.) y que tiene jardín (Ind.) es nuestro ideal.
'*The HOUSE . . . '

In other words, an NP cannot simultaneously be specific and non-specific, or referential and attributive. In the same manner, an NP modified by one reduced relative clause and a full clause can only receive one grammatical interpretation, that is, the one determined by the mood of the full clause, and it can never be ambiguous in the sense discussed here.

(6a) Está visitando la CASA que es espaciosa y con jardín (Ind.)
'He is visiting the HOUSE which is spacious and with a garden.' REFERENTIAL

(6b) Está visitando la CASA que sea espaciosa y con jardín (Subj.)
'He is visiting the HOUSE which is spacious and with a garden.' ATTRIBUTIVE

The same applies to indefinite NPs.

Along the same line of argument, it can be observed that stacked relative clauses must all bear the same mood, both with definite or indefinite antecedents:

(7a) *Cómprame un ABRIGO que sea (Subj.) negro que está (Ind.) rebajado.

(7b) Cómprame un ABRIGO que [sea / es] negro que [esté / está]
rebajado. [(Subj.) / (Ind.)]
'Buy me a COAT which [might be / is] black which [might be / is]
on sale' [NON-SPECIFIC / SPECIFIC]

(8a) *Cómprame el abrigo que sea (Subj.) negro que está
rebajado. (Ind.)

(8b) Cómprame el abrigo que [sea / es] negro que [esté / está]
rebajado. [(Subj.) / (Ind.)]
'Buy me the coat which [might be / is] black which [might be / is]
on sale' [ATTRIBUTIVE / REFERENTIAL]

It has been noticed that non-specific NPs within non-factual, contexts (modal and future contexts, for instance) can only be referred
back to if the counterfactual mood is sustained. As an argument for
the parallelism of the specificity/referentiality distinction, I would
like to indicate that an attributive NP within a modal context has the
same property as its non-specific counterpart. Compare the following examples with respect to the behavior of the NP whose noun is
corbata 'tie':

(9a) *Tráeme una CORBATA que sea roja. Está encima de la
mesa. (Subj.)
'Bring me a TIE which is red. (It) is on top of the table.'
NON-SPECIFIC

(9b) *Tráeme la CORBATA que sea roja. Está encima de la
mesa. (Subj.)
'Bring me the TIE which might be red. (It) is on top of
the table.' ATTRIBUTIVE

(10a) Tráeme una CORBATA que sea roja. Quizás esté encima
de la mesa. (Subj.)
'Bring me a TIE which might be red. Perhaps (it) is on
top of the table.' NON-SPECIFIC

(10b) Tráeme la CORBATA que sea roja. Quizás esté encima
de la mesa. (Subj.)
'Bring me the TIE which might be red. Perhaps (it) is
on top of the table.' ATTRIBUTIVE

If we assume that the subject of the second sentence in the examples
(9a)-(9b) and (10a)-(10b) has been deleted after some sort of pronominalization, we can see that the only sequence which is grammatical is the one in which the non-factual mood is maintained (10a)-(10b)
for both definite and indefinite NPs. That is to say, attributive definite NPs in modal contexts can only be referred back to if the counterfactual mood is maintained. The same principle explains the deviance
of (11) below:

(11a) *Juan traerá a una MUCHACHA que sea rubia a la fiesta,
y es muy guapa. (Subj.)
'John will bring whatever GIRL might be blond to the party,
and (she) is very pretty.' NON-SPECIFIC

(11b) *Juan traerá a la MUCHACHA que sea rubia a la fiesta,
y es muy guapa. (Subj.)
'John will bring that GIRL who might be blond to the party,
and (she) is very pretty.' ATTRIBUTIVE

Compare (11) with (12), in which the non-factual mood is maintained
in the second conjunct by the use of the Future:

(12a) Juan traerá a una MUCHACHA que sea rubia a la fiesta,
y será muy guapa. (Subj.)
'John will bring whatever GIRL might be blond to the
party, and (she) will be very pretty.' NON-SPECIFIC

(12b) Juan traerá a la MUCHACHA que sea rubia a la fiesta,
y será muy guapa. (Subj.)
'John will bring that GIRL who might be blond to the
party, and she will be very pretty.' ATTRIBUTIVE

In Spanish, contrary to what appears to be the case in English
(Kuno 1970), both specific and non-specific indefinite NPs can be
pseudo-clefted (13b; 15b). In a parallel fashion both attributive and
referential definite NPs can also be pseudo-clefted (14b; 16b).

(13a) Juan quiere comer una TRUCHA que esté fresca. (Subj.)
'John wants to eat a TROUT which should be fresh.'
NON-SPECIFIC

(13b) Lo que Juan quiere comer es una TRUCHA que esté
       fresca. (Subj.)
       'What John wants to eat is a TROUT which should be
       fresh.' NON-SPECIFIC

(14a) Juan quiere comer la TRUCHA que esté fresca. (Subj.)
       'John wants to eat that TROUT which will turn out to be
       fresh.' ATTRIBUTIVE

(14b) Lo que Juan quiere comer es la TRUCHA que esté
       fresca. (Subj.)
       'What John wants to eat is that TROUT which will turn
       out to be fresh.' ATTRIBUTIVE

(15a) Juan quiere comer una TRUCHA que está fresca. (Ind.)
       'John wants to eat a TROUT which is fresh.' SPECIFIC

(15b) Lo que Juan quiere comer es una TRUCHA que está
       fresca. (Ind.)
       'What John wants to eat is a TROUT which is fresh.'
       SPECIFIC

(16a) Juan quiere comer la TRUCHA que está fresca. (Ind.)
       'John wants to eat the TROUT which is fresh.' REFERENTIAL

(16b) Lo que Juan quiere comer es la TRUCHA que está fresca.
       (Ind.)
       'What John wants to eat is the TROUT which is fresh.'
       REFERENTIAL

Perhaps an argument which has kept linguists from advocating the
identity between definite and indefinite NPs with respect to their
specificity and referentiality, is that a number of transformational
grammarians have argued that the specific/non-specific distinction
can be found only in future, negative, and opaque contexts (Dean 1968)
(for instance in the complement of such verbs as querer 'want') whereas philosophical discussions of the referential/attributive distinction
do not connect it with those contexts. It has now been established that
specificity is a notion which appears in non-opaque, non-future, non-
negative contexts as well (Karttunen 1969). In connection with this,
I would like to point out that Spanish has specific and non-specific
NPs in all kinds of contexts, as the following surface structures indicate, and referential and attributive NPs in the same contexts. (17)
and (18) exhibit opaque contexts, with the verb want in the matrix.
(19) and (20) present non-opaque, non-negative, non-future contexts.

(17a) Quiero que venga una SECRETARIA que es eficiente. (Ind.)
'I want a SECRETARY who is efficient to come.' SPECIFIC

(17b) Quiero que venga una SECRETARIA que sea eficiente (Subj.)
'I want a SECRETARY who might be efficient to come.'
NON-SPECIFIC

(18a) Quiero que venga la SECRETARIA que es eficiente. (Ind.)
'I want the SECRETARY who is efficient to come.'
REFERENTIAL

(18b) Quiero que venga la SECRETARIA que sea eficiente. (Subj.)
'I want that SECRETARY who might turn out to be efficient
to come.' ATTRIBUTIVE

(19a) Juan se está casando en este momento con una CHICA que
tiene ojos azules. (Ind.)
'At this moment, John is marrying a GIRL who has blue
eyes.' SPECIFIC

(19b) Juan se está casando en este momento con una CHICA que
tenga ojos azules. (Subj.)[4]
'At this moment, John is marrying a GIRL who has blue
eyes.' NON-SPECIFIC

(20a) Juan se está casando en este momento con la CHICA que
tiene ojos azules. (Ind.)
'At this moment, John is marrying the GIRL who has blue
eyes.' REFERENTIAL

(20b) Juan se está casando en este momento con la CHICA que
tenga ojos azules. (Subj.)[5]
'At this moment, John is marrying that GIRL who may
have blue eyes.' ATTRIBUTIVE

As a last argument for the identity of the referential/specific
distinction, I will now turn to a semantic discussion.

In his very famous study on definite descriptions B. Russell (1925)
stated that existence is contextually defined for definite descriptions
or, as he puts it, 'existence is not one among the properties which
things may or may not possess'. This observation, which Russell
incorporates into the logical rules for definite descriptions, means
in linguistic terms that the existence of a referent for a definite NP
depends on the semantic-syntactic context in which it appears. In
other words, definite NPs do not always involve a referent, and the

existence or non-existence of the object described by the NP is derived from the grammatical environment in which that NP appears.
This observation is correct as far as certain natural languages are
concerned. It has nevertheless been ignored by linguists, perhaps
because it has been lost in the heat of the discussion of the truth value
of the example The king of France is not bald, which is where Russell
chooses to make the point about the entailment of existence in definite
descriptions I have just presented. For instance in the UCLA grammar
(Stockwell et al. 1968) it is stated that the feature [+DEF] always involves a referent; along a similar line of reasoning B. Hall Partee
(1972) says that definite noun phrases always include a presupposition
that an object fitting the description actually exists.

It is my contention that definite NPs do not always carry an existential presupposition, that their existential presupposition may fail because of the linguistic environment, and they have this aspect in common with indefinite NPs which may or may not carry an existential
presupposition as well. In other words, I am proposing what Russell
said long ago, that existence is a property which definite NPs acquire
through their linguistic environment. Furthermore, I am proposing
that this behavior is shared by indefinite NPs as well.

It would be beyond the scope of this paper to study linguistic contexts and their import on the existential status of definite and indefinite NPs. I will simply present one set of examples sharing
exisential presuppositions and a second set where those presuppositions fail.

First, in non-modal contexts definite and indefinite descriptions
alike, their specificity being irrelevant, carry an existential presupposition. For example, (19a)-(19b) and (20a)-(20b) share the presupposition that there exists at least one girl with blue eyes. To see
this, consider the felicity conditions of the following examples, non-
specific and attributive respectively. I have not chosen specific and
referential examples because in those cases the existential presupposition is more clearly felt and not normally in question.

(21a) $\neq$ Juan está bailando con una CHICA que tenga ojos azules,
        la cual no existe en este momento. (Subj.)[6]
        '$\neq$ John is dancing with whatever GIRL may have blue
        eyes, who doesn't exist at this moment.' NON-SPECIFIC

(21b) $\neq$ Juan está bailando con la CHICA que tenga ojos azules,
        la cual no existe en este momento. (Subj.)
        '$\neq$ John is dancing with that GIRL who might have blue
        eyes, who doesn't exist at this moment.' ATTRIBUTIVE

The semantic anomaly of (21a) and (21b) is due to the fact that the restrictive relative clause presupposes existence while the non-restrictive clause, appearing at the end of the example, asserts non-existence.

So-called modal contexts affect the existential presuppositions connected with definite and indefinite NPs. For instance, in future contexts, referential and specific NPs retain their existential presupposition while their attributive counterparts lose it, as the felicity of the following examples indicates.

(22a) ≠ Juan bailará con una CHICA que tiene ojos azules, la cual no existe en este momento. (Ind.)
'≠ John will dance with a GIRL who has blue eyes, who doesn't exist at this moment.' SPECIFIC

(22b) ≠ Juan bailará con la CHICA que tiene ojos azules, la cual no existe en este momento. (Subj.)
'≠ John will dance with the GIRL who has blue eyes, who doesn't exist at this moment.' ATTRIBUTIVE

(23a) Juan bailará con una CHICA que tenga ojos azules, la cual no existe en este momento. (Subj.)
'John will dance with a GIRL who may have blue eyes, who doesn't exist at this moment.' NON-SPECIFIC

(23b) Juan bailará con la CHICA que tenga ojos azules, la cual no existe en este momento. (Subj.)
'John will dance with that GIRL who might have blue eyes, who doesn't exist at this moment.' ATTRIBUTIVE

Since a restrictive relative clause in the subjunctive does not presuppose existence within a future context, the non-restrictive clause which follows can deny that existence without creating an anomalous situation: (23a) and (23b). On the other hand, relative clauses in the indicative do presuppose existence within a future context, which together with the negative assertion presented in the non-restrictive clause of (22a) and (22b) creates a deviant sentence.

So far I have shown that the existential presuppositions of attributive and non-specific NPs are contextually defined. This shows that existence is defined in a similar way for both definite and indefinite NPs and argues for the identity of the referential/specific aspect of NPs.

Referential and specific NPs seem to have a referent in all of the environments discussed so far. I would like to show now that existence is also contextually defined for referential and specific NPs, so that Russell's hypothesis is true for Spanish in an expanded form which includes indefinite NPs. I will also illustrate how the assumption that definite NPs always carry an existential presupposition is false even if we speak of referential NPs alone. It is true that most specific and referential NPs carry an existential presupposition but there are ways to block such a presupposition. For instance, consider the following examples:

(24a) Juan quiere pescar un PEZ que según él pesa 5 lbs.,
        y tal pez no existe. (Ind.)
        'John wants to catch a FISH which according to him weighs
        5 lbs., and such a fish does not exist.' SPECIFIC[7]

(24b) Juan quiere pescar el PEZ que según él pesa 5 lbs. y
        tal pez no existe. (Ind.)
        'John wants to catch the FISH which according to him
        weighs 5 lbs., and such a fish does not exist.'
        REFERENTIAL

(25a) ≠ Juan quiere pescar un PEZ que según mi opinión pesa
        5 lbs., y tal pez no existe. (Ind.)
        '≠ John wants to catch a FISH which according to me
        weighs 5 lbs., and such a fish does not exist.'
        SPECIFIC[7]

(25b) ≠ Juan quiere pescar el PEZ que según mi opinión pesa
        5 lbs., y tal pez no existe. (Ind.)
        '≠ John wants to catch the FISH which according to me
        weighs 5 lbs., and such a fish does not exist.'
        REFERENTIAL

The sentences in (25) have an existential presupposition, those in (24) do not. This poses a number of interesting problems which I will not discuss here, however, such as the connection between linguistic specificity and referentiality, and existence. My contention is simply that the meaning of specific indefinite NPs and of referential definite NPs is affected in the same way by the context in which they appear.

It should be obvious at this point that only a portion of the so-called 'referential' definite NPs in natural language do have objective referents. Therefore, it is perhaps more accurate to speak of specific definite NPs in linguistics, keeping in mind that a subset of those are referential as well, in the sense of Donnellan. Referentiality in the sense of having existential import can be determined by the linguistic

context, and is not an intrinsic aspect of specific definite (or indefinite) NPs.

Summary and conclusions. I have argued that the notion of referentiality associated with definite NPs and that of specificity in connection
with indefinite NPs should be combined into one unique aspect of NPs
in general. Furthermore, the distinction between the referential/
specific and the attributive/non-specific belongs to the realm of syntax
and semantics and not to pragmatics because this dichotomy has syntactic and semantic consequences.

My discussion has had a double purpose, given my two different
hypotheses: to show the parallelisms between the referential and the
specific, and to show the syntactic-semantic consequences of these
notions.

The arguments in favor of my double hypothesis are the following:

(1) In surface structure Spanish marks both definite and indefinite
NPs in a similar manner with respect to their specificity: by the mood
of restrictive relative clauses.

(2) A definite or indefinite NP cannot be modified by conjoined restrictive relative clauses or by stacked relatives of different moods.
The result is ungrammatical, not merely infelicitous.

(3) Non-specific definite and indefinite NPs within non-factual
contexts can be referred back to if the counterfactual mood is sustained.

(4) Both definite and indefinite NPs, regardless of their specificity,
can be pseudo-clefted in Spanish.

(5) The specific/non-specific distinction is not limited to future,
negative, and opaque contexts. The referential vs. the attributive
dichotomy is found in the same contexts as the specific/non-specific
difference.

And finally, (6) existential presuppositions are contextually defined for all NPs, definite or indefinite, and these presuppositions
are determined in the same way for referential and specific NPs on
the one hand, and for attributive and specific on the other.

NOTES

*This work was supported in part by Grant S72-0384 from the
Canada Council. I thank Raymond St-Laurent for some interesting
discussions on the English glosses.

[1]In this presentation I will use the following convention to indicate
the mood of the restrictive relative clause modifying the NP under
discussion, and whose head noun I capitalize in Spanish and English
for ease of reference. Ind. = indicative; Subj. = subjunctive.

[2]Glosses are only approximate since English either has different means to make the distinctions discussed here, or does not mark them at all in a formal way.

[3]If we take the terms 'implied' or 'presupposed' in a strict sense, the distinction is then considered as semantic and not syntactic, in a theory where semantics and syntax are components of different nature.

[4]The conditions under which (19b) is appropriate and nondeviant are quite specific and perhaps complex. This may lead speakers to reject (19b) as ungrammatical. (19b) implies that the speaker knows that John is getting married, although he doesn't know what girl he is getting married to, but what he specifically knows is that John likes blue-eyed girls only. (19b) is in some way equivalent to 'If John is getting married at this moment, and it seems he is, then it must be to a blue-eyed girl' (since it is the only kind he likes, for instance).

[5]The comments presented in fn. 4 apply to this example as well, with one difference: sentence (20b) has a presupposition of uniqueness not present in (19b). That is, (20b) presupposes that there is only one girl, unknown, who has blue eyes. This uniqueness presupposition, connected with the definite determiner, is not part of the meaning of (19b).

[6]I indicate infelicitous sentences by $\neq$. I use the term infelicitous not in a pragmatic sense, but in relation to such semantic notions as contradiction, presupposition failure, implication, etc.

[7]The NP un pez que según él pesa 5 lbs. 'a fish which according to him weighs 5 lbs.' in (24a) is specific with respect to Juan (as subject of the main sentence) but not in reference to the speaker. The same is true in (24b). This is made explicit by según él 'according to him'. In (25a) and (25b) the specificity is associated with the speaker because of the presence of según mi opinión 'according to me'.

REFERENCES

Baker, C. L. 1966. Definiteness and indefiniteness in English. Unpublished M. A. thesis, University of Illinois.

Dean, Janet. 1968. Nonspecific noun-phrases in English. Report NSF-20 to the National Science Foundation, Computational Laboratory, Harvard University, Cambridge, Mass.

Donnellan, Keith. 1966. Reference and definite descriptions. The Philosophical Review. 75.281-304.

Karttunen, Lauri. 1969. Problems of reference in syntax. Unpublished Ph. D. dissertation, Indiana University.

Kuno, Susumo. 1970. Some properties of non-referential noun-phrases. In: Studies in general and Oriental linguistics. Ed. by R. Jakobson and S. Kawamoto. Tokyo, TEC Company Ltd.

McCawley, J. D. 1970. Where do noun phrases come from? In: Semantics. Ed. by D. Steinberg and J. Jakobovits. New York, Holt, Rinehart, and Winston.

Partee, Barbara Hall. 1972. Opacity, coreference, and pronouns. In: Semantics of natural language. Ed. by D. Davidson and G. Harman. Dordrecht, D. Reidel.

Russell, Bertrand. 1925. Principia Mathematica. Vol. I, 2nd ed. Cambridge, Cambridge University Press.

Stalnaker, Robert C. 1972. Pragmatics. In: Semantics of natural language. Ed. by D. Davidson and G. Harman. Dordrecht, D. Reidel.

Stockwell, Robert P. et al. 1968. Integration of transformational theories on English syntax. Los Angeles, University of California Press.

REFERENCE AND MOOD IN ITALIAN

MARIO SALTARELLI

University of Illinois

1. Mood. In recent transformational studies the topic of mood has been treated in a variety of ways which reflect the evolution of theoretical interests from morphology to syntax to semantics. The question which puzzles the linguist is the following: what is the theoretical relevance of mood in an explicit grammar which recognizes two levels of representation and a relational set of rules? The answer to this question is couched in terms of the particular empirical considerations entertained in the analysis, along with the general theoretical arguments which can be mustered in support. It is often the case that the position of the new grammarian, vis-à-vis the word and paradigm linguist, is therefore strained. At any one moment his preoccupation with the representational device may curtail, for vested interest reasons, his empirical field of vision; or, conversely, an unenlightened empirical consideration may unduly constrain the grammatical framework.

In Chomsky (1965:170) mood and other inflectional categories are represented as syntactic features in the underlying representation of verbs and nouns. This means that, in the case of mood, every verb would be marked with the feature Indicative, Subjunctive, Imperative, etc. The proper morphophonological form of the verb would then be assigned by rules defined on these categories. Clearly, Chomsky's feature analysis of mood rests squarely on a preoccupation with a grammatical mechanism that would assign the correct verb endings. At its best this theoretical interpretation of mood is the least one can do in an explicit grammar. At its worst it implies that the category mood is an unanalyzable characteristic of verbs, much the same as passive and the like. This theoretical position precludes the possibility that mood might be the result of the interplay of other phrasal or sentential factors.

Evidence from syntax was adduced by Kiparsky (1968:44) to argue that 'a feature analysis of tense, mood, and case cannot be justified for early Indo-European, and that on the contrary there are good reasons to regard tense and mood as constituents rather than features on other constituents.' Specifically, he proposed that mood should be represented as an underlying adverbial constituent. The validity of the proposal is supported by the syntactic behavior of mood in Indo-European in the process of conjunction reduction. Kiparsky's theory has explanatory relevance beyond Chomsky's mere account of inflectional endings. But like Chomsky's it makes the claim that mood is an underlying primitive category, one which is not reducible to a function of other independently needed factors.

Syntactic-semantic considerations in the treatment of mood were first discussed by Robin Lakoff (1968:156) in conjunction with independent and dependent subjunctives in Latin. Drastically departing from earlier transformational accounts she posits that the meaning of subjunctive clauses and their syntactic and morphological behavior is defined by 'meaning-class' properties of the verb in the higher (matrix) sentence. Her account represents a formalization of time-honored views found in Latin and Romance manuals in the case of dependent subjunctives like:

(1a) cupio ne venias
      'I desire that you may not come'

(1b) timeo ut venias
      'I fear that you will come'

where verbs of 'wishing and desiring' especially cupio, opto, volo, malo, and verbs of 'fearing' like timeo, metuo, vereor, 'govern' the subjunctive in the embedded object clause. She generalizes the meaning-class concept to independent subjunctives like (2a-c)

venias
(2a) 'come, you should come [imperative]'

(2b) 'may you come [wish]'

(2c) 'you may come [possibility]'

by positing in this case abstract verbs of Command, Wish, Possibility which belong to the same meaning class as real verbs, but never appear in the surface structure. The virtue of this theory of

REFERENCE AND MOOD IN ITALIAN / 205

mood is that it accommodates in a single idea, within the explicit framework of a grammar of rules, the semantic distinctions passed down to us by earlier classicists: <u>coniunctivus potentialis</u>, <u>dubitativus</u>, <u>optativus</u>, <u>hortativus</u>, <u>concessivus</u>, etc. However, when we explore beyond this data we immediately realize that mood in Latin plays a much more extensive semantic role than Robin Lakoff discussed in her book. The subjunctive in fact distinguishes semantically different types of temporal, relative, and conditional clauses as in (3a–b), (4a–b), and (5a–b), respectively.

(3a) illo die, cum est lata lex de me
      'on that day when the law concerning me was passed'

(3b) cum equitatus noster in agros ejecerat
      'whenever our cavalry advanced into the field'

(4a) qui hoc dicit, errat
      'he who says this is mistaken'

(4b) qui hoc dicat, erret
      'he who should say this would be mistaken'

(5a) si hoc credis, erras
      'if you believe this you are mistaken'

(5b) si hoc dicas, erres
      'if you should say this you would be mistaken'

In these examples item (a) is in the indicative and item (b) is in the subjunctive. (3a) refers to a specific event in the past which actually took place. The day on which the law was passed is 'recorded' as far as the utterer is concerned, in the book of statutes and in his own mind. (3b), on the other hand, refers to an event in the past but not to any one specific cavalry action that one might find in campaign records. In (4a) the utterer has in mind an event in the very near past in which someone made a sort of pronouncement; (4b), on the other hand, refers to an event which is not identified as to any particular time, and consequently the relative pronoun refers to a set of possible people and not to any one in particular. Likewise in (5a) both protasis and apodosis are in the indicative, where it is implied that the utterer has factual evidence or is convinced that the person being addressed holds a certain belief. In item (5b), however, where both verbs are in the subjunctive, the sentence is not identified in the real world of space and time.

206 / MARIO SALTARELLI

Readily available data of this kind shows that the 'governed' theory of mood posited by earlier grammarians and extended and formalized by Robin Lakoff is descriptively inadequate in that it can account for only a subset of mood-antonymous sentences. Thus a characterization of the linguistic use of mood in Latin (and I shall claim in Romance as well) cannot be correctly captured by a meaning-class government theory.

Original semantic observations on Spanish mood by María Luisa Rivero (1971) constitute strong evidence that the 'government' theory must be abandoned even in the cases where it appeared to be on its firmest ground: the dependent clause. Sentences like (6a-c),

(6a) mi primo cree que Juan ganó

(6b) mi primo cree que Juan ganara

(6c) my cousin believes that Juan won

where (6c) is the usual English rendition of Spanish (6a) and (6b), show obviously that modern English has no inflectional mood distinction and most importantly that the subjunctive versus indicative distinction correlates neatly with a presuppositional semantic distinction. In (6a) the speaker conveys a 'positive' presupposition about the event described in the object clause que Juan ganó, i.e. the speaker believes the event to be true. Such is not the case in (6b). Within the framework of a 'governed' theory the only way to capture this semantic distinction with verbs like creer is to give it distinct underlying representations, but substantive arguments in support are not forthcoming.

In this paper I take the position that Rivero's observations about subjunctive v.s. indicative clauses correctly identify their semantic nature. My analysis of Italian will support the position that mood is a clause-propositional characteristic rather than a special constituent of that clause (Kiparsky 1968), a feature of a constituent of that clause (Chomsky 1965), or a feature of a constituent of the higher (matrix) clause. I shall further show that Rivero's presuppositional analysis is reducible to an extended concept of clause-propositional reference (and that the converse is not the case), and that a referential look at the semantic-syntactic behavior of clauses/propositions in discourse reveals that inflectional mood paradigms in Romance are only one reflection of a more comprehensive semantic phenomenon.

2. Mood Italian style. A cursory look at the use of the subjunctive inflection in Latin and modern Italian will show little correlation.

(7a) vale   'farewell'
      cura ut vales

(7b) sta sano

(8a) velim venias   'please come'
      fac venias

(8b) vieni

(9a) ne audeant   'may they not dare'

(9b) non osino

(10a) ne credideris   'do not believe'
      ne dubitaveritis   'do not doubt'

(10b) non credere
      non dubitate

(11a) utinam te videat   'would that I may see you'
      utinam te videret

(11b) voglia Iddio che ti veda
      volesse Iddio che ti vedesse

(12a) velim   'I would like'
      vellem

(12b) vorrei
      vorrei

(13a) oremus!   'let us pray!'

(13b) preghiamo!

(14a) sint haec falsa sane, . . .   'granting that they are false'

(14b) siano pure false
      benché siano false
      ammettiamo che siano false

(15a) quis dubitet?   'who would doubt?'

(15b) chi dubiterebbe?
       chi dubiterá?
       chi vorrá dubitare?

(16a) quid faciam?   'what shall I do?'

(16b) che devo fare?
       che fare?

The above examples (1-16) illustrate the Latin independent subjunctive (items a) and the corresponding Italian rendering (items b). The subjunctive is retained in the case of formal imperative (9), wish (11), and concessive (14), and is replaced in the other imperative forms (7, 8, 10), certain forms of wish (12), hortatory expressions (13), doubt (16), and possibility (15).

Examples (17-20) illustrate the Latin subjunctive in dependent clauses.

(17a) esse oportet ut vivas, non vivere ut edas

(17b) bisogna mangiare per vivere, non vivere per mangiare
       'one must eat to live, not live to eat'

(18a) nemo est tan senex qui se annum non putet posse vivere

(18b) nessuno è cosí vecchio da non credere di poter vivere un
       anno
       'nobody is so old as not to believe he could live one more
       year'

(19a) cum sis mortalis, quae mortalia sunt, cura noctu ambulabat
       Themistocles, quod somnum capere non posset

(19b) giacché sei mortale, cura le cose mortali
       Temistocle soleva camminare di notte, perché (diceva)
       non poteva dormire
       'since you are mortal, mind mortal things'
       'Themistocles used to walk at night, because he couldn't
       sleep'

(20a) Lysander cum vellet Lycurgi leges commutare, proibitus est

(20b) quando Lisandro voleva cambiare le leggi di Licurgo, non
       glielo permisero
       'when Lysander wanted to change Lycurgus' laws, he was
       prevented'

Expressions indicating purpose (17) and result (18) are rendered with
the infinitive, whereas cause (19) and time (20) use the indicative.
Notice, furthermore, that in (21) and (22) the Latin accusativus cum
infinitivo construction is replaced by a finite complement construction
thus resuscitating in Italian a subjunctive/indicative contrast which
did not exist in Latin.

(21a) scio te esse bonum   'I know that you are good'

(21b) so che tu sei buono

(22a) spero te valere   'I hope that you are well'

(22b) spero che tu stia bene

In comparing Latin subjunctive clauses in Italian the point which I
consider relevant to the scope of this paper is the apparently unrestricted variety of inflectional paradigms which replace the subjunctive yet conveying the same presuppositional semantic differences.
This suggests to me that the relation which unites the semantic characteristic of mood and its morphological inflection must be a very loose
one.   Evolutionary theories offer no principled explanations on why
the use of the subjunctive is much more stable in Spanish than it is in
Italian.   Note in particular

(23a) dile que se vaya   'tell him to leave'

(23b) digli di andarsene

(24a) se lo digo cuando venga   'I will tell him when(ever)
                                   he comes'
       se lo digo cuando viene   'I tell him when he comes'

(24b) glielo dico quando viene

that in indirect imperatives (23) Spanish wants a finite object clause
in the subjunctive where Italian requires an infinitival clause, and in
temporal clauses (24) Italian lacks the subjunctive/indicative opposition.   Yet Italian requires the subjunctive in the second term of comparative expressions (25) where Spanish does not.

(25a) es más alto de lo que creía   'he is taller than I thought'

(25b) è più alto di quanto credessi

The tentative conclusion I would like to draw at this moment is that semantic mood distinction is a clause-wide characteristic of all dependent clauses regardless of inflectional endings, and that the subjunctive/indicative correlations found in various degrees in Romance represent only one piece of systematic surface evidence for the phenomenon. The underlying semantic characterization of mood could not then be in terms of abstracted inflectional categories like the classical Imperative, Hortatory, Prohibitive, Deliberative, Concessive, Optative, Volitive, Potential, etc. types of subjunctive. It must be so since sentences of these types remain in the same semantic equivalence class regardless of the diachronic or dialectal inflectional mutations. Neither could the underlying semantic characterization of mood be in terms of the extended theory of 'government'. The meaning-class of predicates governing the subjunctive, it must be assumed, would have an erratic and unstable definition in order to capture the discrepant use of mood in Italian and Latin; and, more crucially, it could not account for the fact that in spite of morphological and syntactic evolution the utterances remain in the same semantic equivalence class. It seems to me that an accurate semantic characterization of mood can best be achieved by a formalization of the clause-wide semantic oppositions discovered by María Luisa Rivero. But how do you formalize presuppositional import in an explicit theory of language in a way that can be tested? The kind of presuppositional information that we are dealing with here is 'the speaker believes the complement clause (its cognitive information) to be true, or he holds no such belief'. In the next section I attempt to show that this kind of presupposition is reducible to an independently motivated clause-reference marking, thus eliminating the need for separate categorical structure.

3. Reference analysis.
Consider (26).

(26a) cerco una ragazza coni capelli biondi

(26b) cerco una ragazza che abbia i capelli biondi (Subj.)

(26c) cerco una ragazza che ha i capelli biondi (Ind.)
       'I am looking for a girl with blond hair'

(26a, b) and (26a, c) but not (26b, c) constitute semantically equivalent classes. That is, the nominal complement in (26a) <u>con i capelli biondi</u> is ambiguous between the subjunctive relative clause (26b) <u>che abbia i capelli biondi</u> and the indicative relative clause (26c) <u>che ha i capelli biondi.</u> They are in fact used in mutually exclusive discourse situations.

(27) cerco una ragazza con i capelli biondi

(27a) --perché i capelli neri stonano con il mio cappotto di cammello
       'because black hair doesn't match my camel coat'

(27b) --perché deve tingerseli neri
       'because she has to dye them black'

(27a) is a syntactically appropriate sequel to (26a), which can be replaced by the subjunctive form (26b) only. Likewise (27b) follows syntactically (26a), which is now replaced only by the indicative form (26c). The mutually exclusive use of the result clauses (27) indicates that the cognitive content of the object clauses in (26) (and not just the head noun or its determiner) may be interpreted in either one of two unique ways with different results in the everyday world of space and time. I shall informally characterize the semantically relevant distinction as follows:

(28) Given any clause (sentential or otherwise) in a linguistic situation, it will evoke an image which is either 'identified' or 'unidentified' in the world of space and time.

I believe that this distinction systematically correlates with the subjunctive versus indicative opposition, and guess that millennia of linguistic tradition focusing on inflectional regularities has shielded the grammarian's eye from the all-pervasive conversational nature of this semantic factor. As a first approximation, I would like to suggest that an appropriate formalization of (28) is in terms of clause/proposition referential indices, an extension of the independently motivated device discussed in Karttunen (1968, 1971). This means that, in the same manner that nouns and noun phrases must be referentially marked for cognitive-semantic reasons and consequent syntactic phenomena, propositional clauses describing events and images are also referentially marked in the underlying representation of utterances for the correct definition of conversational well-formedness discussed in connection with the unique sequencing of (26) and (27) and formulation of rules for assigning the desired inflectional form. Thus the underlying semantic structure of (26b) would differ from (26c) in that the object clause (and every other major clause in it) is 'unidentified' in the former but 'identified' in the latter.

Notice that there are cooccurrence restrictions for this referential category, determining well-formedness as well as the application of syntactic rules. In (29a-b)

(29a) cerco una ragazza con cui giocare
                          possa giocare
                          *devo giocare
    'I am looking for a girl with whom to play'

(29b) cerco una ragazza con cui devo giocare
                          *possa giocare
                          *giocare
    'I am looking for a girl with whom I am supposed to play'

ragazza and cui are not only understood as coreferential in (29a) they must both be referentially 'unidentified' and in (29b) they must be both 'identified', which means that a feature of referential 'identification' plus a function of identity are basic to relative clause formation and their semantic well-formedness. Observe further that the referential feature I am proposing also controls syntactic rules of infinitive formation and modal verb choice.

Another argument in support of a referential identification feature is offered by the behavior of the so-called 'personal a' in Spanish, whereby personal or personalized direct objects are introduced by the particle a.

(30a) fueron a buscar un médico experimentado que conociera
       bien las enfermedades del país.
       'They went to look for an experienced doctor who would
       know well the diseases of the country.'

(30b) fueron a buscar a un médico extranjero, que gozaba de
       una gran reputación.
       'They went to look for a foreign doctor who enjoyed a
       great reputation.'

We see in (30) (data from Ramsey 1956:43) that it is not the case that every personal object takes the particle a. Rather it is used only with referentially identified personal objects, as corroborated by the use of the subjunctive versus the indicative in their relative clauses. The semantic conclusion one can draw is that personification is here intended by the language user as one particular being, as opposed to a class of them.

As in Latin and Spanish, Italian uses the subjunctive in predicate complement constructions like (31-33), but to a lesser extent and in a different way.

(31a) credo di essere stanco (Inf.)
       credo che (io) sono stanco (Ind.)
       *credo che (io) sia stanco (Subj.)
       'I think I am tired'

(31b) credo che (tu) sia stanco (Subj.)
       credo che (tu) sei stanco (Ind.)
       *credo di essere stanco (Inf.)
       'I think you are tired'

Comparing sentences (31a) and (31b) we notice a syntactically curious fact. (31a) can be expressed in the infinitive and in the indicative but not in the subjunctive, (31b) can be expressed in the subjunctive and in the indicative but not in the infinitive. In other words, the subjunctive and the infinitive exclude each other. For reasons analogous to Rivero's (1971:306) insightful observations in Spanish, the selection of the subjunctive versus indicative mood distinction cannot be attributed, without artificiality, to the subordinating verb <u>credere</u>. If we turn our attention to the referential identification characteristics of the complement clauses we see that in (31a) the indicative as well as the infinitive construction of the predicate 'being tired' conveys a reality positively identified as a fact of the real world by the utterer. In (31b) on the other hand, the subjunctive and the indicative constructions of the predicate 'being tired' conveys a conviction that it is a fact in the latter case but only a possibility in the former. What still needs to be explained is why the subjunctive is not possible in (31a) and why the infinitive is not possible in (31b). The explanation is to be found in the fact that the complement clause is in the same person as the utterer in (31a) but not in (31b). In (31a) an 'unidentified' (subjunctive) construction would lead to a natural contradiction. How could the speaker waver as to his own 'being tired'? At any given moment he is positively either tired or not tired or somewhere in between, even if only 'fuzzily' identified. The reason for the lack of the infinitival construction has to do with the blocking of the operation of the set of rules responsible for infinitive formation. These rules involve (recoverable) deletion of the subject of the complement clause, pruning and predicate raising. In (31a) the infinitival construction is possible because the only (naturally) logical interpretation is one of 'identified reference'.

In (31b), on the other hand, the speaker has no control over the identified/unidentified nature of the complement. Therefore either

the subjunctive or the indicative is a possibility. The infinitival construction is not possible in this case because the definite subject pronoun deletion would not be recoverable. I wish to emphasize that it
is not the unidentified reference (or Rivero's noncommittal presupposition) that blocks infinitive formation in Italian. Cases like (32)
illustrate this phenomenon.

(32a) dille di andarsene
       dille che se ne andasse/vada
       'tell her to leave'

(32b) dígale que se vaya
       *dígale irse

I have shown that verbs like credere, and the impersonal sembra
'it seems' cooccur either with unidentified or identified complements.
There are verbs of wish, command, doubt, like volere, ordinare,
dubitare, etc. which can only cooccur with unidentified complements,
and verbs of factual knowledge like sapere, scrivere, etc. which can
obviously cooccur only with identified complements, as can be observed in (33).

(33a) vuole che le truppe se ne vadano
       'he wishes that the troops leave'

       ordina ai soldati di sparare
       'he tells the soldiers to shoot'

       dubito che se ne andranno vadano
       'I doubt they will leave'

(33b) sa che Maria è arrivata
       *sa che Maria sia arrivata
       'he knows that Mary arrived'

       scrive che è piovuto
       *scrive che sia piovuto
       'he writes that it rained'

It should be obvious that the class of verbs that cooccur with
'unidentified' complements must not be confused with the list of
verbs that cooccur with the subjunctive. One can say in most cases
that the latter will be a subset of the former. The membership of
that list may vary widely in modern Italian, depending on the dialectal background, the social-professional-economic status, and the

amount of textbook instruction one has received. A study was conducted in Rome's <u>scuole medie</u> (grades 6, 7, and 8) to test the use of the subjunctive. It turned out that the list membership increased with each higher grade of schooling. We inferred that the subjunctive is used in everyday language much less than the school tradition prescribes.

The extensive use of the Latin independent clause subjunctive has been only minimally retained in Italian, as we discussed in connection with examples (7-16). Within the framework of the referential theory that I am proposing, there is no theoretical need for hypothesizing abstract verbs as required by R. Lakoff's governed theory of mood, whose empirical validity has been placed in serious jeopardy by Rivero's (1971) presuppositional observations. Those clauses remain correctly characterized as 'referentially unidentified', as in the case of the subordinate clauses which we have just discussed.

Consider furthermore temporal, spatial, and if-clauses in (33a-e):

(33a) glielo dico quando viene
       *glielo dico quando venga
       'I'll tell him when he comes'

       ti scrivo dove dici (tu)
       *ti scrivo dove dica/dirai
       'I'll write where you say'

(33b) glielo dico quando viene/verrá
       *glielo dico quando venga
       'I'll tell him whenever he comes'

       ti scrivo dovunque (tu) dica/dirai
       *ti scrivo dovunque (tu) dici
       'I'll write wherever you say'

(33c) se prendi l'autostrada, arriva prima
       'If you take the toll road, you'll get there faster'

(33d) se prendessi l'autostrada, arriveresti prima
       'If you took the toll road you would get there faster'

(33e) se non piovesse, andremmo in campagna
       'If it didn't rain, we'd go to the country'

(33a) and (33b) are identified and unidentified time and space clauses. They behave semantically and, Michael Geis (1970) wants to argue, syntactically like relative clauses. Notice, in fact, that in (34)

(34a) --ma non so quando (viene)
'but I don't know when'

--ma non so dove (dici)
'but I don't know where'

(34b) --che è domani mattina
'which is tomorrow morning'

--che è Bloomington, Ind.
'which is Bloomington, Ind.'

(34a) and (34b) would be a dishonest sequel to (33a) and (33b), respectively. Only (33a)-(34b) and (33b)-(34a) would be acceptable matchings. In (33c) the se clause is not hypothetical, but a necessary/ positive prerequisite to get there faster, a confirmed reality in today's world of the automobile. In (33d, e) the protasis describes a hypothetical occurrence. The speaker knows that the content is not 'identified' in the real world: the driver decided not to take the toll road and it is raining.

Let us look finally at the use of the subjunctive in comparative clauses.

(35a) è più alta di quanto tu creda
'she is taller than you think'

è più alta di quanto tu credessi
'she is taller than you thought'

è più alta di quanto egli creda
'she is taller than he thinks'

è più alta di quanto egli credesse
'she is taller than he thought'

*è più alta di quanto io creda
*'she is taller than I think'

è più alta di quanto io credessi
'she is taller than I thought'

(35b) è alta quanto tu credi
'she is as tall as you think'

è alta quanto tu credevi
'she is as tall as you thought'

è alta quanto egli crede
'she is as tall as he thinks'

è alta quanto egli credeva
'she is as tall as he thought'

*è alta quanto credo
*'she is as tall as I think'

è alta quanto credevo
'she is as tall as I thought'

There are two puzzling points in the paradigm (35). First, what is the explanation for the subjunctive in the comparison of 'majority' and the indicative in the comparison of 'equality'? Second, why is there a gap in Italian as well as in English in the case of the first person present forms?

The answer to the first question follows directly from the referential theory I have proposed. The second term of comparison in (35a) is referentially unidentified. Since the utterer is asserting a degree of height greater than the degree of height believed by the subject of the second terms, he knows for a fact that the latter proposition is not a fact of the real world; consequently the subjunctive is used. In (35b), on the other hand, the second terms of comparison is referentially identified, and therefore the indicative is used. In fact, the utterer is now asserting a degree of height equal to the degree of height believed by the subject of the second term, he knows then that this proposition refers to a fact of the real world.

The answer to the second question follows from the logical principles of contradiction and tautology. Its resolution supports further the proposed theory of clause/propositional referential marking. The grammatical gap in (a) represented a cognitive-semantic contradiction, and therefore not used in natural language. The utterer would be asserting (and therefore believe to be true) one proposition and at the same time believe that a different one is also true, an unbearable cognitive-semantic strain. (I dedicate this argument to the primordial honesty of the human mind, before it entered politics). In a similar way in (b), the same two propositions create a cognitive-semantic tautology in a comparison of equality, and therefore the construction is not used in natural languages.

218 / MARIO SALTARELLI

4. Conclusions. I have shown that an analysis of mood is not co-
extensive with an analysis of the subjunctive versus the indicative.
Rather the subjunctive-indicative is just one, though systematic, surface reflection of an all-pervasive clause/propositional phenomenon.
Complement clauses evoke images in the mind of the speaker which
are either 'identified' or 'unidentified' in the world of space and time.
It is suggested that this semantic characteristic of propositions (I
believe also correctly observed by María Luisa Rivero) with conversational as well as syntactic consequences is best formalized in terms
of the independently motivated mechanism of referential indices.

REFERENCES

Chomsky, N. 1965. Aspects of the theory of syntax. Cambridge:
MIT Press.
Geiss, M. 1970. Time prepositions as underlying verbs. Papers
from the Sixth CLS Meeting. 235-49.
Karttunen, L. 1968. What do referential indices refer to? Mimeo-
graphed.
_____. 1971. The logic of predicate complement constructions.
Mimeographed.
Kiparsky, P. 1968. Tense and mood in Indo-European syntax.
Foundations of Language. 4.30-57.
Lakoff, R. 1968. Abstract syntax and Latin complementation.
Cambridge: MIT Press.
Ramsey, M. M. 1956. A textbook of modern Spanish. Revised by
R. K. Spaulding. New York, Holt, Rinehart and Winston.
Rivero, M. L. 1971. Mood and presupposition in Spanish.
Foundations of Language. 7.305-36.

IN CHAOS OR INCHOATIVE?
AN ANALYSIS OF INCHOATIVES
IN MODERN STANDARD ITALIAN[1]

DONNA J. NAPOLI

Harvard University

1.0 The problem

Many instances of clitic reflexive pronouns which do not involve reflexivity occur in various languages, among them Italian. The particular use of such pronouns studied here is seen in (1):

(1) Io mi ammalai. 'I got sick.'
    Roberto si ammalò. 'Robert got sick.'

These sentences, unlike reflexive sentences, cannot be derived from a deep structure with two coreferential NP, one in subject and the other in object position, since such a structure does not express the meaning of (1) nor is it even grammatical:

(2) *Io ammalai me. 'I sickened me.'
    *Roberto ammalò Roberto. 'Robert sickened Robert.'

Such sentences have been called inchoatives with various meanings assigned to the term, such as 'changes of state', 'inceptiveness', and predicates which are 'experienced' by the subject rather than 'emanating' from that subject. These definitions, while they describe semantic features common to many verbs that can appear in inchoative structures, are not precise standards for judging whether or not a sentence is inchoative. For example, cadere 'fall' and raffreddare 'chill' may both be used with subjects that 'experience'

219

the predicate, cominciare 'begin' and iniziare 'initiate' both involve 'inceptiveness', aumentare 'increase' and congelare 'freeze' both describe 'changes of state', yet in all these pairs the first verb cannot appear with reflexive pronouns but the second can. Instead of such semantic features, we will define inchoatives by their syntactic properties. We argue that the reflexive pronouns of (1) are transformationally introduced, that the surface subject of (1) originates in deep object position and the deep subject node is empty, and that there is a rule moving the deep object into subject position and leaving behind a copy, thus creating the structural description for the transformational rule REFLEXIVE.

1.1 Phrase structure rules versus REFLEXIVE. The clitics seen in (1) have a full paradigm for person and number:

(3) Io mi ammalai. 'I got sick.'
    Tu ti ammalasti. 'You got sick.'
    Lui si ammalò. 'He got sick.'
    Noi ci ammalammo. 'We got sick.'
    Voi vi ammalaste. 'You (all) got sick.'
    Loro si ammalarono. 'They got sick.'

The surface subject of such sentences may be either gender (cf. Lei/Lui si ammalò 'She/He got sick'). In composite tenses the auxiliary used is essere (cf. Maria si è svegliata 'Mary woke up'). Past participles agree in person, number, and gender with the clitic, which in turn so agrees with the surface subject. In inchoatives embedded under fare 'make' and lasciare 'let' (among other verbs), the clitic does not appear (cf. Ho fatto ammalar (*si) Giorgio 'I made George sick'), just as the reflexive pronoun does not so appear (cf. Ho fatto graffiar (*si) Giorgio 'I made George scratch himself').

This clitic may be introduced by one of two means: a transformational rule or a phrase structure rule (PS-rule). If it is introduced by a T, that T must be cyclic in order to account for its occurring before the cyclic rule of Equi-NP Deletion in a sentence such as:

(4) Mi ha pregato di ammalarmi prima del matrimonio. [2]
    'He begged me to get sick before the wedding.'

If the clitic of inchoatives is introduced by a PS-rule, this rule must have the form:

(5a) $S \rightarrow NP$ clitic VP[3]

That clitic is not free; it must match the subject for person, number, and gender:

(5b) S → NP $\begin{bmatrix} \alpha\,\text{person} \\ \beta\,\text{number} \\ \gamma\,\text{gender} \end{bmatrix}$ clitic $\begin{bmatrix} \alpha\,\text{person} \\ \beta\,\text{number} \\ \gamma\,\text{gender} \end{bmatrix}$ VP

But again not all possible clitics are allowed, since for a third person masculine singular subject, for example, the possible clitics are gli (dative), lo (accusative), and si (reflexive), but only si is acceptable. Thus we have:

(5c) S → NP$_i$ reflexive pronoun$_i$ VP

But now there are two rules producing reflexive pronouns: the PS-rule (5c) and the T REFLEXIVE (which we do not discuss in detail here, but which, in brief, converts the second of two coreferential NP within the same simplex S into a reflexive pronoun, and applies cyclically). Since any grammar with two mechanisms to produce one form (in this case, reflexive pronouns) is costly, we wish to eliminate one mechanism: precisely the PS-rule, since its use is limited to inchoatives while REFLEXIVE applies to reflexive as well as inchoative structures. We note that REFLEXIVE adequately accounts for all the features of these clitics noted above. What is more, the PS-rule presents the problem of accounting for the inadmissibility of the clitic with simple verbs having no accusative, dative, or prepositional object (cf. *Si va(nno), *Si sbadiglia(no)) in a non ad hoc manner. However, REFLEXIVE does not encounter this problem, since REFLEXIVE applies only when the VP contains some NP (whether accusative, dative, or object of a preposition). There is, however, one major disadvantage of REFLEXIVE not found with the PS-rule: it must account for the inadmissibility of non-clitics in inchoatives (*Roberto ammalò sé) in some non-obvious way, while the PS-rule generates only clitics. We will offer an explanation using REFLEXIVE which does account for this property.

1.2 The embedded S proposal. Lakoff (1965) and Roldán (1971) have proposed that inchoatives have an embedded sentence subject, which is a stative sentence, and an abstract matrix verb:

(6)

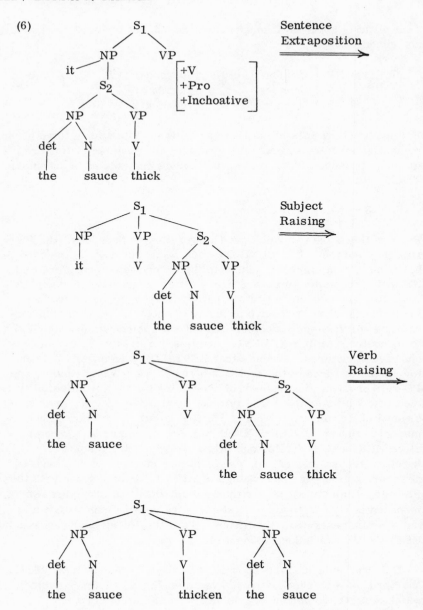

Sentence
Extraposition
⟹

Subject
Raising
⟹

Verb
Raising
⟹

Surface Structure:
<u>The sauce thickens.</u>

Presumably the foundation for this analysis is based on the semantic property of 'change of state'. No syntactic evidence for the embedding is given, however, and there is evidence that such embedding is doubtful. First, there are no T's which may apply on S_2. This could be explained if Lakoff's Verb Raising were precyclic, thus destroying the S_2 node and therefore the S_2 cycle. However, Verb Raising cannot be precyclic since Lakoff orders it after the two cyclic rules Sentence Extraposition and Subject Raising. Second, Fodor (1970) has shown that when two verbs are present in a given deep structure and both are semantically compatible with time adverbs, we should be able to have two adverbs in that structure, one referring to each verb. In inchoatives both the state (the lower verb) and the change (the abstract matrix verb) are semantically compatible with time adverbs. Yet we never find two such adverbs in inchoatives (cf. *Alle otto il ghiaccio si è fuso per due ore 'At eight o'clock the ice melted for two hours').

1.3 The simplex S proposal. Since there is syntactic evidence against embedding, and since the surface form of inchoatives is simplex, we propose a simplex S source for inchoatives. Within this S we must determine the roles of the surface constituents. We noted with (2) above that the deep structure for inchoatives cannot have coreferential subject and object for semantic considerations. Syntactically, as well, such a structure is inadequate. We see in (7a) below that were we to accept such a deep structure, the selectional restrictions on the subject of infiammare are allowed to be violated in NP_i V NP_j precisely when i=j. This explanation is not only ad hoc, it also is not true for other reflexive structures such as Giorgio si guarda ('George looks at himself'), where the selectional restrictions may not be violated (*La carta si guarda 'The paper looks at itself'). Instead we propose an analysis explaining the above facts naturally.

1.3.1 The surface subject: The deep object. That the surface subject originates in deep object position can be argued on three counts: (1) the surface subject is the logical object, (2) most verbs found in inchoatives require objects when used actively and non-inchoatively, and (3) the selectional restrictions on the object of an active non-inchoative verb and on the surface subject of this same verb used in an inchoative sentence are very similar (if not identical).

First, when talking of 'logical' roles we are not referring to any precise criteria, since we know of none. Instead, we mean simply that the NP il fieno has the same relationship to the V infiammare 'ignite' in (7a), an inchoative, as it has in (7b), an active non-inchoative sentence:

(7a) Il fieno si infiammò.
      'The hay caught fire.'

(7b) Il fiammifero infiammò il fieno.
      'The match ignited the hay.'

We would be missing a generalization if we failed to generate il fieno 'the hay' from the same underlying source in both (7a) and (7b). While the source of il fieno in (7a) is at issue, we can rely on the most common derivation of active sentences to derive il fieno in (7b) from underlying object position.

Second, most verbs which appear in inchoatives cannot appear in active non-inchoative intransitive sentences:

(8a) (inchoative) La porta si è aperta.
      'The door opened.'

(8b) (active, non-inchoative) Ho aperto la porta.
      'I opened the door.'

(8c) (active, non-inchoative) *Ho aperto.
      'I opened.'

We can explain (8b) and (8c) by subcategorizing aprire in the lexicon as occurring in the frame [. . . ___ +NP . . .], that is, as requiring an object. Since aprire in (8a) has the same meaning as in (8b), that of changing the state of some NP from (more nearly) closed to open, we assume that aprire is the same lexical item in all of (8). Thus, aprire requires a deep object in (8a) as well as in (8b). The only candidates are la porta and si. But we have already argued (in 1.1) that si is transformationally introduced, thus there must be some NP underlying si. The only possible NP is la porta. We are led to the conclusion that la porta must be the deep object of aprire in (8a).[4]

Third, consider the following sentences:

(9a) *Sveglio il rumore.
      'I wake the noise.'

(9b) Il rumore mi sveglia.
      'The noise wakes me.'

(9c) *Il rumore si sveglia.
      'The noise wakes up.'

(9d) Apro la porta.
      'I open the door.'

(9e) *La porta apre la scatola.
      'The door opens the box.'

(9f) La porta si apre.
      'The door opens.'

Svegliare in active non-inchoative sentences accepts inanimate subjects but rejects inanimate objects. However, in inchoatives it rejects inanimate surface subjects. Aprire in active non-inchoative
sentences accepts inanimate non-instrumental objects, but rejects
such subjects. However, in inchoatives it accepts inanimate non-
instrumental surface subjects. In both cases the selectional restrictions on the surface subject of inchoatives are the same as those on
the object of the same verbs used in active non-inchoative sentences.
Again, in order to explain this fact the grammar must derive surface
subjects of inchoatives from the same underlying source as surface
objects of active non-inchoatives. Assuming that the active non-
inchoative sentences above have surface roles of constituents very
similar to deep roles, we derive the surface subjects of inchoatives
from underlying object position.

1.3.2 The deep subject. Looking at an inchoative such as (7a),
we have already argued that il fieno originates in object position but
not in both object and subject position. Since there are no NP other
than il fieno and si in the surface structure of (7a), we have no obvious candidate for the deep subject. In fact, we argue that there is
no deep subject and cite as evidence restrictions on instrumental
phrases, manner adverbs, and purpose clauses:

(10a) Il fieno si infiammò per il fulmine.
       'The hay caught fire because of the lightening.'

(10b) *Il fieno si infiammò deliberatamente.
       'The hay caught fire deliberately.'

(10c) *Il fieno si infiammò per spaventare la mamma. [5]
       'The hay caught fire in order to scare mommy.'

In (10a) we have an instrumental per-phrase which cannot cooccur in
an S with an agentive NP (cf. *Carla infiammò il fieno per il fulmine).
The fact that per il fulmine can occur in (10a) supports the claim
that there is no agentive NP in the deep structure. [6] In (10b) the

manner adverbial <u>deliberatamente</u> cannot occur without an animate agentive NP (cf. *<u>Il fulmine infiammò il fienc deliberatamente</u> but <u>Carla infiammò il fieno deliberatamente</u>). Thus (10b) must not have an animate agentive NP in deep structure. Likewise, in (10c), we have a purpose clause which requires an animate agentive NP as its own subject, and therefore as some constituent of the higher S (since its own subject has been deleted by Equi-NP Deletion under identity with some NP in the matrix). The unacceptability of (10c) is due precisely to the lack of just such an NP.

While the facts shown in (10) illustrate only that no agentive NP can be present in the deep structure, we can conclude that no subject is present in the deep structure since the verbs which may appear in inchoative sentences (for a partial list see Section 3 below), if they have deep subjects, require agentive subjects.

2.0 A solution

We have argued thus far that inchoatives employ REFLEXIVE, that they have a simplex deep structure, that their deep subject node is empty, and that their surface subject originates in deep object position. We need an analysis which will move the deep object into subject position and create the structural description for REFLEXIVE. We propose the following deep structure and analysis:

(11) Surface: Roberto si ammala facilmente.
      Deep: ammalare facilmente Roberto.

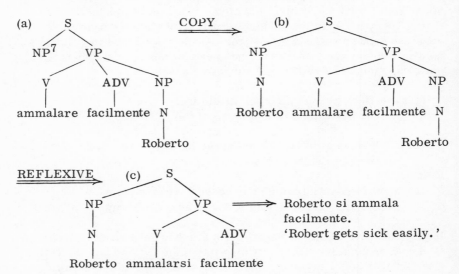

The deep structure in (11a) follows from the discussion in Section 1 above. The transition from (11b) to (11c) to surface structure presents no new theoretical problems. The only step to be clarified is the one from (11a) to (11b), labeled COPY.

2.1 COPY. There are two logical possibilities for the internal mechanism of COPY: either it merely copies the object into subject position, or it moves the object into subject position leaving behind a copy. Many linguists have proposed copy rules for similar constructions (Langacker 1970, Fillmore 1968), but no one to my knowledge has specified exactly how the rules work. We assume the position that COPY has two parts: movement and copy. There are two reasons for this. First, the verbs which can appear in inchoatives in various languages seem to form a (very) rough semantic class. Therefore, we would like to offer an analysis which will be applicable with minor variations to languages other than Italian. Looking at the English inchoative construction, we note that it does not occur with reflexive pronouns (John awoke, Mary got sick, The door opened). Lakoff (1965) has claimed that the sentences in (12) are inchoatives:

(12a) John hurt himself when he fell down.

(12b) John dirtied himself.

From this data Lakoff claims that the reflexive does appear, though rarely, in some inchoatives in English. However, (12) does not present inchoatives, but rather real reflexives. We can see this by noting that if the context explicitly excludes the possibility of reflexivity, the reflexive pronoun cannot occur:

(13a) *John hurt himself when a tree fell on him.

(13b) *John dirtied himself when Mary poured coffee on him.

    (cf. John got hurt when a tree . . .
    John got dirty when Mary . . .)

The reflexive clitic of inchoatives in Romance, however, does not imply the possibility of true reflexivity:

(14a) Giovanni si fece male quando un albero cadde su di lui.

(14b) Giovanni si sporcò quando Maria versò del caffè su di lui.

228 / DONNA J. NAPOLI

Given these facts, there is no evidence that English has a copy at any stage in the derivation of an inchoative S. Thus inchoative in English probably involves a simple movement rule. If Italian COPY is a movement rule plus a copy formation, the Italian derivation differs from the English by only one step, the extra copy formation.

Second, there are other instances of copies in Italian, and all of them are coordinated with movement rules. For example:

(15) (Left Dislocation) Tua sorella, lei è andata in cerca di guai.
'Your sister, she went looking for trouble.'

(Right Dislocation) L'ho vista proprio qui, tua sorella!
'I saw her right here, your sister.'

(Focus on verb) Il cane lo sento (, ma non lo vedo).
'I hear the dog, but I do not see it.'

Certainly the examples of (15) suggest many questions about focusing and topicalization which cannot be answered here. It suffices our purposes to note that all copies in Italian are associated with movement rules (although not all movement rules call for copies). Thus, if COPY is a movement rule as well as a copy rule, it is consistent with the other data we know about copies.

2.2 The explanatory power of this analysis

2.2.1 Intransitive versus transitive. In the opening of this paper we noted that cadere does not appear in inchoatives, but raffreddare does. We now have a ready explanation: cadere is an intransitive verb (cf. Maria cade (*il fazzoletto)), thus it cannot appear in the deep structure (11a); raffreddare, on the other hand, is a transitive verb, (cf. Il ghiaccio raffredda l'acqua), therefore it can appear in (11a).

2.2.2 Complex versus simplex. In Section 1.0 we noted also that cominciare does not appear in inchoatives, but iniziare does. From studies done by Perlmutter (1970) and Newmeyer (1970), we assume that cominciare can appear in only two deep structures: an intransitive one with a sentential NP subject, and a transitive one with a sentential NP object. Let us consider the following two sentences:

(16a) La lezione (*si) comincia alle nove.

(16b) La lezione si inizia alle nove.
'The lesson begins at 9 o'clock.'

From arguments in Perlmutter (1970) we conclude that active sentences with <u>cominciare</u> whose subject is inanimate must have the former deep structure; that is, a sentential NP subject. The possible deep structures for (16a) are:

(17a)

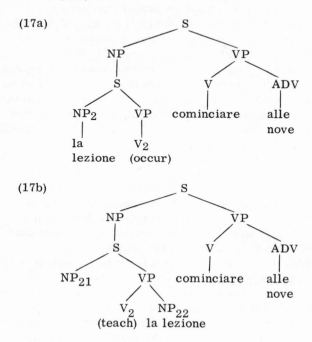

(17b)

The difference between (17a) and (17b) is the role the NP <u>la lezione</u> plays in the embedded S. (Note that V_2 in both structures could be filled by many verbs. There is a transformation which deletes V_2. See Newmeyer (1970), Ross (1973), and Karttunen (1968) for justification of this kind of V deletion.) If (17a) is the correct deep structure, V_2 deletes and NP_2 raises into subject position. COPY never applies so we do not get a reflexive pronoun in surface structure. If (17b) is the correct deep structure, NP_{22} moves into the empty NP_{21} node, leaving a copy (by COPY); REFLEXIVE applies putting a reflexive clitic on V_2; then V_2 deletes along with its clitic. At this point the derived lower subject raises into matrix subject position and again we are left with no reflexive pronoun in surface structure.

Iniziare, on the other hand, is a transitive verb which easily falls into the deep structure of (11a). Thus, (16b) has the regular inchoative derivation.

2.2.3 No copy. A third pair of verbs noted in the opening of this paper is <u>aumentare</u> and <u>congelare</u>; the former allows no reflexive pronouns, the latter does. One basic difference between them is that noted between <u>cadere</u> and <u>raffreddare</u> in 2.2.1 above: <u>aumentare</u> can appear in intransitive sentences (<u>La folla aumenta</u> 'the crowd grows'), while <u>congelare</u> requires a transitive frame (<u>Il vento mi congela</u> 'the wind freezes me'). However, <u>aumentare,</u> unlike <u>cadere,</u> is not restricted to intransitive frames (cf. <u>Lo stato aumenta le tasse</u> 'The state increases the taxes'). There are at least two possible analyses for this behavior. Either <u>aumentare</u> is listed in the lexicon as occurring in both transitive and intransitive frames, or one of the frames is basic and the other is transformationally derived. A drawback of the first analysis is that it fails to predict the fact that the selectional restrictions on the object of <u>aumentare</u> used transitively and on its subject used intransitively are the same.

The second analysis could easily handle this fact by saying either that (1) the transitive form is basic and the intransitive is derived from it by movement of the object into subject position, or (2) the intransitive form is basic and the transitive one is derived from it by movement of the subject into object position. Both solutions have problems. The first must explain why, if <u>aumentare</u> appears in transitive deep frames, it does not undergo COPY when no deep subject is present (cf. <u>La folla (*si) aumenta</u>). <u>Aumentare</u> will have to be marked as an exception to the part of COPY that leaves a copy. The second solution calls for some complex structure in order to account for the appearance of a subject in the surface form of transitive sentences. The subject would originate as the matrix subject; the matrix verb would be an abstract cause verb; and the matrix object would be the intransitive sentence with <u>aumentare</u>:

(18)

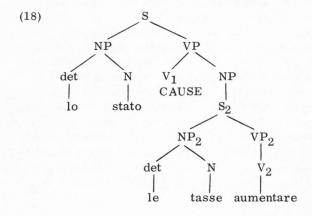

NP_2 would move to the right of VP_2 under S_2 and V_2 would then be incorporated into V_1 by some sort of verb raising. (This is similar to Lakoff's (1965) analysis of causatives; however, he would make S_2 complex, as well, having a stative sentence as its subject and an abstract verb INCHOATIVE as its predicate. (See (6) above.)) While this analysis explains the non-occurrence of reflexive clitics with aumentare, (18) does not seem to me to reflect the semantic value of the sentence. In my understanding of Italian aumentare, and of the English counterpart, increase, there is a true transitive reading not described by the causative structure of (18).

Which analysis is correct cannot be determined without a thorough discussion of the nature of transitive and intransitive structures, a discussion which would carry us beyond the scope of this paper.

2.2.4 Variations. There are some inchoative sentences in which the reflexive clitic is optional:

(19a) La gelateria (si) chiude troppo presto.

and, in some varieties of Italian,

(19b) La lezione (si) inizia alle nove.

There appears to be a strong correlation between these facts and the phenomenon of Unspecified NP Deletion (UNPD). (This is the rule which deletes unspecified objects of verbs such as mangiare, Mangio alle otto, but not tagliare, *Taglio prima di cena. Which verbs undergo UNPD is probably an idiosyncratic fact to be handled in the lexicon (see Chomsky 1965:87).) We see that chiudere is marked (-UNPD):

(20) *Chiudiamo molto lentamente. (cf. Mangiamo molto presto.)
     'We close very slowly.'   'We eat very early.'

except in one of its lexical meanings, that of closing a store:

(21) Chiudiamo (il negozio) alle trè.
     'We close (the store) at 3 o'clock.'

Likewise, it requires the reflexive clitic with inchoatives:

(22) La porta si chiude.
     *La porta chiude.
     'The door closes.'

However, here again with the lexical meaning of closing a store it is
an exception, optionally appearing with the reflexive clitic, as in
(19a).

Likewise, in most varieties of Italian, iniziare is (-UNPD) (cf.
*Iniziamo 'Let's initiate') and requires a reflexive clitic in inchoatives
(cf. *La lezione inizia). However, in at least one variety of Italian
iniziare is (+UNPD) (cf. Iniziamo!) and in this variety iniziare may
optionally take a reflexive clitic in inchoatives, as in (19b).

It appears that, while the optional rule deleting the NP underlying
the reflexive clitic may not be identical to UNPD, it is at least correlated with this rule. Since UNPD is a rule applying only to transitive
verbs, we have one more fact consistent with the analysis in (11).

2.2.5 No non-clitic form. One problem our analysis must explain
is why we never find a non-clitic form for the reflexives of inchoatives
(*Roberto ammala sé). First, we must note that non-clitic object pronouns occur usually only[8] when they are assigned stress or contrast.
Since stress and contrast are of primary importance to the meaning
of a sentence, we assume that such features are present in the deepest level of any linguistic structure. In Italian, when an NP with contrast is moved, the contrast goes with it (using intonation as a signal
for contrast, we have underlined the element receiving the highest
intonation peak):

(23a) Vedo il cane, non il gatto.
 'I see the dog, not the cat.'

(23b) Il cane vedo, non il gatto.
 'The dog I see, not the cat.'

Let us now look at an inchoative sentence which has contrast in it:

(24) Roberto si ammala più spesso di Maria.
 'Robert gets sick more often than Mary.'

At some point, the underlying structure for (24) is:

(25a)

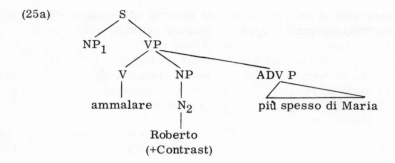

(We do not detail the underlying structure for the comparative clause since the structure of comparatives is not at issue here.) COPY moves N_2 into the NP_1 node, taking the feature of contrast with it, and leaving behind a copy:

(25b)

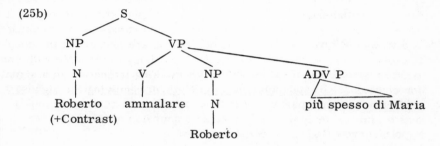

REFLEXIVE applies generating only clitic reflexives, since the derived NP object can never have the features of contrast or emphasis.

3.0 Inventory

A list of verbs which can occur in the inchoative derivation shown in (11) would include the following but certainly would include many others as well:

(26a)

accorciare	annebbiare
accumulare	annoiare
addormentare	annuvolare
adirare	arrabbiare
allungare	arricchire
ammalare	assopire
ammansare	atterrire
ammorbidire	

(26b) illanguidire   infiammare
       impadronire   ingrassare
       impaurire   innamorare
       impazientire   intiepidire
       impermalire   invogliare
       impoverire   irritare
       incollerire   istupidire
       inerpicare

(26c) agitare   gonfiare
       alterare   guarire
       amareggiare   meravigliare
       commuovere   offendere
       disgustare   rafforzare
       disinteressare   rattristare
       divertire   spaventare
       emozionare

4.0 Extensions

The phenomenon of inchoative is not isolated. Middle voice sentences such as Gli appartamenti in quella zona della città si affittano molto presto 'The apartments in that area of town rent very quickly' have a similar analysis. For further discussion of this point see Napoli Furrow (1973).

5.0 Conclusion

We have shown that inchoative is a productive syntactic process of Italian. The deep structure of inchoative sentences is a simplex S with an empty subject node (or no subject node at all); the surface subject originates in deep object position; and REFLEXIVE produces the proper clitic after COPY has moved the object NP into subject position and formed a copy.

NOTES

[1] I would like to thank Paolo Valesio, Dwight Bolinger, Michael Freeman, David Nasjleti, Judith Aissen, and Emily Norwood for their suggestions and criticisms.

[2] It is also logically possible that this T is pre-cyclic. However, it must be ordered after at least one other pre-cyclic rule, that of Predicate Raising (PR) found with matrix verbs such as fare, lasciare, and optionally with many verbs of perception (see Aissen 1972). Since there are very few pre-cyclic rules known and since the question of

pre-cyclic rules being ordered with respect to each other has not even been posed, it would be very surprising if this rule were both pre-cyclic and ordered after PR. Also, such an ordering has many of the disadvantages of the PS-rule discussed below.

[3]Actually, the proper PS-rule is VP → Clitic V (NP) (NP) (ADV) etc., since the clitic is attached to the V, not to the VP. However, this PS-rule has the same disadvantages as (5) in the text above.

[4]Note that we have already discarded the possibility that la porta is both deep subject and deep object of aprire (cf. (2) and (7)).

[5]In (10) as in all other examples in this paper, the surface subject must be read as a nominative. A test for such a reading is pronominalization, where cases are overly marked. If, instead of nominative, the initial NP is read as an accusative in (10), we have a different structure from inchoatives, the indefinite si structure. For a discussion of indefinite si sentences, see Napoli Furrow (1973).

[6]Lakoff (1968) has argued that selectional restrictions between agents and instrumental phrases are not valid. Bresnan (1969) has rebutted this argument. We are assuming Bresnan's position.

[7]Whether inchoatives have empty delta subject nodes or no subject node at all in deep structure will not be determined here.

[8]There are cases where non-emphatic and non-contrastive pronouns in object position may not cliticize. See Wanner (1972) for a discussion of these cases. None of them, however, are relevant to inchoatives.

REFERENCES

Aissen, Judith. 1972. Pre-cyclic rules. Unpublished manuscript, Harvard University.

Bresnan, Joan. 1969. On instrumental adverbs and the concept of deep structure. Quarterly Progress Report No. 92, Massachusetts Institute of Technology.

Chomsky, Noam. 1965. Aspects of the theory of syntax. Cambridge, MIT Press.

Fillmore, Charles. 1968. The case for case. In: Universals in linguistic theory. New York, Holt, Rinehart and Winston.

Fodor, Jerry. 1970. Three reasons for not deriving 'kill' from 'cause to die'. Linguistic Inquiry. 1.429-38.

Karttunen, Lauri. 1968. What do referential indices refer to? RAND Corporation Report, Santa Monica, California.

Lakoff, George. 1965. Irregularity in syntax. New York, Holt, Rinehart and Winston.

_____. 1968. Deep and surface grammar. Bloomington, Indiana, Indiana University Linguistics Club.

Langacker, Ronald. 1970. Review of Spanish case and function. Language. 46(1). 167-85.

Napoli Furrow, Donna J. 1973. SI: Its role in reflexive, inchoative, and indefinite subject sentences in modern standard Italian. Unpublished doctoral dissertation, Harvard University.

Newmeyer, Frederick. 1970. On the alleged boundary between syntax and semantics. Foundations of Language. 6. 178-86.

Perlmutter, David. 1970. The two verbs begin. In: Readings in transformational grammar. Ed. by R. Jacobs and P. Rosenbaum. Waltham, Massachusetts. 197-19.

Roldán, Mercedes. 1971. Spanish constructions with se. Language Sciences. 18. 15-29.

Ross, John. 1973. To have have and to not have have. In: Festschrift for Archibald Hill. Ed. by E. Polomé and W. Winter. Austin, University of Texas Press.

Wanner, Dieter. 1972. The mis-placed clitics of Italian. Preliminary version, University of Illinois manuscript.

PREPOSITIONS AND PROPOSITIONS: SOME REMARKS ON FRENCH INFINITIVES

MARK E. LONG

Indiana University

One of the more interesting irregularities of French syntax is the distribution of infinitives preceded by prepositions. Such infinitival constructions are not peculiar to matrix verbs which are subcategorized for prepositional phrases. They may likewise occur with verbs which take direct objects or no objects at all. [1] In such cases, moreover, there can be no sentential interpretation for the pronouns y and en, which normally correspond to prepositional phrases or locatives. Compare the following sets of sentences:

(1a) Ce général s'offense d'être pris pour un intellectuel.
    'This general is offended at being taken for an intellectual.'

(1b) Il s'offense de ma conduite.
    'He is offended at (by) my conduct.'

(1c) Il s'en offense.
    'He is offended at it.'

(2a) J'avais oublié de lire cet article.
    'I had forgotten to read that article.'

(2b) *J'avais oublié de cet article.
    'I had forgotten that article.'

(2b') J'avais oublié cet article.
    '[Same].'

(2c) *J'en avais oublié.
      'I had forgotten it.'

(2ć) J'avais oublié de le faire.
      '[Same].'

(3a) Il m'a forcé à tuer ce garçon.
      'He forced me to kill that boy.'

(3b) *Il m'a forcé à cet homicide.
      'He forced me into that murder.'

(3c) *Il m'y a forcé.
      'He forced me into it.'

We might choose to call the de following oublier or the à after
forcer an 'infinitival particle', rather than a preposition in the usual
sense. I will in fact use this term, if only for convenience's sake,
during the remainder of the present paper.[2] Such a change of labels,
however, does not constitute an explanation, nor does it explain why
infinitival particles may co-occur with some matrix verbs (regretter,
refuser), but not with others (oser, savoir, vouloir).

It is not clear, as a matter of fact, whether every restriction on
French infinitival particles may be accounted for in some principled
way.[3] All I will claim in this paper is that such particles are definitely excluded after a particular semantic class of verbs. As a
consequence, differing semantic functions of certain verbs may be
distinguished by the presence or absence of infinitival particles in
surface structure. Having justified these claims, I will go on to discuss their implications for a generative account of predicate complementation in French.

Let me begin by attempting to clarify certain semantic notions.
A considerable number of matrix verbs express judgments with regard to their complements. Some of these, like regretter, are
emotive, that is, they express 'a subjective, emotional, or evalua-
tive reaction' to a fact or an event (Kiparsky and Kiparsky 1968:363).
There are other verbs, however, which involve judgments concerning
the truth-value of propositions.[4] The point at issue with such verbs
is not a complement's relevance on some subjective level, but rather
its truth or falsity. In cases of this latter sort, we may speak of
'propositional' predicates, or (more precisely) of verbs which may
function propositionally.

One criterion for assigning verbs to the propositional class is provided by tags of the form: (a) mais c'est vrai, (b) mais c'est là un
fait, or (c) mais c'est évident. These seem most appropriate after

negative statements[5] which involve verbs of speaking, thinking, or knowing:

(4a) Il n'affirme pas que Jean parle allemand, mais c'est vrai.
'He doesn't maintain that John speaks German, but it's true.'

(4b) Elle ne croit pas que Jacques soit malade, mais c'est vrai.
'She doesn't believe that Jim is sick, but it's true.'

(4c) Il ne sait pas que deux et deux font cinq, mais c'est vrai.
'He doesn't know that two and two are five, but it's true.'

Emotive verbs, on the other hand, seem to clash semantically with assertions of truth-value. The following example appears highly questionable:

(4d) ??Il ne regrette pas que la porte soit fermée, mais c'est vrai.
'He isn't sorry that the door is shut, but it's true.'

It seems inappropriate to comment on truth-value for complements of regretter. This may be partly because this particular verb is factive. Note, however, that savoir is likewise factive, and yet sentence (4c) poses no difficulties. On the other hand, truth-value tags seem problematic even with non-factive verbs, where the latter are emotive:

(4e) *?Jean ne veut pas que je parte, mais c'est vrai.
'John doesn't want me to leave, but it's true.'

Propositional verbs have various other interesting formal properties. [6] Of primary interest to us here is the fact that no French verb used propositionally will permit the use of infinitival particles. Thus the verb croire allows only a bare infinitive, as in:

(5a) Je crois avoir réussi.
'I think I passed.'

Similarly for dire in:

(5b) Il dit être victime de la Mafia.
'He says he's a victim of the Mafia.'

These are equivalent, respectively, to Je crois que j'ai réussi and Il dit qu'il est victime de la Mafia. Infinitives with particles are impossible in these cases:

(5a') *Je crois d'avoir réussi.
  '[Same as 5a].'

(5b') *Il dit d'être victime de la Mafia.
  '[Same as 5b].'

Note that, while this restriction is basically valid only for those verbs which take direct objects, there is some tendency to extend the bare infinitives to verbs with oblique objects as well, when these are used propositionally. Consider the following set of sentences:

(6a) Elle se souvient de sa visite.
  'She remembers her visit (his visit).'

(6b) Elle s'en souvient.
  'She remembers it.'

(6c) Elle se souvient (d')être allée chez l'accusé.
  'She remembers having gone to the defendant's home.'

The preposition in (6c) is optional, at least in writing.

As further evidence that the presence or absence of infinitival particles is a mark of semantic function, consider the case of verbs which may be used either with propositions or with embedded commands. Such verbs often show alternations of Prep and Ø before infinitives. This is true of dire, as may be seen in the following examples (adapted from the Grammaire Larousse 1964:119):

(7a) Elle nous avait dit ne pas souffrir.
  'She had told us she wasn't suffering.'

(7b) Elle nous avait dit de ne pas souffrir.
  'She had told us not to suffer.'

In the first case the complement represents a statement, in the second a request or command. When dire is not used propositionally, its infinitives must be preceded by de:

(8a) Il dit à Jean-Pierre de monter dans ce taxi.
  'He's telling J. P. to get in that taxi.'

(8b) Le colonel dit à Jean-Pierre de démolir ces bâtiments.
      'The colonel is telling J. P. to demolish those buildings.'

It should be noted in passing that the propositional/imperative
distinction noted here may also be indicated by a contrast of indicative
and subjunctive, as in:

(9a) Mathilde écrit à Hélène qu'elle vienne la voir.
      'Matilda is writing for Helen to come and see her.'

(9b) (compare: . . . qu'elle viendra la voir)
      '[Matilda is writing to Helen] that she will come and see her.'

(10a) Le colonel dit à Jacques qu'il démolisse ces bâtiments.
       'The colonel is telling Jim to demolish those buildings.'

(10b) (compare: . . . qu'il démolit ces bâtiments).
       '[The colonel is telling Jim] that he is demolishing those
       buildings.'

It is, I think, apparent that the distribution of French infinitival
particles is dictated to some degree by semantic functions of matrix
verbs. Moreover, there are at least some instances in which these
particles may serve to mark semantic distinctions involving what is
apparently a single verb. This last fact is of considerable importance for a generative analysis of French infinitives. It means that,
for verbs like dire, the infinitival particle cannot simply be inserted
optionally by transformation (as is apparently suggested in Ruwet
1968:292), [7] since such an optional insertion would change meaning.
To the contrary, sentence pairs like (7a) and (7b) must be the surface
result of two distinct deep structures, only one of which is to contain
an infinitival particle.

One possible means of distinguishing these two deep structure
representations would be to claim the existence of two verbs dire, of
which one functions propositionally and the other imperatively. Such
a solution, however, would force us to treat the dual function of dire
as a lexical accident, whereas such ambivalence in fact seems to
characterize a large number of verbs. In addition to the greater
part of the verbs of speaking, one might cite examples like the following:

(11a) Il m'apprend que ma femme est infidèle.
       'He informs me that my wife is unfaithful.'

(11b) Il m'apprend à jouer du violon.
     'He's teaching me to play the violin.'

(12a) Jacques oublie qu'il a d'autres chats à fouetter.
     'Jim forgets that he has other fish to fry.'

(12b) Jacques a oublié de fouetter les chats. [8]
     'Jim forgot to fry the fish [lit. 'whip the cats'].'

(13a) Il sait avoir profité de sa jeunesse.
     'He knows that he took advantage of his youthfulness.'

(13b) Il sait profiter de sa jeunesse.
     'He knows how to take advantage of his youthfulness.'

In these instances as well, we have alternations between propositional and non-propositional functions, where the former are never marked by infinitival particles while the latter may be. [9] It would seem more reasonable to regard this type of semantic ambivalence as a regularity of the language, characteristic of certain classes of matrix verbs, and not as some kind of homophony, which must be described separately for each verb affected. [10]

Another possibility for sentences like (7a) and (7b) is a transformational solution, whereby the two distinct types of infinitive phrases would be derived from two distinct sentence types in deep structure. Such a solution seems the more plausible when we recall the contrasts between subjunctive and indicative in (9)-(10) above. We might wish to say, then, that sentence pairs like those in (7) differ in terms of the markers AFFIRMATION and IMPERATIVE, which have been proposed for deep structure representations on altogether independent grounds (for example, in Dubois and Dubois-Charlier 1970:133-38). In this way, the phrase-marker:[11]

(14)

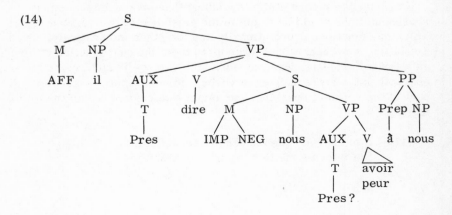

has the possible surface realizations:

(14a) Il nous dit de ne pas avoir peur.
       'He's telling us not to be afraid.'

(14b) Il nous dit que nous n'ayons pas peur.
       '[Same].'

Such a deep structure tree will contrast with:

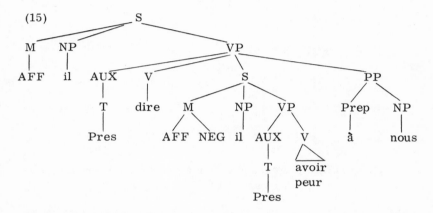

(15)

whose surface forms would be:

(15a) Il nous dit ne pas avoir peur.
       'He's telling us that he's not afraid.'

(15b) Il nous dit qu'il n'a pas peur.
       '[Same].'

The two phrase-markers, then, differ primarily in terms of the
complements' semantic markers (IMPERATIVE vs. AFFIRMATION)
and of their deep structure subjects (<u>nous</u> vs. <u>il</u>).
     To arrive at the surface structures corresponding to these phrase-
markers, we will need a number of transformational rules. Most of
these seem to be rules already required for generative analyses.
Thus, (14b) could be derived by a special case of the SUBJUNCTIVE
transformation (cf. Ruwet 1968:266), whereby all embedded imperatives are obligatorily marked subjunctive. The sentences with infinitives are slightly more problematic. Presumably, a more or
less standard solution would derive them via EQUI-NP-DELETION.
However, since the erasing NP is different in the two cases and since
the dative PP is at least possible in both, there will presumably have

to be two rules of EQUI-NP-DEL, with specification of AFF or IMP
in the embedded S:

(16) T (opt): EQUI-NP-DEL I

$$X - V - IMP \text{ (NEG)} - NP - VP \text{ (ADV)} - à - NP - Y$$
$$1 \quad 2 \qquad 3 \qquad\quad 4 \qquad 5 \qquad\quad 6 \quad 7 \quad 8$$

$$\Longrightarrow 1 - 2 - \qquad 3 \qquad - \emptyset \; - \quad 5 \qquad - 6 - 7 \quad 8$$

CONDITION $4 \equiv 7$

(17) T (opt): EQUI-NP-DEL II

$$X - NP - AUX - \begin{bmatrix} V \\ +Prop \end{bmatrix} - AFF \text{ (NEG)} - NP - AUX - V - Y$$
$$1 \quad 2 \quad\;\; 3 \qquad\quad 4 \qquad\qquad 5 \qquad\quad 6 \qquad 7 \qquad 8 \quad 9$$

$$\Longrightarrow 1 - 2 \;\; - \;\; 3 \;\; - \;\; 4 \quad\;\; - \quad 5 \qquad - \emptyset \; - \; 7 \; - 8 - 9$$

CONDITIONS: $2 \equiv 6$ and either (a) 8 is [-ACTIVE] or (b)
7 contains PERFECT.

Subsequent transformations could add infinitive markers to AUX in
both cases and insert the particle de in the output of (16).

Limitations of time will not permit me to discuss all the problems
raised by this solution or all the refinements which might be introduced into its formulation. Rather, I will focus my attention on one
problem which I consider a major one, the conditions on (17). It
seemingly is the case that propositional verbs are limited to perfec-
tive and/or stative infinitives. This constraint recalls those which
exist for the transformation RAISE-TO-OBJECT in English (see UESP
1968:594-95 for discussion). Thus these examples appear acceptable:

(18a) Elle m'avait dit s'intéresser aux questions de la psychologie.
'She had told me she was interested in problems of psychology.'

(18b) Elle affirme l'avoir rencontré le jour même de
l'assassinat.
'She affirms that she met him on the very day of the
murder.'

(18c) Gaston m'avait dit devoir aller ailleurs.
'Gaston had told me that he had to go somewhere else.'

The following sentences, however, appear to be ungrammatical, even where there is a progressive reading for the infinitive:

(19a) *Elle affirme chanter (en ce moment).
'She affirms that she is singing (right now).'

(19b) *Jacques m'avait dit partir pour Reims le lendemain.
'Jim had told me he was leaving for Rheims the next day.'

(19c) *Le comte avoue monter à cheval.
'The count admits to mounting horses.'

Such restrictions are partly accounted for by the conditions on (17). Unfortunately, there are other cases which suggest that the behavior of propositional verbs in this respect is in fact quite idiosyncratic. Thus, Maurice Gross (1968:82) finds only the infinitives avoir, être, pouvoir, and devoir acceptable following the matrix verb constater. He thus would presumably question the grammaticality of:

(20) Marie-Claire constate ne pas souffrir. (cf. 7a)
'Marie-Claire notes that she isn't suffering.'

There are, on the other hand, propositional predicates which allow the presence of active infinitives. This is especially true for verbs of thought or belief:[12]

(21) Il croit travailler dur.
'He thinks he's working hard.'

With the verbs of speaking, moreover, judgments can be quite variable, so that:

(22a) ?Il dit être président.
'He says he's president.'

is sometimes found less acceptable than:

(22b) Il dit être président de la République.
'He says he's the President.'

These hesitations are perhaps not altogether surprising, given the rather bookish flavor of bare infinitives after propositional verbs (see, for example, Sandfeld 1943:88-91).[13]

Not only are there many constraints on propositional infinitives, but some propositional verbs do not seem to take infinitives of any sort:

(23a) ?Le météo signale avoir constaté une brusque
dépression atmosphérique.
'The weatherman reports having noted a sudden drop in atmospheric pressure.'

(23b) ??Il oublie habiter chez sa vieille tante.[14]
'He forgets that he lives in the home of his elderly aunt.'

(23c) *Il répète avoir rencontré Michel en sortant de chez lui.
'He repeats that he met Mike as he left his house.'

(23d) *Mathilde écrit à Hélène avoir déménagé.
'Matilda writes to Helen that she moved away.'

The transformational solution we have proposed will thus not allow us to account for examples (20)-(23). The alternative solutions we might wish to choose will depend upon our attitude toward such examples. If we consider the problematic sentences syntactically ill-formed, we might follow one of the following three courses:

(A) block the derivation of such examples (and (19) as well) by means of a syntactic filter (or a set of output constraints);

(B) assign rule features to the matrix verbs, assuring that EQUI-NP-DEL II (17) will operate only under the conditions appropriate for a given verb;

(C) state selectional restrictions between a given matrix verb and the verb in its sentential complement.

Of these solutions, (A) seems the least appealing. A filter is an extremely powerful device and would in the present case need to be especially complex and arbitrary in form.[15] As for solution (B), I am not persuaded that rule features are sufficiently motivated as part of generative formalism, particularly when--as here or in certain treatments of RAISE-TO-OBJECT (UESP 1968:595, 615)-- they would in fact be 'condition-on-rule' features.[16] For those who share my aversion, there remains only (C), the solution involving selectional restrictions on lexical insertion for matrix verbs. Since the restrictions in question exist only for infinitives, however, these last must somehow be distinct from clausal complements (que + S) at the point of lexical insertion. In more or less standard theory, this will imply that infinitival complements are distinct from clauses in deep structure. Such a distinction might take the form of some ad hoc marker for subordinate S's which are to undergo EQUI-NP-DEL. [17] If, on the other hand, we wish to limit the domain of selectional restrictions to simplex S's, it might appear more reasonable to generate infinitives directly in the base as VP's, letting their subjects be interpretively supplied by semantic rules. This formalism might also help explain why it is that matrix verbs should impose essentially semantic constraints on infinitival phrases, but not on full S complements.

It is indeed possible that we will wish to claim that sentences like (20) and (22)-(23) are semantically, rather than syntactically, ill-formed. In that event, only some form of solution (C) seems possible within the Katz-Postal hypothesis, since semantic interpretation must take place at the deep structure level. Once again, infinitives would need to be distinct from clausal complements in deep structure. This is true independently of the question as to whether semantically ill-formed utterances should be blocked entirely or merely marked as deviant at the point of semantic interpretation.

Before concluding, I would like to return to the question of deep structure representation of infinitives with and without particles. If we choose to generate infinitives as VP's in the base, then we will have to insert infinitival particles (or some roughly equivalent markers) at this level as well. It is not clear where such particles should be attached. We must, however, insure that infinitives with particles are not later analyzed as PP's. It might seem reasonable to generate infinitival particles within VP's (presumably under AUX). This formalism, however, would cause generation of particles in main S's and clausal complements as well. It would thus seem preferable to make particles sister constituents of their matrix verbs and of following infinitives. It should make no difference, in either case, whether particles are considered to be prepositions, so long as they and their complements are not dominated by the node PP.

The following, then, are the deep structure analyses of the type I would propose for (14a) Il nous dit de ne pas avoir peur and (15a) Il nous dit ne pas avoir peur:

(14)

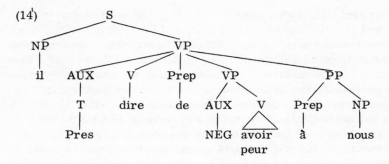

(15)

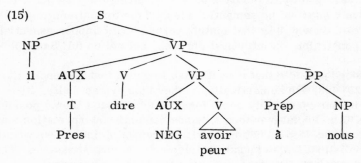

Such deep structures will imply strict subcategorization features of the following types for <u>dire</u>:

(24a) [+ ___ VP (PP)]

(24b) [+ ___ de VP (PP)]

Verbs like <u>croire</u> would share feature (24a), while <u>regretter</u> would have only (24b). The two different structures could be related to differing semantic uses of <u>dire</u> by some interpretive convention such as the following:

(25) Where a matrix verb marked [- ___ PP] enters into the construction [___ Prep VP], it must be assigned a non-propositional reading. Otherwise, mark the sentence as semantically deviant.

Some co-reference rule will also be necessary, in order to specify the understood infinitival subject in each case.

NOTES

[1]The verbs I am speaking of here are those which are subcategorized [+ ___ NP] (oublier) or [+ ___ NP S] (forcer), but not [+ ___ PP].
I have not found any instances of the construction Prep + Infinitive after
verbs which take only predicate complements in object position (oser,
pouvoir, etc.).

[2]In thus adopting the term 'particle', I do not wish to imply that
such occurrences of à and de involve lexical items which differ from
the prepositions of the same form. Indeed, numerous semantic studies,
such as that of Vlado Draškovič (1966), suggest that à and de are far
from being simple infinitive markers, as is often claimed. Certainly,
there seems to be a notion of GOAL associated with à + Inf after verbs
such as apprendre, or of SOURCE for de + Inf following regretter and
related emotives.

[3]In particular, there are verbs such as aimer which may occur
with or without infinitival particles (Sandfeld 1943:108-10).

[4]I am using 'proposition' in more or less its usual philosophical
sense, i.e. as an equivalent of Gottlob Frege's Gedanke (literally
'thought'--see Church 1956:25-27). Of his term Frege writes:
'Without wishing to give a definition, I call a thought something for
which the question of truth arises' (1918:8). Thus a proposition is the
object of a truth-value judgment, whether this judgment is expressed
verbally or occurs in the speaker's mind, whether it remains hypothetical or is assumed to be correct.

It should be emphasized that my use of the term 'propositional'
does not coincide with that of the Kiparskys (1967:392). Rather, I
consider verbs like savoir or se rendre compte to belong to this
class as well. Such verbs, though factive in the strict sense of the
term, are frequently problematic with regard to what is considered
the normal syntactic behavior of factive predicates (see, e.g.
Kiparsky and Kiparsky 1968:348-49). Indeed a subset of factive propositional verbs, verbs of coming-to-knowledge (Givón 1972:46), cease
to be factive in certain circumstances and thus are termed 'semi-
factive' by Karttunen (1971).

[5]This test is subject to two further constraints. First, the main
verb cannot be in the first person; otherwise, a semantic anomaly is
created, in that the speaker makes a judgment and then affirms the
contrary (??Je ne crois pas que Jacques soit malade, mais c'est
vrai). Also, the matrix verb should be in the affirmative where it
is semantically negative (as with nier, douter).

[6]Some additional properties include the following: (i) the ability
to take indirect questions (Il n'a pas dit si elle viendrait ou non/
Savez-vous où elle est partie?); (ii) participation in nominals of the
form DEF + N + que S (la croyance que la terre tourne;

l'affirmation que Jacques est chauve--compare: ?le regret que Marie
soit enceinte); (iii) replacement of complement S by oui or non (Il
croit que oui; Je te dis que non). To these French cases we may perhaps add the ability (in English) to enter into constructions with the
so-called second passive (iv):

$$\text{John is} \begin{cases} \text{said} \\ \text{believed} \\ \text{known} \\ \text{?regretted} \\ \text{*wished} \end{cases} \text{to have died in the crash.}$$

It should be emphasized that not all propositional verbs exhibit these
forms of behavior. Rather, the behavior--with the possible exception
of (iv)--is claimed to be limited to a subset (or subsets) of propositional verbs.

[7]Actually, Ruwet seems to be claiming that insertion of de is
either obligatory, or else does not apply, in the case of any given
verb. This at least is the implication of his questioning the grammaticality of: Pierre dit être malade. In any case, it does not appear to have been Ruwet's purpose, in the paragraph cited (1968:292),
to give a full account of conditions on the infinitive transformation.

[8]Similar cases involving the English verb forget are cited and discussed in UESP (1968:551). There the non-propositional reading is
accounted for by the presence of SUBJUNCTIVE in the underlying
complement S.

[9]One problem which seems to defy solution is that of determining
when a non-propositional predicate will or will not require infinitival
particles (contrast the non-propositional uses of savoir, vouloir with
those of apprendre, oublier). Such behavior may well be idiosyncratic and will thus require specification for each non-propositional
verb. (See also note 3 above.)

[10]As an alternative to the lexical splitting of verbs like dire, we
might propose a distinction between simple use of dire propositionally and a complex predicate composed of (a) dire itself--in more or
less its propositional sense--and (b) an abstract verb expressing
responsibility for performance of an act (where this last is represented by a complement S or de + VP in surface structure). The
sentence Je lui ai dit de partir would thus be assigned an underlying
phrases marker somewhat like the following:

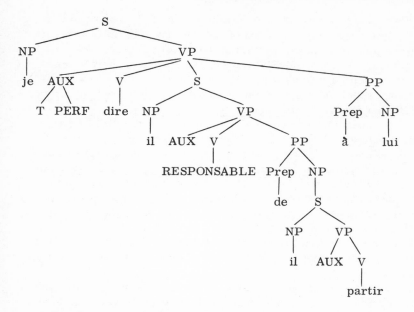

One possible problem here is the difficulty of explaining why there should be no pronominal form for the sentential PP. Perhaps this might be attributed to the depth of embedding. It is likewise not clear to what degree this analysis could be extended to other types of non-propositional verbs, or whether its abstractness is sufficiently motivated. At any rate, use of an abstract intermediate S would not apparently be incompatible with other solutions presented in this paper (though it might render certain of their features superfluous).

[11]I am not concerned, at this point, with the question of whether some S's are in fact dominated by NP, as suggested in Rosenbaum (1967). If the use of semantic markers and the generation of particles in the base (suggested below) are both found unworkable for formal reasons, it might be decided to call imperative complements of dire 'VP complements', letting only propositions be 'NP complements'. Unfortunately, both types meet at least some of Rosenbaum's criteria for NP complements (What Bill told John was to go to the drugstore). Also, I do not think that all cases of infinitival particles could be handled in this way, since many verbs (such as regretter) take particles and yet also allow direct objects and non-propositional sentential readings for le.

[12]Many of the same problems we are discussing here also arise for English verbs of speaking. In particular, these participate in the second passive but do not allow the accusative-infinitive construction (at least on the surface)--see UESP 1968:586-87.

[13]Historically, propositional infinitives are of learned origin in French, resulting from imitation of Latin accusative-infinitive constructions and first appearing during the Middle French period (Gamillscheg 1957:459-60). It is perhaps because of their learned status that such infinitives never acquired particles in French (although they apparently have them in Italian: cf. Ho creduto di fare bene; Dicono di aver fame; Dice di no; Credo di sì).

[14]Most speakers find propositional infinitives decidedly strange following oublier. Nonetheless, Maurice Gross seemingly has no problem with Jean a oublié y être allé (1968:86). Similarly Sandfeld offers an example from Estaunié, J'oublie être un vieil homme (1943: 89). As we have already noted, there is much hesitation as to the correct use of propositional infinitives generally. In any case, it is important that there is apparently no hesitation as to the exclusion of infinitival particles in such cases.

[15]It is in fact difficult to see how a filter could function in this instance without the use of rule features. Thus (A) is perhaps only a special case of (B).

[16]By this last term I mean that such features do not simply state whether certain lexical items must participate in a given transformation. Rather they specify the conditions under which a transformation may (or may not) apply to those items.

[17]One might, for example, wish to follow Jackendoff (1972:181-82) in assigning empty-node subjects to embedded S's which are to become infinitives. In such an event, however, it is not clear how the structural characteristic 'empty-node subject' could be referred to in a selectional restriction for a matrix verb.

REFERENCES

Church, Alonzo. 1956. Introduction to mathematical logic. Vol. I. Princeton, New Jersey.

Draškovič, Vlado. 1966. Infinitiv iza predloga à i de kao dopuna finitnom glagolu u francuskom jeziku (University of Belgrade). Includes a detailed summary in French: L'infinitif précedé des prépositions à ou de comme complément du verbe en français. 237-52.

Dubois, Jean and Françoise Dubois-Charlier. 1970. Éléments de linguistique française: Syntaxe. Paris.

Frege, Gottlob. 1918. The thought. Reprinted in: Logic and philosophy: Selected readings. Ed. by Gary Iseminger. New York, 1968.

Gamillscheg, Ernst. 1957. Historische französische syntax. Tübingen.

Givón, Talmy. 1972. Implications, presuppositions, and the time-axis of verbs. Available from the Indiana University Linguistics Club.

Grammaire Larousse du français contemporain. Ed. by J.-Cl. Chevalier, with M. Arrivé, Cl. Blanche-Benveniste, Jean Peytard, et al. Paris, 1964.

Gross, Maurice. 1968. Grammaire transformationnelle du français: Syntaxe du verbe. Paris.

Jackendoff, Ray S. 1972. Semantic interpretation in generative grammar. Cambridge, Mass.

Karttunen, Lauri. 1971. Some observations on factivity. Papers in Linguistics. 4.55-69.

Kiparsky, Carol and Paul. 1967. The semantics of subordinate clauses. In: Actes du Xe Congrès International des Linguistes. Vol. II. Bucharest, 1970. 391-97.

_____. 1968. Fact. Reprinted in: Semantics: An interdisciplinary reader in philosophy, linguistics, and psychology. Ed. by D. Steinberg and L. Jakobovits. New York, 1971. 345-69.

Rosenbaum, Peter S. 1967. The grammar of English predicate complement constructions. Cambridge, Mass.

Ruwet, Nicolas. 1968. Introduction à la grammaire générative. Paris.

Sandfeld, Kristian. 1943. Syntaxe du français contemporain. Vol. III. L'Infinitif. Geneva, 1965.

UESP = UCLA English Syntax Project, headed by Robert P. Stockwell, Paul Schachter, and Barbara Hall Partee. 1968. Integration of transformational theories on English syntax. University of California, Los Angeles. 2 vols.

ON RESTRICTIVE AND NONRESTRICTIVE RELATIVE CLAUSES, WITH REFERENCE TO FRENCH AND ROMANIAN

THOMAS PAVEL

University of Ottawa

In this paper I will first argue that if grammar has to reflect semantic properties, then restrictive and nonrestrictive relative clauses cannot be derived from the same origin. I will then examine the behavior of RR and NRR with regard to a certain number of determiners and quantifiers, and will propose an explanation of their distributional restrictions in French and Romanian. Finally, I will show that in Romanian the definite article reacts differently, according to whether the object NP is followed by a NRR or a RR clause.

1. I will not examine the arguments brought against the analysis of RR as a S dominated by a NP. It is true that neither the Art-S analysis (Chomsky 1965) nor the NP-S analysis (Ross 1967) is able to capture the hierarchy of dependencies inside the noun-phrase containing a relative clause. Janet Dean (1967) has pointed out, however, that restrictive relative clauses modify the matrix noun, not the matrix NP as a whole. This remark, showing that the determiner modifies a noun already modified by the relative clause, opened the way towards a more accurate representation of syntactic dependencies inside the NP's:

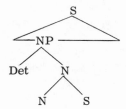

What are the arguments in favor of analyzing the NRR's and the RR's as being derived from the same underlying structure?

It has been claimed (Thompson 1971) that the underlying structure of (1) is a structure like (2):

(1) I met the girl who speaks Basque

(2) (I met girl) (girl speaks Basque)

The difference between (1) and (3)

(3) The girl I met speaks Basque

could be explained as simply a reflection of the presuppositions the speaker has about what the hearer already knows. The conjunct to be relativized is the one which contains the information known by the hearer.

When the head noun is associated with a numeral, however, it seems that NRR and RR clause sentences may have different representations. (4) and (5),

(4) Three boys who had beards were at the party.

(5) Three boys, who had beards, were at the party.

which have to be derived from conjunctions, are said to be different because underlying (4), the numeral is associated with neither of the conjuncts, while underlying (5), it appears in both.

Let us call (3) the 'inverse RR clause sentence' of (1). The inverse RR (NRR) clause sentence of a RR (NRR) clause sentence is a sentence whose main predicate is identical to the main predicate of the original sentence, the NP's and their assignment to predicates being identical in the two sentences. It seems to me that the similarity between the meanings of a RR clause sentence and its inverse sentence is only an apparent one. Consider the following French sentences where the head noun is modified by a generic definite article:

(6) Le soldat qui oublie son devoir doit être puni.
     'The soldier who forgets his duty must be punished.'

(7) Le soldat qui doit être puni oublie son devoir.
     'The soldier who must be punished forgets his duty.'

It is unlikely that (6) and (7) have the same origin, namely something like:

(8) (GENERIC soldier) (soldier forgets his duty)
     (soldier must be punished)

Using the if-then representation for sentences with generic head nouns we can paraphrase (6) and its inverse sentence as follows:

(9) Si un soldat oublie son devoir, il doit être puni.
     'If a soldier forgets his duty, he must be punished.'

(10) Si un soldat doit être puni, il oublie son devoir.
      'If a soldier must be punished, he forgets his duty.'

I see no way in which a grammar could not have to account for the semantic and syntactic differences between (9) and (10), or (6) and (7).

The choice of the conjunct to be relativized is crucial for the meaning of the sentence. This is true not only for generic head noun sentences, but also for sentences like (11) and (12):

(11) Je comprends les professeurs qui parlent français.
      'I understand the professors who speak French.'

(12) Les professeurs que je comprends parlent français.
      'The professors I understand speak French.'

Extending the if-then representation to non-generic articles, we could argue that the underlying structures for (11) and (12) are something like:

(11a) (LES x) (Si (x est un professeur et x parle français)
       ALORS (je comprends x))

(12a) (LES x) (Si (x est un professeur et je comprends x)
       ALORS (x parle français))

It is obvious that (13) and (14) differ in the same way as (11) and (12):

(13) Je comprends la fille qui parle basque.

(14) La fille que je comprends parle basque.

Therefore

(15) (LA fille) (je comprends la fille) (fille parle basque)

cannot be the underlying structure of both (13) and (14). Maybe (15) could be improved by adding some device indicating the conjunct which has to become a RR. This would split (15) into:

(15a) (LA fille) (je comprends fille) (fille parle basque)$_{RR}$

which is at the origin of (13) and

(15b) (LA fille) (je comprends fille)$_{RR}$(fille parle basque)

from which (13)'s inverse sentence, namely (14), could be derived.
On the other hand, deriving a NRR sentence and its inverse sentence from the same conjunction seems less problematic. Consider

(16) The boy, who had a beard, was at the party.

(17) The boy, who was at the party, had a beard.

Let us assume that one of the conjuncts from which (16) and (17) are supposed to be derived is false (i.e. that the boy was not at the party). Obviously this should affect the truth-value of both (16) and (17). The underlying representation of both (16) and (17) could be (18):

(18) (The boy was at the party)(the boy had a beard)

Sentences with generic determiners, which are said to be underlying implications, react in a similar way to changes in the truth-value of one of the conjuncts:

(19) L'homme, qui est un animal raisonnable, cherche
naturellement le bonheur.
'Man, who is a rational animal, naturally seeks
happiness.'

(20) L'homme, qui cherche naturellement le bonheur, est un
animal raisonnable.
'Man, who naturally seeks happiness, is a rational
animal.'

(21) could be thought as a representation of both (19) and (20):

(21) $(\forall x)(H(x) \supset A(x)) \wedge (H(x) \supset S(x))$, where

$H(x)$ = x is a man

$A(x)$ = x is a rational animal

$S(x)$ = x naturally seeks happiness

If one of the conjuncts is false, i.e. if man does not seek happiness,
both (19) and (20) will become false. I am aware, however, that
there is a semantic difference between (19) and (20). It seems to me
that the predicate of the main sentence is, in both cases, felt as some
sort of consequence of the predicate in the RR. (19) and (20) each
have at least one reading very close to (22) and (23):

(22) L'homme, en tant qu'animal raisonnable, cherche
naturellement le bonheur.

(23) L'homme, en tant qu'il cherche naturellement le bonheur,
est un animal raisonnable.

Even so, both (22) and (23), which are not the only readings of (19)
and (20) seem to become false if one of the conjuncts is false. We do
not know very much about the logical properties of such metaphysical
attributions as those introduced by qua 'in so far as'; however, we
can assume that (22) cannot be represented as:

(24) $(\forall x)((H(x) \wedge A(x)) \supset S(x))$

Let us sum up. On the one hand, deriving the RR from conjunctions would imply the introduction of some device indicating the conjunct which has to be relativized. This device has strong semantic
consequences and thus has to appear in the underlying form of the RR
clause sentence, in order to account for the difference between a RR
clause sentence and its inverse RR clause sentence. On the other
hand, even if the semantic difference between a NRR clause sentence
and its inverse is to be represented by some device present in the
underlying form, this device cannot have the same semantic properties

as the one which accounts for RR clause sentences and their inverse
sentences.

2. Up to now only RR and NRR clause sentences with generic and
definite determiners have been analyzed. The consideration of a
larger class of determiners and quantifiers in connection with the
nouns as modified by relatives shows that the syntactic behavior of
NRR's is again different from that of RR's. Consider the following
examples in French and Romanian:

(25) Chaque garçon qui pleure reçoit un sou.
      'Each boy who weeps receives a copper.'

(26) *Chaque garçon, qui pleure, reçoit un sou.
      'Each boy, who weeps, receives a copper.'

(27) Un cîine care latră nu muşcă.
      'A dog which barks doesn't bite.'

(28) *Un cîine, care latră, nu muşcă.
      'A dog, which barks, doesn't bite.'

(29) Am vorbit cu toţi băieţii care au sosit.
      'I spoke to all the boys who arrived.'

(30) Am vorbit cu toţi băieţii, care au sosit.
      'I spoke to all the boys, who arrived.'

(31) Cîţiva băieţi care au sosit poartă pălării noi.
      'Some boys who arrived have new hats.'

(32) Cîţiva băieţi, care au sosit, poartă pălării noi.
      'Some boys, who arrived, have new hats.'

(28) is ungrammatical insofar as un (a) is employed as a generic
determiner. The sentence is fully grammatical if un is the indefinite article (a). (30) has two readings in Romanian:

(33) (I spoke to all the boys together)(all the boys arrived
      together)

(34) (I spoke to each boy)(all the boys arrived together)

but (35) cannot be considered as a reading of (30):

(35) *(I spoke to each boy)(each boy arrived)

It seems to me that after amîndoi (both), the NRR cannot be read distributively. (37) and (38) are possible readings of (36) but not (39):

(36) Am vorbit cu amîndoi băieţ ii, care au venit.
'I spoke to both boys, who arrived. '

(37) (I spoke to both boys together)(both boys arrived together)

(38) (I spoke to each boy)(both boys arrived together)

(39) *(I spoke to each boy)(each boy arrived)

Finally, the NRR cannot appear after a NP whose DET is no, French aucun, Romanian niciun.

(40) *Niciun băiat, care a venit, n-a adus mîncare.
'No boy, who came, brought anything to eat. '

McCawley (1968) pointed out that in order to assign deep structures to both readings of (41), i.e. (42) and (43)

(41) Those men went to Chicago

(42) Those men went each to Chicago

(43) Those men went together to Chicago

it is necessary to subcategorize noun phrases into two types which he calls joint and nonjoint. Adjuncts like together are allowed only by joint NP's; each can determine only a nonjoint NP. Verbs like (to be) erudite require a nonjoint subject, while go allows either a joint or a nonjoint subject, and (to be) similar allows only a joint subject.

Our NRR cases, when definite or indefinite articles and quantifiers like all, each, or no are involved, may be explained using this [± joint] subcategorization. (25)-(40) and other possible examples show that the noun phrase in the NRR is always interpreted as [+joint], while the NP in the main sentences of the correct examples is always unmarked with respect to the [± joint] features.

Following a suggestion made by Lakoff (1970), I will call [unmarked joint] or [u joint] a NP which can be interpreted for the most part as being [+ joint], but which also allows, in some cases, the [- joint] reading. The NP's in the main sentences of (30) or (36) are

[u joint]. A sentence containing a NP which is [marked joint] or
[m joint] is interpreted only as [- joint]. This is the case for NP's
with adjuncts like chaque or un (generic). We will consider that
NP's with definite or indefinite articles or generic le are [u-joint].
Aucun, niciun are to be considered as [-joint]. Examining again examples (25)-(40) we notice that

(a) when the NP in the main sentence is [u joint], the reading
    which interprets the NP of the NRR clause as [- joint] is
    incorrect: (35), (39).

(b) when the NP in the main sentence is [- joint], the NRR
    clause sentence is blocked: (26), (28), (40).

As we have already pointed out, the NP in the NRR is always [+ joint].
To block both incorrect sentences like (26) or (28) and incorrect readings of well-formed sentences like (35) or (39), we have to set up a
cooccurrence restriction demanding that the NP in the NRR have, besides the referential identity with the NP in the main sentence, the
same determiner as the main NP, but always with the [+ joint] reading. Obviously, this will be possible only with [u joint] determiners.
   On the other hand, no such restriction is needed by restrictive
relativization where, as it has been shown, the only restriction is
that unique reference NP's cannot be relativized. But this is a trivial
consequence of a well-known logical property of RR's: the NP followed
by a RR refers to a subset of objects referred to by the same NP
without the RR.
   The importance of the [± joint] features for the behavior of the
NP's in the main sentence and in a subordinate clause is not limited
to NRR clause sentences. Consider, for example (44):

(45) Ces hommes ont préféré partir.
      'These men preferred to leave.'

which derives from something like (45), after the Equi-NP deletion
transformation has applied:

(45) (Ces hommes ont préféré)(ces hommes partir)

It may be argued that (44) is ambiguous in at least four ways as it
can have each of the following readings:

(46) Those men together preferred those men together to leave.

(47) Those men together preferred each of those men to leave.

(48) Each of those men preferred those men together to leave.

(49) Each of those men preferred each of those men to leave.

If these four readings are all indeed correct interpretations of (44), we could assume that Equi-NP Deletion is not blocked by lack of concord between the [± joint] features, if the feature is present in the noun's matrix. However, (50) cannot be interpreted as (48):

(50) Chacun de ces hommes a préféré partir.

but

(51) Ces hommes ont préféré partir ensemble.

may have both (46) and (48) as readings. It is worthwhile to notice that the same NP adjuncts which block the nonrestrictive Relativization impose a nonjoint interpretation on the NP in the embedded sentence in the Equi-NP Deletion SD:

(52) {Chacun de ces / Chaque / Aucun} homme(s) (n')a préféré partir.

At the same time the NP's which allow the NR Relativization, i. e. the [u joint] NP's, permit both a joint and a nonjoint interpretation of the embedded NP in the Equi-NP Deletion SD:

(53) {Tous ces / Quelques-uns de ces / Certains de ces etc.} hommes ont préféré partir.

While in the sentences of (52), both NP's have to be interpreted as nonjoint, in the sentences of (53) the two NP's may be similar or different with respect to this feature.

3. The syntactic behavior of the Romanian Definite Article with regard to NRR and RR clause sentences reinforces our arguments against a common origin of the two types of sentences.

The postposed definite article in Romanian is sensitive, among other things, to the position of the NP-object with regard to the end of the sentences.

It is known, first of all, that object NP's with animate nouns are subject to an optional transformation which obtains (55) from (54) by introducing the preposition PE (PE-Transformation):

(54) Am văzut copilul cu ochi albaştri.
      'I saw the child with blue eyes.'

(55) L-am văzut pe copilul cu ochi albaştri.
      (same meaning as (54))

Although correct, (54) seems pedantic; in fact, the only constructions actually used are similar to (55).

After the PE-Transformation has applied, object NP's with animate nouns are no longer distinguishable from Prep-P. All nouns
preceded by a large class of prepositions (pe, la, spre, din, sub
. . . but not cu, înaintea, înapoia . . .) are subject to the ART-
DEF-Deletion Transformation if the definite article is the only ad-
junct of the PREP-NP. Consider (56)-(59):

(56) L-am văzut pe copilul cu ochi albaştri.
      'I saw the child with blue eyes.'

(57) L-am văzut pe copil.
      'I saw the child.'

(58) Am mîncat din farfuria roşie.
      'I ate from the red dish.'

(59) Am mîncat din farfurie.
      'I ate from the dish.'

It is true that for some animate nouns, there are dialectal variants,
such as:

(60) ! Am văzut-o pe femeia.
      'I saw the woman.'

(61) ! L-am întîlnit pe omul.
      'I met the man.'

but this kind of sentence is felt to be strongly unacceptable at a certain social level, not necessarily too high. (! symbolizes 'social
unacceptability'). (60) and (61) may be related to

(62) L-am văzut pe bunicul.
      'I saw grand-pa.'

(63) Am văzut-o pe mama.
      'I saw mummy.'

as opposed to

(64) L-am văzut pe bunic.
'I saw the grandfather.'

(65) Am văzut-o pe mamă.
'I saw the mother.'

Some animate nouns like mamă (mother), tată (father), bunic (grandfather), împărat (emperor) may not lose their definite article even
when the SD for ART-DEF-Deletion is met, if they are understood as
proper nouns. We can explain (60) and (61) as extensions of this correct use.

Notice also that if the NP object preceded by a preposition is at the
end of a sentence conjoined with another sentence, the ART-DEF
Deletion must apply:

(66) L-am văzut pe băiat şi i-am dat o prăjitură.
'I saw the boy and I gave him a cupcake.'

It may be worthwhile to notice that the definite article in this
position reacts differently if the object NP is followed by a NRR or
a RR clause:

(67) L-am întîlnit pe băiatul care tocmai îşi cumpărase
o prăjitură.
'I met the boy who had just bought himself a cupcake.'

(68) L-am întîlnit pe băiat, care tocmai îşi cumpărase o
prăjitură.
'I met the boy, who had just bought himself a cupcake.'

The RR blocks the ART-DEF Deletion Transformation, while the
NRR requires it. If we compare (66) and (68) we see that NRR and
conjunctions have the same effect upon the applicability of this
transformation. On the other hand, (67), (56), and (58) are similar.
This reinforces the hypothesis concerning the derivation of NRR's
from conjunctions and the analysis of RR's as adjuncts of the noun
in the noun phrase.

REFERENCES

Chomsky, Noam. 1965. Aspects of the theory of syntax. Cambridge, Mass., MIT Press.

Dean, Janet. 1967. Determiners and relative clauses. Unpublished paper, Massachusetts Institute of Technology.

Lakoff, George. 1970. Irregularity in syntax. New York, Holt, Rinehart and Winston.

McCawley, James D. 1968. The role of semantics in grammar. In: Universals in linguistic theory. Ed. by E. Bach and R. T. Harms. New York, Holt, Rinehart and Winston.

Ross, John. 1967. Constraints on variables in syntax. Unpublished Ph. D. dissertation, Massachusetts Institute of Technology.

Smith, Carlota S. 1964. Determiners and relative clauses in a generative grammar of English. Language. 40.37-52.

Thompson, Sandra Annear. 1971. The deep-structure of relative clauses. In: Studies in linguistic semantics. Ed. by Ch. J. Fillmore and D. T. Langendoen. New York, Holt, Rinehart and Winston.